OXFORD POLITICAL THEORY

Series editors: Will Kymlicka, David Miller, and Alan Ryan

REFLECTIVE DEMOCRACY

OXFORD POLITICAL THEORY

Oxford Political Theory presents the best new work in contemporary political theory. It is intended to be broad in scope, including original contributions to political philosophy, and also work in applied political theory. The series contains works of outstanding quality with no restriction as to approach or subject matter.

REFLECTIVE DEMOCRACY

ROBERT E. GOODIN

OXFORD
UNIVERSITY PRESS

OXFORD

UNIVERSITY PRESS

Great Clarendon Street, Oxford OX2 6DP

Oxford University Press is a department of the University of Oxford.
It furthers the University's objective of excellence in research, scholarship,
and education by publishing worldwide in

Oxford New York

Auckland Bangkok Buenos Aires Cape Town Chennai
Dar es Salaam Delhi Hong Kong Istanbul Karachi Kolkata
Kuala Lumpur Madrid Melbourne Mexico City Mumbai Nairobi
São Paulo Shanghai Taipei Tokyo Toronto

with an associated company in Berlin

Oxford is a registered trade mark of Oxford University Press
in the UK and in certain other countries

Published in the United States
by Oxford University Press Inc., New York

British Library Cataloguing in Publication Data

Data available

Library of Congress Cataloging in Publication Data

Data available

ISBN 0-19-925617-9

1 3 5 7 9 10 8 6 4 2

Typeset by Newgen Imaging Systems (P) Ltd, Chennai, India
Printed in Great Britain
on acid-free paper by
TJ International Ltd, Padstow, Cornwall

For Diane

PREFACE

I missed the 'fall of the Wall': my second son was in the process of being born. But none of us political philosophers could fail to feel its reverberations.

Which is not to say that any of us knew quite what to make of it, immediately. The first flush of mindless triumphalism soon gave way to despair over the release of long-repressed ethno-nationalist score-settling; and many of the 'new democracies' were democratic in form only (and decreasingly that, all too often). While constitutional lawyers busied themselves with the tasks of statecraft, advising on basic institutions for the new democracies, political sociologists continued probing the suitability of the sociological and psychological soil for sustaining these political transplants. Those have proven to be rich sites for new political theorizing, fully as rich as all the other first-order political movements and events that have done so much to reinvigorate political philosophy in our lifetimes.

Beyond more specific issues of sustainable institutional design (on which I have written in the past and hope to do much more), broader issues of democratic theory were suddenly back at the centre of the political philosophical agenda. Of course, democratic theory was never considered a 'settled' subject, and questions of power and participation and inclusion have always been simmering away. But as the catch-cry of 'democratization' began echoing around the world, what had long simmered away on political philosophers' back burners suddenly shifted to the forefront. Suddenly all of us—not just those specializing in the subject—had to confront questions of what it was to democratize a society, both others' and our own.

These issues were pressed upon me with particular force when the incoming President of the International Political Science Association, Carole Pateman, invited me to serve as the Program Chair for that Association's XIVth World Congress, meeting in Berlin in August 1994 to discuss the theme of 'Democratization'. Working with her and our Berlin colleagues—Gerhard Göhler and Hubertus Buchstein, Hans-Dieter Klingeman and David Soskice, Claus Offe and Peter Wagner, and many others—on preparations for that event not only kept my mind focused on issues of democratization but helped me see more clearly their many different aspects. The contributions of the several thousand participants in that Congress, which as Program

Chair I monitored more assiduously than as a mere Congress-goer I ever would have done, helped all the more.

The upshot is the following set of reflections on democratic theory. I would not claim that it adds up to a wholly 'new' theory of democracy. I would not claim that it is connected as closely as one might have wished to the real-world political events occasioning it. All I would care to claim is that it represents a rethinking of democratic theory, inspired by real-world events and attempting, however obliquely, to come to grips with some of the challenges that they pose.

ACKNOWLEDGEMENTS

The arguments contained in this book have been trialled before a great many audiences in various places, over the past decade or more. I should begin by recording my diffuse debts to those audiences in Amsterdam, Austin, Buffalo, Canberra, Kirchberg, New Orleans, Oslo and San Francisco. I should record more specific thanks, for help on one or more chapters, to Louise Antony, Veit Bader, Brian Barry, Rainer Bauböck, Akeel Bilgrami, Luc Bovens, Geoff Brennan, David Braddon-Mitchell, John Broome, James Chase, Josh Cohen, David Copp, Martin Davies, Andy Dobson, Dave Estlund, Cynthia Farrer, John Ferejohn, David Firth, Jim Fishkin, Andreas Føllesdal, Dick Flathman, Barbara Fried, Archon Fung, Amy Gutmann, Jerry Gaus, David Gauthier, Diane Gibson, Bernie Grofman, Russell Hardin, Dan Hausman, Jim Hawthorne, Aanund Hylland, Bruce Headey, Frank Jackson, Will Kymlicka, Peter Laslett, Mick Laver, Keith Lehrer, Saul Levmore, Christian List, Ian McAllister, Iain McLean, Gerry Mackie, David Miller, Knud Midgaard, Nick Miller, Simon Niemeyer, Martha Nussbaum, Claus Offe, Johan Olsen, Josh Parsons, Carole Pateman, Philip Pettit, John Quiggin, Peter Railton, Martin Rein, Stein Ringen, Mathias Risse, Bo Särlvik, Stew Saunders, Debra Satz, Michael Smith, Rob Sparrow, Cass Sunstein, Abram de Swaan, Folke Tersman, David Thacher, Mariam Thalos, Dennis Thompson, Ulf Torgersen, Avi Tucker, Jeremy Waldron, Albert Weale, and Iris Young. My particular thanks go to John Dryzek, who not only commented on virtually all of the chapters separately as they were being written but also advised on the overall shape of the book as a whole, as at later stages did Niki Lacey and anonymous readers for OUP. I am indebted to Geoff Brennan for permission to reuse in Chapter 4 material from an article we co-authored, and to Christian List for similar permission in respect of Chapter 5. None of them, of course, bear any responsibility for the arguments or interpretations contained herein. Finally, I am grateful to Dominic Byatt for taking it all off my hands and for seeing it so efficiently into such pretty print.

I am grateful to publishers and co-authors for permission to reprint material from the following:

Robert E. Goodin, 'Communities of Enlightenment', *British Journal of Political Science*, 28 (July 1998), 531–58, by permission of Cambridge University Press.

Robert E. Goodin, 'Democracy, Preferences and Paternalism', *Policy Sciences*, 26 (1993), 229–47, by permission of Elsevier Publishers.

Robert E. Goodin and Geoffrey Brennan, 'Bargaining Over Beliefs', *Ethics*, 111 (Jan. 2001), 256–77, by permission of Geoffrey Brennan and the University of Chicago Press.

Christian List and Robert E. Goodin, 'Epistemic Democracy: Generalizing the Condorcet Jury Theorem', *Journal of Political Philosophy*, 9 (Sept. 2001), 276–306, by permission of Christian List and Blackwell Publishers.

Robert E. Goodin, 'The Paradox of Persisting Opposition', *Philosophy, Politics and Economics*, 1 (2002), 109–46, by permission of SAGE Publishers.

Robert E. Goodin, 'Democratic Deliberation Within', *Philosophy and Public Affairs*, 29 (Winter 2000), 79–107, by permission of Princeton University Press.

Robert E. Goodin, 'Enfranchising the Earth, and its Alternatives', *Political Studies*, 44 (Dec. 1996), 835–49, by permission of Blackwell Publishers.

Robert E. Goodin, 'Inclusion and Exclusion', *Archives Européenes de Sociologie*, 37 (Dec. 1996), 343–71, by permission of the journal's editors and publishers.

Robert E. Goodin, 'The Politics of Inclusion', in Peter Koller and Klaus Puhl (eds.), *Current Issues in Political Philosophy: Justice and Welfare in Society and World Order* (Vienna: Verlag Hölder-Pichler-Tempsky, 1997), 133–46, by permission of Verlag Hölder-Pichler-Tempsky.

CONTENTS

CHAPTER 1

Introduction

Democracy is a much-contested concept. Fundamentally, though, it is a matter of making social outcomes systematically responsive to the settled preferences of all affected parties.[1]

Voting is the classic mechanism for ensuring systematic responsiveness of that sort. The democratic credentials of any polity altogether lacking some such electoral check would be very threadbare indeed. But while voting might constitute a necessary condition of democratic rule, it is not necessarily sufficient. It may not even be what matters most in ensuring the sort of systematic responsiveness towards one another which characterizes a genuinely democratic polity.

Voting is an external act. Here I shall be focusing more on the internal acts that precede and underlie it. For political outcomes to be democratic in a suitably strong sense, people's votes ought to reflect their *considered* and *settled* judgements, not top-of-the-head or knee-jerk reactions. Democratic citizens are supposed to act *reflectively*. They are supposed to ponder long and hard what they want and why, and what really is the right way for the larger community to assist them in achieving those goals. Democratic citizens are supposed to come to some joint determination of what they *collectively* ought to do. In the course of that, they are expected to reflect seriously upon what others want and why, and how those others' goals might articulate with their own. Democratic citizens are supposed to act *responsively*, taking due account of the evidence and experience embodied in the beliefs of others. Democratic citizens are supposed to act *responsibly*, taking due account of the impact of their actions and choices on all those (here or elsewhere, now or later) who will be affected by them.

---

[1] May 1978; Saward 1998: ch. 3. See similarly Pennock 1979: ch. 7.

Such are the familiar pieties of democratic citizenship. Those pieties are standardly glossed with passing embarrassment in modern democratic theory. Such is the lasting legacy of the 'empirical theory of democracy' that lay at the heart of 'behavioural revolution' in mid-century American political science. Its teaching was that, nice though it would be if those criteria were met, they really must be seen as ideal standards to which we dare not hold real-world agents in real-world regimes.[2] We must not put ourselves in the position of having to deny people the vote simply because they could not pass a political literacy test—or a 'moral competence' test of the sort just sketched, either. The realpolitik of democracy cautions us against probing too deeply behind the sheer act of voting.[3]

That excess of political realism threatens to sell democracy short, in my view, both as a normative ideal and as a social practice. People do 'come to terms' with one another in all those ways that democratic theory demands, virtually every day. The way they do that is not so much through formal negotiations as through informally internalizing and anticipating the perspectives of one another, and adjusting their own behaviour accordingly. My suggestion is that the same sort of 'mental mediation' that people practise in their everyday dealings with one another can go some considerable way towards easing the interpersonal burdens of democratic deliberation as well.

Voting inevitably remains the ultimate act of political legitimation in a democracy. But democratic theorists can and should, I suggest, be more sensitive to what precedes and underlies it, accepting internal-reflective deliberations of a suitable sort as broadly on a par with (indeed, in certain crucial respects of a cloth with) the sort of external-collective deliberations that look so impractically demanding in modern polities.

Situating the Project

Let me begin by situating my project within the more familiar traditions of democratic discourse.

---

[2] Represented in collections such as Dahl and Neubauer (1968) and Cnudde and Neubauer (1969). The legacy is evident in empirical studies of 'democratization' in our own day (cf. Diamond 1999).

[3] This is the take-home message of the 'behavioural revolution', expressed most forcefully by Converse (1964) and anticipated by e.g. Dewey (1927) and Lippmann (1955). For attempts by normative theorists to try to accommodate behavioural findings without altogether relinquishing their democratic ideals, see Thompson 1970; Yankelovich 1991; Marcus and Hanson 1993.

Democracy had long been equated with populism—'popular rule' to its friends, 'mob rule' to its critics. Against the background of that populist presupposition, democratic theory progressed in three broad waves over the course of the twentieth century.[4]

The first wave was one of *democratic elitism*. Democratic elitists rejected those received populist theories of democracy as impractical because, among other things, they imposed unrealistic demands on the time and attention of ordinary citizens. At mid-century, the received wisdom was decidedly Schumpeter's: in a representative democracy, voters are rightly relegated to choosing among packages of policy proposals which have been formulated by political parties, which are accountable to the people at elections alone.[5] Democracy, for democratic elitists, consisted simply in the competitive struggle for people's votes in periodic elections—and (for the democratic pluralists who strove so mightily to differentiate themselves from democratic elitists) in the competitive struggle among interest groups for the attention of elected and unelected officials in between elections.[6]

The second wave of democratic innovation, very much counterpoised to the first, extolled the virtues of *participatory democracy*. Partly that was a matter simply of boosting the sheer numbers of people involved, both in the formal political process and also at other key sites where social life is shaped. Partly, too, participatory democracy was a matter of boosting the nature and level of people's involvement— among other things, centrally extolling the virtues of cooperative rather than artificially adversarial modes of problem-solving.[7] In both respects, participatory democracy was largely a story of the progressive development of the human capabilities of participants, broadening and deepening the social perspectives and moral capacities of those engaged in the participatory enterprise.[8] Democracy, for participatory democrats, consisted in empowering and encouraging people to engage meaningfully in the collaborative tasks that constitute social life on a daily basis.

The third and most recent wave of innovation in the theory of democracy, building on the last, proceeds under the banner of *deliberative democracy*.[9] Democracy in this mode is to be deliberative in contradistinction to many opposites: adversarial, ill-considered,

---

[4] The first two of which are effectively recounted in Macpherson 1977.

[5] Schumpeter 1950; cf. Dahl 1956: ch. 3 and Bachrach 1967. On 'accountability', see Day and Klein 1987; Goodin 2000*a*.   [6] Dahl 1961; Polsby 1980.

[7] Mansbridge 1980; Goodin 1996*e*.   [8] Dahl 1970; Pateman 1970; Macpherson 1973.

[9] Cohen 1989, 1996; Manin 1987; Gutmann and Thompson 1996; Bohman 1996; Bohman and Rehg 1997; Elster 1998*a*.

individualistic, self-interested, aggregative. Correspondingly many political programmes travel under this banner. Some self-styled 'deliberative democrats' seek salvation in reformed representative institutions,[10] others in judicial deliberations or constitutional moments,[11] still others in idealized deliberations among mass publics[12] or oppositional groups.[13]

The hallmark of the 'deliberative turn' in contemporary democratic theory, across all those variations, is to see 'democratic legitimacy ... in terms of the ability or opportunity to participate in effective deliberation on the part of those subject to collective decisions'.[14]

The great challenge facing such models of directly deliberative democracy—or participatory democracy, either—is this: how can we realistically involve the *entire* community of people affected by a decision in *meaningful* deliberations over that decision?

Face-to-face deliberation, it seems, is necessarily the province of small groups.[15] Robert Dahl long ago offered the following back-of-the-envelope calculation as a *reductio ad absurdum* of participatory—and, by extension, directly deliberative—democracy. Suppose that we regard political outcomes as democratically legitimate if and only if everyone affected by them has had a chance to have a say on them (the 'deliberative test of legitimacy', outlined above). Suppose, accordingly, we allocate each person ten minutes' speaking time (a bare minimum for meaningful participation, it would seem). Suppose, furthermore, that we devote fully ten hours a day to such deliberations (a generous allocation, by any standard). Under those conditions, it would take a modest-sized group of merely sixty people one whole day to reach one single decision.[16]

Contrary to the claims of enthusiasts, new technology is no solution.[17] Imagine we are conducting the deliberation on the internet. We still need to spend a certain amount of time reading what one another

---

[10] Bessette 1994; Uhr 1998.   [11] Ackerman 1991.
[12] Dryzek 1990; Fishkin 1991, 1995.   [13] Dryzek 1996, 2000; Young 2000.
[14] Dryzek 2000: 1.

[15] Groups of seven people, on one account: 'That number of men can sit around a small table, talk with each other informally without waste of words or any display or pretence, provide an adequate diversity of points of view and modes of dealing with the subject at hand, and yet be prompt and efficient in the despatch of business' (Lindsay 1929: 22, quoting C. W. Eliot).   [16] Dahl 1970: 67–8.

[17] Budge (1996: 1) e.g. writes that 'the new challenge of direct democracy lies in the startling fact that it is now technically possible. Public policy can be discussed and voted upon by everyone linked in an interactive communications net. Such nets are spreading through the world, so they can easily carry debates among the citizens of any one state. This destroys the killer argument habitually used to knock direct democracy on the head, that it is just not practical in modern mass societies to bring citizens together to discuss public policy. The existence of electronic communications means that physical proximity

has written. Suppose we spend a mere ten minutes reading what each other has written, and we do not come to a decision until we have all read what each other has written. Then the force of Dahl's point remains. A group of sixty people spending ten-hour days on the task can still reach only a single decision a day.

Were we trying to involve more people or to make more decisions, whether in person or on the internet, the situation would become quickly hopeless. In groups of hundreds (much less thousands or millions) which are trying to resolve many matters, there would seem simply to be no realistic scope for democracy in this directly deliberative mode.[18]

If we want to make the deliberative ideal practical in those circumstances, we apparently face an unpalatable choice. Either we have to reduce the number of people deliberating, thus involving less than the entire community; or else we have to reduce the breadth or depth of the deliberation, thus making the deliberation less meaningful in some sense or another. Representative institutions (parliaments or citizens' juries or deliberative polls or planning cells[19]) are flawed in the first respect. Mechanisms channelling public attention (such as mass media or referenda[20]) are flawed in the second.

Thus, the problem with which democratic elitists began at the turn of the last century returns to haunt democratic theory in its most recent incarnations. How can we constructively engage people in the public life of a mass democracy, without making wildly unrealistic demands on their time and attention?

That problem becomes particularly acute when we appreciate that we are inevitably dealing with people who often take no direct interest in political affairs, as such. Furthermore, they have no rational reason to do so, at least from a narrowly instrumental perspective. After all, the odds are minuscule that any one person's vote or voice will make any great difference to the ultimate outcome among a large group of people; so it is perfectly rational for voters not to go to any great trouble or expense informing themselves.[21]

---

is no longer required. Mass discussion can be carried on interactively when individuals are widely separated.'

[18] There are fewer 'distinct perspectives'—'discourses', in Dryzek's (2001) terms—than there are people. But in the absence of any 'spokespersons' authorized to negotiate among them, the same multitudes are left to reconcile the various perspectives for themselves.

[19] Cf. Fishkin 2000.

[20] Page 1996; Key and Crouch 1939; Budge 1996; Scarrow 2001.

[21] Downs 1957. Of course, as I have argued elsewhere, the fact that their vote is individually inconsequential simply liberates people to vote on the basis of whatever (nonconsequential) moral values they might harbour (Goodin and Roberts 1975; see also

Much has recently been done to liberate voters from that condemnation to rational ignorance.[22] Theories show how rational choice under conditions of low information is perfectly possible, just so long as people cue on reliable signals from others who are better informed. They can, for example, simply take their cues from whichever political party or newspaper seems most nearly in line with their considered views, whenever they do take the trouble to form such views.[23]

The problem with those solutions is that the elites from whom the mass public is supposed to be taking its cues are themselves acting under instruction from the very masses whom they are supposed to be cuing. If the elites are to appeal democratically to their electors, then they must, to some greater or lesser extent, mirror the mass public, in all its flaws. Democratic elitism might moderate the rational ignorance of the mass public, at the margins. But in so far as it is democratic, democratic elitism can only moderate and not eliminate that phenomenon. Nor, more especially, can it eradicate the short-sighted pursuit of narrow personal and sectional interests that typically ensues from judging public issues on the basis of information incidentally acquired in pursuit of one's own more personal affairs.[24]

One illustration of the damage that could be caused by such short-sightedness among electors, and their representatives in consequence, is the so-called 'political business cycle'. On this account, governments (in so far as they are able) heat up the economy in the run-up to an election. Electors reward them with another term in office; once re-elected, the government then has to cool down the inflationary pressures it introduced in the run-up to the last election.[25] The result is a wholly artificial boom–bust cycle, politically rather than economically induced. The trick works, politically, precisely because of the ignorance and short-sightedness of the electorate in cuing on 'how things are going just now'. But governments taking political advantage of it end up mimicking that short-sightedness in their own economic policy in consequence.

Brennan and Lomasky 1993). That might seem cold comfort to those of us who believe that the structure of morality is itself essentially consequentialist. But of course a person might make it a matter of principle to vote for that party which, if elected, would produce the best consequences—and she might vote in that way as a matter of moral principle, even knowing that her own vote will play little or no role in bringing about those consequences (the election of that party, and through that the implementation of those policies).

[22] Wittman 1995.
[23] Popkin 1991; Page and Shapiro 1992; Lupia 1994; Lupia and McCubbins 1998.
[24] Downs 1957.   [25] Nordhaus 1975. Cf. Hibbs 1987; Alesina and Rosenthal 1996.

Whether or not there really is a political business cycle is a much-debated issue. It may well be that that argument presupposes more capacity than governments actually have to fine-tune the economy in just those ways. But whether or not that particular phenomenon is real, the example none the less serves as a useful illustration of how the unreflectiveness of voters might evoke analogous misbehaviour among politicians attuned to them, thus infecting the whole political process.

The Project

Mass political preferences might be unreflective in several respects. They might be *ill-considered*: half-baked, knee-jerk, top-of-the-head, not thought through. They might be unreflective in the connected sense of being *narrow*. Among the things that unreflective agents might have failed to think through are the full ramifications, either for themselves or others, either for the short term or especially the long term.

Here I shall be attempting to identify deliberative democratic methods for evoking more *reflective preferences* as inputs into the political process. Properly crafted deliberative processes can produce preferences which are more reflective, in the sense of being:

- more *empathetic* with the plight of others;
- more *considered*, and hence both better informed and more stable; and
- more *far-reaching* in both time and space, taking fuller account of distant periods, distant peoples and different interests.

The key innovation I shall be offering is, in the first instance, a theoretical one. What is required is a new way of conceptualizing democratic deliberation—as something which occurs *internally*, within each individual's head, and not exclusively or even primarily in an interpersonal setting. It happens in interpersonal settings, too, of course. Indeed, that is a central plank in my argument on this score. The philosophy of mind and language teaches us that, even in face-to-face conversation, much of the work in making sense of what the other is saying to you goes on inside your own head. You have to imagine yourself in the place of the other in trying to decode what she seems to be trying to tell you.[26] If that is what goes on in ordinary interpersonal discussions, then the same sort of mentally imagining oneself in the place of others might

---

[26] These philosophical propositions, discussed more fully in Ch. 9 below, are broadly corroborated by social psychological research (Krauss and Fussell 1996; Chaiken *et al.* 1996).

well occur in the absence of any actual other. A suitably informed imaginary might serve the same internal-discursive purpose.

Seeing democratic deliberation as being inevitably a largely internal mental process—and potentially more so still—we are led to see as democratically more central than we might otherwise have done a wide range of political arrangements designed to inform the political imagination.

- *Cultural* institutions and policies matter. Harriet Beecher Stowe's *Uncle Tom's Cabin* famously helped people imagine what it might like to be a slave, thus fuelling the Abolitionist movement, and E. M. Forster's *Passage to India* likewise helped Britons imagine what it might be like to be a colonial subject, encouraging sympathy with demands for decolonization.[27] The power of modern media is surely as great, or greater, than the power of traditional literary forms in this regard.
- Policies and institutions that facilitate *social mixing*—having people whose social circumstances are radically unlike your own living nearby, going to school with you or your children, riding public transportation alongside you—can again serve as an aid to the political imaginary. It is inevitably easier to project yourself into their place if you observe them at close quarters over a protracted period, and that might be true even if you know little more than what you observe through casual interactions.
- *Consultative* procedures, even of an apparently toothless sort, could also actually have far more democratic bite than we might ordinarily suppose. Members of committees which are obliged to read other people's submissions, even if the members of those committees are empowered then to ignore those submissions, might find themselves 'putting themselves in the place of the other' and being more responsive to the petitioner's concerns than we might expect from the power relations inscribed in those formal rules of procedure.[28]

---

[27] From the ordinary deliberative democrat's perspective, perhaps, 'storytelling' of this sort is 'just another form of communication'. ('Communication' is a sufficiently expansive category that perhaps everything is.) The point here is just that virtually no face-to-face interaction was required for these stories to have had the power they did.

[28] Scandinavian procedures of this sort are discussed more fully in Ch. 8 below. See similarly Taylor's (1984) account of how being forced to fill out Environmental Impact Statements makes the US bureaucracy more environment-conscious, or Risse's (1999) discussion of how discursive engagement alters the behaviour of renegade regimes violating human rights of their citizens.

Precepts of Reflective Democracy

The main message of my model, and its main differences from more traditional models of democracy, might be encapsulated in a few brief precepts, which will be illustrated and elaborated over the course of this book.

Inputs Matter, Not Just Outputs

Hard-headed political realists teach us to look behind the homilies and pieties, the myths and illusions, of politics. They tell us to focus on the 'bottom line'—on the actual outputs of the political process, on 'who gets what, when, how'.[29]

Everyone knows that inputs matter too, of course. But the way they matter is standardly supposed to be through their impact on outputs. In systems models of political life, the political system is depicted as 'transforming' inputs into outputs. In standard 'systems theories' of political science, inputs are used to 'explain and predict' outputs.[30] In practice, political activists deploy their inputs so as to 'evoke' their desired outputs. In all those ways, inputs are clearly seen to matter, but in a purely derivative way. They matter, but only because they matter to the outputs. The ultimate focus in all those exercises remains on the 'bottom line', just as political realists would want.

Standard democratic theory lifts our focus above the bottom line, by a bit. It tells us to be concerned with process and procedure, not merely with substantive outcomes. Getting the right answer in the wrong way (for example, having a dictator impose by *fiat* exactly the same law which would have been enacted through free and fair democratic procedures) is not something that democratic theory would ever endorse.

Democratic proceduralism focuses on how inputs are processed, once they have been put into the political system. Moving a step or two further back, yet again, democratic theory also often raises questions about where the inputs came from (insisting, for example, that everyone affected should be able to have a say) and sometimes raises questions about the quality of those inputs (insisting, for example, that inputs should be tolerably well-informed).

True enough, all that can be found somewhere or another in received democratic theory. But it is, I think, fair to say that the further you move back from the bottom line, the less central those issues are to

---

[29] Lasswell 1950.   [30] Easton 1965.

democratic theory as we have come to understand it. Thus, ordinary democratic theory regards it as absolutely essential that everyone's input (vote) gets counted in democratic aggregations, and almost as essential that everyone affected should get to have input (a vote). Upon what basis people vote, however, is usually regarded as their own business, not a proper concern (anyway, certainly not a central concern) of democratic theory. Democracy is supposed to take people's votes as given, and simply aggregate them fairly into some overall social choice. So too, it is typically supposed, with democratic theory itself.[31]

Not so, say I. One of my central arguments in this book is that inputs themselves can be more democratic or less democratic. To the extent that people practise 'democratic deliberation within', their own inputs will encapsulate the concerns of many other people as well. A person who has internalized the perspectives of others, balancing them with her own, will have already partially performed the bottom-line democratic aggregation inside her own head. Her own input will therefore be 'more democratic', even just in the standard vote-aggregating sense of the term.

The more general point is just this. Democratic theory is not really being true to its own primary concerns when it is sucked by political realism into an exclusive focus on the 'politics of the bottom line'. Realpolitik is not democratic theory, however important it is for democratic theory to be realistic. The bottom line is not the be all and end all, from a democratic perspective.

Thoughts Matter, Not Just Acts

This fixation on the 'politics of the bottom line' leads us not only to focus on outputs to the exclusion of inputs. It also leads us to focus substantially on the 'end stages' of the political process—voting, and the aggregation of votes into electoral outcomes.

That has been true of political scientists ever since the behavioural revolution swept the last century. Psepheologists study 'the vote' as the one hard political datum available to political scientists. Students of political behaviour treat 'how people vote' as the principal piece of political behaviour to be explained. Students of electoral systems take the rules for aggregating votes into electoral outcomes as their prime locus of concern.

---

[31] 'Deliberative democrats' being the exception, here, given their emphasis upon how discussion is supposed to winnow and reshape preferences (Sunstein 1991).

In fixating in these ways on 'the simple act of voting', political scientists are not alone. In many ways, they thereby mimic long-standing concerns of democratic theory itself. Voting has long been regarded as the consummate act of democratic citizenship. For literally centuries, extending the franchise was the great democratic project. 'Free and fair elections' remain among its greatest contemporary aspirations. An inclusive franchise and regular elections are rightly regarded as *sine qua non* of liberal democratic politics worldwide.[32]

All of those are undeniably indispensable elements of democratic rule. All of my discussions presuppose them; none of my mechanisms can claim any democratic legitimacy without them. But fixating in such ways on those simple acts of voting and aggregating votes can blind us to important cognitive processes that precede and shape those ultimate political acts.

Students of political behaviour, of course, offer rich explanatory accounts of the socio-psychological determinants of people's votes. But those tend to be causal accounts, empirical in orientation and often ill-suited to addressing (except negatively[33]) the normative concerns of democratic theory in consequence. Clearly, that is not true of all such accounts; and some studies do indeed examine the behaviour of the reasoning voter in light of the requirements of normative theory.[34] While empirical political scientists have occasionally gone some way towards accommodating their studies to the requirements of normative democratic theory, democratic theorists themselves have often remained largely aloof from the enterprise of examining the processes preceding the all-important bottom-line processes of casting and counting ballots.

Here I shall try to refocus democratic theory, at least in part, on processes preceding the vote. More unconventionally still, I shall be concerned primarily with the processes that occur within the heads of individual voters, rather than within the formally political realm. Various elements of the democratic process (free speech, free association, free entry of new parties, and such like) have always been regarded as essential elements of the democratic competition. What are less often noticed, and to which I shall here direct most of my attention, are the more 'internal reflective' concomitants of democratic political discussions.

---

[32] Gastil 1991.   [33] After the fashion of Converse (1964).
[34] Page and Shapiro 1992; Marcus and Hanson 1993.

Premises Matter, Not Just Conclusions

Deliberative democracy is standardly contrasted with 'aggregative democracy'.[35] Political realists advocate a 'politics of the bottom line' in the sense of focusing on outcomes of the political process, 'who gets what, when, how', and on votes as primary determinants of that. Aggregative democrats practise a slightly different 'politics of the bottom line', yet again. They ask us to focus on each voter's *own* bottom line, and not to look beyond that. The bottom line, for each voter, is her vote. That represents her overall conclusions, her all-things-considered, summary judgement of what should be done, politically. Aggregative democrats take each voter's vote as given, and then proceed to aggregate all those votes into some collective decision.

When deliberative democrats complain about 'aggregative' forms of democracy, their complaint is usually aimed at the mechanistic meat-grinder aspect of the aggregation of votes into collective decisions. 'Adding is not reasoning', the slogan goes. Merely counting votes is a poor substitute for deliberating together about what really is the right thing to do.

That is an important point. But the problem is not just what gets overlooked in the process of aggregating votes—what gets lost in the internal workings of the political adding machine, as it were. The problem is equally, or more, what is necessarily sacrificed in rendering people's opinions suitable for entering into that adding machine in the first place.

The logic of aggregation requires simple, fixed points that can then be processed. Aggregation eschews messy arguments. What it wants from each of us, by way of an input, are our own clear conclusions. Different people's conclusions differ. That is why an aggregation procedure is required to render a determinate collective decision. But in reaching such a decision through processes of aggregating, aggregations are performed on people's bottom-line conclusions—their votes, not their reasons.

Here is another way of putting the contrast. The ordinary deliberative-democratic objection is that aggregative democracy does a disservice to persons, of roughly the same sort that critics of utilitarianism complain about in terms of its failing to respect the 'separateness of persons'.[36] Merely adding up the numbers on each side of the question is a crass way of going about things. The further objection here in view is that, beyond that, aggregative democracy does a disservice

---

[35] Miller 1992; Dryzek 2000: 5.   [36] Rawls 1971: sec. 30.

to arguments themselves. By fixating on each person's bottom-line conclusions, and coming to a collective decision on the basis of operations performed on those alone, aggregative democracy ignores the reasoning that led people to their conclusions.

That is a mistake, too, importantly different from the first. Premises matter, not just conclusions. Democrats trying genuinely to respond to one another need to ask not merely *what* people want, but *why*. What they are asking, through that further question, is not for some psycho-social explanation but rather for people's self-conscious rationales.

Democratic theorists need to ask that further question, in the first instance, simply in order to come to some sensible plan of joint, collective action that will accommodate the real concerns of all. They also need to ask that question in order to decide whether other people's preferred action plans really best serve their own expressed concerns. Democrats would not launder preferences lightly. But there are sometimes compelling reasons to suppose that that can and should be done, in good democratic faith.[37]

The Mute Matter, Not Just the Vocal

Deliberative democrats have been stung by the criticism that what they are advocating is essentially just a 'seminar room' model of democracy or, worse still, the democracy of a 'gentleman's club'.[38] In response, they have begun explicitly embracing 'unruly' forms of democratic contention.[39] Shouting and rioting, breaching the law and breaking windows, are all now to be seen as potential contributions to deliberative democratic processes.

At the same time as enfranchising the unruly, however, we ought also spare a thought for the mute.[40] The proposition is familiar, in certain standard connections. Silence does not necessarily betoken consent, consent theorists learnt to their chagrin. Regimes derive no legitimacy from abstentions, dictators keep learning to their cost.

What I have more in mind here, however, are not those who are mute by choice but those who are mute by something approaching necessity. Among them are the 'socially excluded' within our own societies. Some of them (aliens, the homeless) are officially denied

---

[37] As argued in Ch. 3 below, and other places before (Goodin 1986, 1991).

[38] Sanders 1977; Dryzek 2000; ch. 3.

[39] Young 2000: ch. 2; 2001; Dryzek 2000: ch. 4; Estlund 2001.

[40] Which is to say, it is important to 'listen' (Bickford 1996)—even to those incapable of speaking.

a vote. And even where they are formally enfranchised, the socially excluded typically lack the social wherewithal to give effective voice to their concerns.

Proceeding up the scale of the 'necessarily mute', foreigners have no voice or vote within our political community, however much they might be affected by our actions and choices. They lack a vote simply by virtue of the standard, place-based criterion of citizenship. Pragmatically as well as legally, those who are most in need of a voice—those who are most adversely affected by our actions and choices—are all too often least well situated to register their concerns with us. Action at a distance (our harming them) turns out to be considerably easier in the modern world than voice at a distance (their complaining effectively to us about those harms).

Future generations are perhaps the paradigm case of the 'necessarily mute'. They will clearly be affected, for better or worse, by the current generation's actions and choices. But being as yet unborn, they are unavoidably incapable of giving voice to their own concerns in our current deliberations.

The same is equally true of other non-human interests, in so far as non-humans can have interests at all. That is a contentious issue, perhaps; and it is beyond the remit of the present book to argue it at any length. But suppose that at least certain sorts of non-human primates, and possibly even a wide range of animals and ecosystems, do indeed have interests. And suppose (as seems all too likely) those interests, if interests they are, will indeed be affected by our community's actions and choices. Again, those interests deserve a seat at the table, from the perspective of any democratic theory that allocates seats at the table on the basis of affected interests. But again, non-human agents are necessarily mute, incapable of coming to the table and directly communicating their own concerns to us.

Supposing that all those mute interests deserve a hearing, my model of 'democratic deliberation within' seems clearly better equipped than any alternative democratic procedure to give them provide that. It is undeniably hard to imagine ourselves into the place of a homeless person or a Kurdish peasant, much less into the place of an orangutan or of people a thousand years from now. Still, imperfect though our imagination might be, we will almost certainly be more successful in our imaginings than such agents would be in speaking for themselves in the councils of state. Thus, I claim that my model of 'democratic deliberation within' is better able to accommodate mute interests than is the standard model of deliberative (still less any other sort of) democracy.

The Plan of Action

All of those propositions are developed and defended in the later chapters of this book. Before coming to them, however, there is a pair of necessary preliminaries to which I must first attend. Both derive from the fact that my model of 'democratic deliberation within' is essentially a preference-based model of liberal democracy, with all the baggage that that entails.

First, models of liberal democracy like mine crucially presuppose that people's preferences are substantially 'autonomous'. Individuals are basically regarded as independent and autonomous agents of the sorts discussed in Chapter 2. Were they otherwise—were strong communitarian claims correct, and were individuals purely artefacts of their communities—the nature and task of democracy would take a very different and more collectivist form.

Thus, one necessary preliminary is to defend the autonomy of individuals' preferences against communitarian claims to the contrary. Chapter 2 is devoted to sorting out what is true and attractive, and what is implausible and unattractive, in communitarian claims to the contrary. My conclusion there is that those elements of the communitarian critique which are true and attractive are perfectly compatible with individual preferences displaying the sort of autonomy that my larger model requires; and those communitarian claims which would be incompatible with my model are implausible or undesirable, anyway.

Secondly, models of liberal democracy like mine presuppose that people's preferences carry a substantial measure of 'authority'. They require us to take a respectful attitude towards the preferences and perspectives of one another. Were we not—were people's preferences devoid of any authority—there would be no grounds for the liberal democratic project of ensuring systematic responsiveness of public policy to the expressed will of the people.

But just as not all preferences are completely autonomous, so too are not all preferences completely authoritative. Paternalists have something of a point, just as do communitarians. In sorting out what is true and appealing in the paternalist challenge to the authority of people's preferences, and what is not, it turns out once again that the most compelling challenges can be comfortably (indeed, arguably ideally) accommodated within my larger model of 'democratic deliberation within'.

Here, in a nutshell, is how the argument of Chapter 3 goes. Certainly we ought take seriously what others say they believe and what they say they want. But part of taking them and their claims seriously is actually reflecting on their assertions. It is neither respectful, nor required, nor even permitted by my model for us simply to register which box they ticked on a form (the ballot paper). It is essential to attend to their arguments and reasons, not just to their 'bottom lines'. Reflecting upon others' arguments and reasons may sometimes lead us to conclude that their expressed preferences would ill serve their own aims. Being an indirect and mediated mode of democratic responsiveness, my model of 'democratic deliberation within' is capable of responding reflectively to their aims in this way. That is in stark contrast to the ways in which more traditional models of democratic aggregation would simply take preferences and votes as read, aggregating them unreflectively into a social choice.

Those two chapters thus defend the basic liberal model of preference-respecting democracy against two classic challenges it always has to face. That done, I then turn to the more constructive portion of my argument. My larger aim is to shift more attention towards the internal deliberative aspects of political judgement and action. Those deliberations involve a blend of both facts and values. Political action, like all intentional action, represents a conjunction of beliefs and desires, broadly understood. Democratic politics is essentially a matter of coordinating people's actions, of blending their diverse beliefs and desires or values into collective decisions for joint action.

My model of democratic deliberation thus has two basic elements: beliefs and values.[41] The latter have tended to be much more discussed than the former, with the evaluative component generally eclipsing the cognitive component in previous democratic theory. That seems to me doubly unfortunate. First, it is untrue to much of what political argument is all about. Political disagreements are driven by disputed facts as often as by contested values, and political bargaining is very often of the sort described in Chapter 4: over how we collectively are to proceed in the absence of settled agreement on the facts of the matter.

Secondly, it is unfortunate for democratic theory to ignore issues of facts and beliefs, because democracy has so very much to contribute to resolving those issues. As I show, in one way in Chapter 5 and in another in Chapter 6, democratically pooling the independent opinions of several agents can be a very powerful device indeed for resolving issues of sheer fact. The views of only minimally competent people,

---

[41] Moral realists may be right in asserting that moral propositions can have truth value, too. But that metaphysical truth, if truth it be, is politically of no assistance: 'even among those who accept the proposition that some views about justice are true and others false, disagreement will persist as to which is which' (Waldron 1999*b*: 3).

when pooled with one another in even just modest-sized electorates, prove rationally compelling.[42]

Were factual disputes all there were to politics, then, there ought rationally be little politics and less dispute. A quick democratic vote usually should rationally settle those things decisively, even in the minds of those who were initially powerfully of some other view.

So why does democratic opposition persist—and why do we think it is right that it should persist—even in the face of decisive democratic majorities? Why is deliberation required, rather than mere aggregation of people's votes?[43] As Chapter 7 suggests, that is principally because issues of fact are intertwined with differences over values. Mechanical aggregation of people's votes should rationally suffice to resolve issues of purely the former sort, but it necessarily leaves differences of the latter sort untouched. To resolve them, mechanisms of some other kind are required.

Coming to terms with others' perspectives in the round—their values as well as their beliefs—is the task of 'democratic deliberation within', as developed in Chapter 9 and illustrated in the other three chapters in that part of the book. The democratic aim is to get people to respond empathetically to others in a wide range of differing social situations. Confronting all those diverse others and coming fully to terms with their beliefs and values cannot realistically be done in person in any actual interpersonal deliberative setting, in any large and extended society. But something like that might be done internally, by populating one's imaginary with exemplars rendered vivid by representations of a literary or artistic or autobiographical nature. Projecting oneself into the place of others, and imagining how the choice would look from their perspective, might then reshape our own 'overall' assessment of the options in turn.

Such exercises can never wholly substitute for mechanical aggregations of people's votes. The latter will remain crucial for democratically legitimating political outcomes. But internal deliberations involving an extended imaginary might serve as a crucial supplement, helping to make the inputs into those mechanical aggregations more genuinely

---

[42] The test of competence is minimal indeed: voters merely have, on average, to be better than 'random' at assessing the facts of the matter correctly. The requirement of size is minimal as well: often a few hundred voters is all that is required to yield virtual certainty; the number of people in a town or small city would virtually always be more than enough.

[43] Grofman 1993: 1582–3. Why do we think that it is better for the constitutionality of an enactment to be determined by Supreme Court justices deliberating over it rather than through a sheer vote on an undebatable point of order raised by a Senator, as can also be done (Tushnet 2001)?

'democratically deliberative', more fully taking account of a broad range of social perspectives. And, as argued in Chapters 10 and 11, 'democratic deliberation within' constitutes the best (and maybe the only) way of taking fully into account the perspectives of all those whose social, biological, or temporal location effectively excludes them from the ordinary political process.

Things Left Undone

My aim in this book is to elaborate my concept of, and arguments for, people's political preferences being made more reflective, and to show how democratic deliberation as an internal mental process might aid in that. In the course of these arguments, I shall be building on various earlier work on how to motivate people to behave morally in politics, helping them to move beyond narrow self-interest to think more seriously about the interests of other people, other times, and indeed other species.[44] In all this, I shall be drawing upon the theoretical and conceptual resources not only of political theory itself but also adjacent fields of philosophy, psychology, and so on.

All this theoretical and conceptual work, however, is only part of what must eventually be a larger task. Theories of this sort obviously need ultimately to be underpinned by, and tested against, evidence of a more *empirical* character. While I shall occasionally allude to empirical evidence in passing, undertaking a full-scale empirical inquiry into these issues must be deferred to some subsequent occasion.[45] Clarifying the basic theoretical issues is task enough for the present book.

Abstract theoretical work also needs ultimately to bridge to some more specific *institutional* recommendations. No doubt part of good government is to get right the relations among all the parts of the

[44] Mansbridge 1990. I have previously attempted to address these issues in various ways in various contexts (e.g. Goodin 1992b, 1996c, 1999b, c; Goodin et al. 1997). I would like to think, but cannot guarantee, that those earlier views are broadly consistent with my present approach.

[45] One way of assessing the extent to which mass political preferences actually are more or less reflective might be to look at the 'time horizon' that they encompass. Unreflective voters of the sort modelled in the literature on the political business cycle are myopic: they vote for or against the party in power, depending just on how things are going around the time of the election itself. Reflective voters, in contrast, would vote for or against the party in power depending on how things went across its entire period in government. Thus, if voters are unreflective, the best predictor of election outcomes ought to be the government's standing in the polls in the immediate pre-election period; if voters are reflective, the best predictor of electoral outcomes ought to be the average of the government's standing in the polls across its entire period in government.

political apparatus, mixing and matching components so they articulate well both among themselves and with the larger social and political environment. But in much larger part, the art of good government must be bottom–up rather than top–down: it must involve the search for institutions which will bring out the best in citizens themselves, encouraging them to encourage their political representatives in turn to take a longer term, more expansive, more considered view of things.

No purely mechanical devices are likely to prove utterly reliable in evoking those more reflective and public-interested approaches to political decisions.[46] Still, there might be ways of organizing large-scale political institutions and practices that facilitate those sorts of conversations, other ways that frustrate them. For a simple example, an agreement to agree (with the terms of the agreement left to later discussions) is a device which is standardly used in intergovernmental negotiations to good effect; and it is a model which might well be generalized beyond that specific context.[47] But fuller development of those institutional-design considerations, too, must be deferred to some future occasion.

[46] Goodin 1996c.   [47] Gibson and Goodin 1999.

Preference Democracy

The model of reflective democracy that I shall be propounding in this book is fundamentally liberal democratic. It assumes autonomous individuals who come together to make some joint decisions. It assumes that those individuals bring to bear independent perspectives of their own which are ordinarily worthy of respect.

Both those assumptions are of course subject to challenge. Communitarians would query the extent to which individuals are independent and autonomous in the way that that model of liberal democracy requires. Paternalists and perfectionists would query the extent to which their own perspectives and preferences really are as worthy of respect as that model of liberal democracy would accord them.

Those are familiar and long-standing disputes within political philosophy. Many books have been written around them. Still, those constitute important foundational challenges to the entire enterprise upon which I am embarked in developing a new variant of liberal democratic theory. So even if I cannot in the context of the present book address them fully, it is only proper that I give some indication at the outset of how I would hope to finesse those issues.

CHAPTER 2

The Autonomy of Preferences

Democracy is first and foremost a matter of making collective decisions. Not only are there different ways of making collective decisions, however. There are also different ways of conceptualizing the collectivity whose decisions those represent.

This book is predicated on a fundamentally individualistic understanding of democracy. The analysis presupposes individuals who are autonomous then coming together to make collective decisions. Democracy, on this view, is essentially a matter of treating those autonomous individuals with equal consideration and respect.[1]

Rival views posit communities as fundamental and individuals as epiphenomenal. Seeing individuals as less autonomous casts collective decision-making in a correspondingly different light: less a matter of merging the views of independent individuals, and more a matter of discovering what is appropriate to the 'true nature' of the pre-existing social entity. Communitarian writers from Rousseau forward have regarded such processes of discovery as the very essence of democracy.

In the midst of the Cold War, that distinction between individualist and collectivist views of democracy marked the ideological divide between the 'liberal democracies' of the West and the 'people's democracies' of the East.[2] Even as that dispute was waning geopolitically, the distinction was reborn within Western political theory through the renewal of communitarian critiques of liberalism. In according primacy to communities over autonomous individuals, those self-styled communitarians also offered a correspondingly 'communitarian' view of democracy as discovering what 'we' want and believe, in

---

[1] In ways that admit of many different specifications: this formulation is obviously intended to be agnostic among the range of possible ways of fleshing out the basic democratic individualist formula. [2] Naess *et al.* 1956.

a sense of 'we' that is intended to be far stronger than that represented by the convergent wills of autonomous individuals within ordinary Enlightenment liberal models.[3]

Accordingly, my first task in this book is to defend the Enlightenment model of social life, and the form of democratic individualism that flows from it, against these new communitarian challenges. I begin by briefly characterizing the sort of notions of liberal autonomy that underlie the Enlightenment model, and counterposing that even more briefly to the new communitarian rivals. I proceed to describe the sort of 'community'—a 'community of interests'—which makes most immediate sense in terms of that Enlightenment model, showing that it is rather more expansive than communitarian caricatures of it might often lead us to suppose. I then go on to discuss various other sorts of 'community' to which new communitarian writing sometimes points. Next I sketch the sort of accommodation that I propose the liberal Enlightenment model can make to those various forms of communitarian challenge, which in my view incorporates all that we need to or should want to of the communitarian model. I then proceed to reapply all this to democratic theory proper, showing what difference these rival understandings of the nature of community make to how we understand democratic deliberation.

Democratic Autonomy: Enlightenment and its Alternatives

The Enlightenment model underlying the liberal theory of human agency is a seductive one.[4] It depicts rational (or anyway reasoning) individuals choosing goals and plans and projects for themselves, with those autonomous individuals then coming together, of their own volition, in pursuit of shared interests and common goals. This founding fiction of the modern social world is well captured in the words one Renaissance writer has God as saying to Adam:

I have given you... neither a predetermined place nor a particular aspect nor any special prerogatives in order that you may take and possess these through your own decision and choice. The limitations on the nature of other creatures are contained within my prescribed laws. You shall determine your

---

[3] The most extended treatment of democratic theory by an unambiguously communitarian thinker is found in Sandel (1996), although many others influenced by this tradition develop similar themes.

[4] The liberal–communitarian debate in political theory finds echoes in the agency–structure debate with contemporary social science. Wendt (1987) has proposed a reconciliation of that latter controversy which is broadly similar to that which I here propose for the former.

own nature without constraint from any barrier, by means of the freedom to whose power I have entrusted you ... I have made you neither heavenly nor earthly, neither mortal nor immortal, so that like a free and sovereign artificer you might mould and fashion yourself into that form you yourself shall have chosen.[5]

From Pico della Mirandola through Kant and the early Rawls, this vision of modern man as a 'sovereign artificer' has reigned supreme throughout mainstream Western moral and political thought.[6]

There have, of course, always been dissenting voices and indeed whole dissenting traditions. From Burke, Vico, and Herder to Hegel and his heirs, a long line of philosophers have tried to put that sovereign artificer firmly in his social place.[7] Within the contemporary carve-up of the social sciences, the whole discipline of sociology was founded with that as its principal motivation and its major continuing concern.[8] Feminists remind us that the 'sovereign artificer' was always principally a model of modern man: women had always been presumed to be 'situated' in a set of social relations (some constraining, others caring) which denied them the independence of a 'sovereign artificer'.[9] Postmodernists more generally tell us that all knowledge—and most certainly knowledge of the self—is socially situated.[10]

Familiar old Hegelian themes have recently been refashioned into a full-dress 'communitarian critique' of liberalism and, through it, of the Enlightenment conception of man as a whole.[11] In place of the socially

---

[5] Pico 1486, at para. 3, pp. 224–5; here I use Hollis's (1981) revised translation of the passage. In a hauntingly unconscious echo of this passage, Sandel (1982: 177) describes the model that his communitarianism opposes in almost identical terms: 'Freed from the dictates of nature and the sanction of social roles, the deontological subject is installed as sovereign, cast as the author of the only moral meanings there are. As inhabitants of a world without *telos*, we are free to construct principles of justice unconstrained by an order of value antecedently given ... And as independent selves, we are free to choose our purposes and ends unconstrained by such an order, or by custom or tradition or inherited status. So long as they are not unjust, our conceptions of the good carry weight, whatever they are, simply in virtue of our having chosen them. We are "self-originating sources of valid claims" ...'.

[6] Kant 1784: esp. sec. 2. Rawls 1971, 1980. Adorno and Horkheimer 1979.

[7] Culminating, latterly, in Taylor 1978, 1989.   [8] Nisbet 1966: ch. 3; Hollis 1977.

[9] Brennan and Pateman 1979; Pateman 1980, 1988; Gilligan 1982; Lloyd 1993.

[10] Ironically, although its opposition to universalizing metanarratives puts postmodernism in opposition to Enlightenment philosophy as a whole, its specifically poststructuralist propositions can equally well be pressed into the service of Enlightenment liberalism's denial that the sovereign artificer's actions and volitions are structurally determined. See e.g. White 1991; Benhabib 1992a; Nicholson 1990; Barrett and Phillips 1992; Bock and James 1992; and Benhabib *et al.* 1995.

[11] I use the term advisedly, on the advice of the feminist critique just canvassed: the Enlightenment conception was indeed a conception of *man*, and man alone.

'unencumbered self' of Enlightenment mythology and Kantian ethics, we are asked to substitute a 'socially embedded' self. In place of the autonomous individual, we are asked to substitute an agent constituted and constrained in important respects by communal attachments and cultural formations.[12]

Liberal democrats can endorse many sorts of community as genuine 'communities of enlightenment'. What cannot be accepted—in the name of enlightenment or the Enlightenment, of liberalism or liberal democracy—is what I dub a 'community of subsumption'. In those sorts of communities, people cease to be sovereign artificers at all; their preferences cease to be autonomous in the ways required by liberal democracy. But those are very special, and especially unattractive, sorts of community which we have independent reasons to want to reject.

Communities of Interests

Let us begin, however, with the standard way in which the sovereign artificers of Enlightenment fantasies—the sovereign individuals of capitalism, the possessive individualists of pre-capitalist formations[13]—might constitute themselves into communities. *Ex hypothesi*, there are no affective sentiments binding them together. *Ex hypothesi*, each is indifferent to the well-being of the other. *Ex hypothesi*, each is pursuing his or her own goals to the exclusion of all else.

Despite their utter indifference to one another in all those respects, such individuals do none the less find themselves embedded in 'communities of interests'. They share certain concerns which can be better pursued jointly than separately. Each finds that others have something s/he wants or needs. Without coordination, they find themselves cutting across one another unnecessarily, or they find themselves missing opportunities for mutually beneficial collaboration.

That story is as familiar as Hobbes and Locke and the Scottish Enlightenment. Sometimes those stories are presented in terms of an overarching social contract;[14] other times they are couched in terms of

---

[12] Sandel 1982, 1984*b*; MacIntyre 1988; Taylor 1989. Michael Walzer, sometimes included among communitarians, constitutes a more ambiguous case, as is evident from his *Thick and Thin* (1994). The general outline of the communitarian argument will be taken as read. It has been reviewed effectively in many other places already, e.g. Gutmann 1985; Kymlicka 1990; Mulhall and Swift 1996; Frazer and Lacey 1993; see also key contributions compiled in Sandel (1984*a*) and Avineri and de-Shalit (1992).

[13] Abercrombie *et al.* 1986; Macpherson 1962; Goodin 1976*b*.

[14] Hobbes 1651; Locke 1690.

more diffuse conventions underlying social institutions or particularized exchange relations.[15] What all those stories none the less have in common is that they all depict a 'community of interests' arising among individuals without any antecedent communal sentiments. Interests, and interests alone, here beget community.

Those are minimal communities, to be sure.[16] People do not care about one another, or about the bonds linking them to one another, except in the most instrumental fashion. Still, contrary to the standard caricature, such a community of interests is not just something akin to a 'spot market', with people collaborating as long as it is in their interests to do so and ceasing to collaborate the moment it ceases to be in their interests. For a start, communities of interest are more stable than that might make them seem. Everyone situated in a community of interests has an interest in that community existing and enduring. It is ordinarily in people's interests to frame their interests in such a way that they can be pursued collaboratively, simply because (thanks to the division of labour) interests which can be pursued collaboratively can usually be pursued further and more effectively. Furthermore, once people have begun interest-based collaboration, it is (thanks to hysteresis and path-dependence) usually in their interests for the collaboration to continue.[17]

In an ongoing community of interests, all participants also have an interest in protecting their own reputations as reliable and trustworthy actors.[18] It is in their interests, narrowly construed, for others to be prepared to include them in cooperative ventures. When involved in interactions, it is in their interests to be trusted to play cooperatively, so others can dare to play cooperatively with them in turn. In a mere community of interests, the value that each attaches to trustworthiness is purely instrumental. One values being trusted oneself, merely because one wants to be included in cooperative ventures on terms that are advantageous. One values being able to trust others, merely because that makes those ventures more advantageous for oneself.

The benefits to self-interested, maximizing agents of acquiring a reputation for reliably reciprocating the actions of others have been famously demonstrated through game-theoretic models and computer tournaments.[19] More conclusively, ethnographic evidence reveals

[15] Smith 1776; Hume 1739, 1777*a*.

[16] In a way even more minimal than many other of Michael Walzer's (1994: ch. 1) 'thin, minimal moralities', not all of which are of a strictly instrumental sort.

[17] Elster 1976; North 1990; Hausner *et al.* 1995.

[18] Goodin 1976*a*; Kreps and Wilson 1982; Kreps 1990; Gambetta 1994*a,b*.

[19] Axelrod 1984, 1986.

those to be standard practices among even the most aggressive max-
imizers of the capitalist economy, ranging from managers of small
businesses to traders on the New York Stock Exchange and the
Chicago Mercantile.[20] As one businessperson explains, 'If something
comes up, you get the other man on the telephone and deal with the
problem. You don't read legalistic contract clauses at each other if you
ever want to do business again. One doesn't run to lawyers if he wants
to stay in business because one must behave decently.' Another says,
more succinctly, 'You can settle any dispute if you keep the lawyers
and accountants out of it. They just do not understand the give and
take needed in business.'[21]

In 'face-to-face' societies, then, ordinary prudence would dictate
behaviour which is substantially indistinguishable from Golden Rule
ethics of a community where all love their neighbours as themselves.[22]
Self-enforcing considerations of reputation and trust evoke cooperative play from the most rational egoist, so long as the group is
sufficiently small and stable for everyone's reputation to be sufficiently
well known to everyone else.[23] Among larger or more fluid groups of
more anonymous players, reputation will obviously count for less and
external sanctions for more. But while in the absence of such sanctions each rational egoist would be tempted to cheat on all others, each
would also welcome a system of sanctions made binding on all. Being
able to open yourself up to being sued for breach of contract is actually
empowering, for without such institutions rational egoists would be
unable to make deferred-performance contracts with one another.[24]
By similar logic, so is all the familiar coercive apparatus of the state
arguably in the interests of broadly prudential egoists.

Most of the other institutions of modern society might, to some
greater or lesser extent, be seen similarly as manifestations of the
need for external sanctions to underwrite mutually rewarding trusting
and trustworthy behaviour in the context of a large and fluid society.
Ranging from secret societies and organized religions to families and
firms and social clubs, many of the most central institutions of modern
society might be regarded as mere communities of interest. That is not

[20] Baker 1984; Leblebici and Salanick 1982.

[21] Macaulay 1963: 61. See, more generally, Granovetter 1985; Goodin 1996e.

[22] It is not that calculative egoism masquerades as high-minded moralism, or that people's
'real' motives there are much more base than they allow. Where prudence and principle
point so consistently in the same direction, the issue of differentiating the motives simply
does not arise—certainly not in any practically meaningful way for agents themselves, and
given that fact it cannot coherently arise for outside commentators on their actions either
(Goodin 1989a; see similarly MacIntyre 1967; Mills 1940).   [23] Laslett 1956.

[24] Schelling 1960: 43; Hardin 1982: 260.

to say that that is necessarily all there is to the story, nor is it to say that that is how people involved in those institutions would necessarily prefer to tell the tale to themselves. It is simply to say that 'community of interest' considerations provide one reason (among many, perhaps) for people to create and sustain such institutions and norms.

In short, much of social life—including many of the things we most naturally describe as our sundry communal attachments—can be analysed on the model of mere 'communities of interests' which would be generated by the Enlightenment's sovereign artificer in even his most self-seeking mode. Which is simply to say: we do not need to assume any great mutual affection to get from there to here. That may have been present, too, and if it was the evolution was no doubt that much easier. But then the outcome would be overdetermined, and 'the' (one true) explanation correspondingly underdetermined.

Other Kinds of Communities

Communitarian critics of Enlightenment liberalism, then, cannot simply say that it neglects community. Clearly it does not. Clearly it offers some account (after its possibly peculiar fashion) for the phenemenon. If self-styled communitarians want to berate Enlightenment liberalism on that score, they have instead to specify what it is about community that is importantly left out of (or misleadingly represented within) that standard Enlightenment account of community as a community of interests.

There is, of course, much that is apparently left out of that account. There are several other senses in which people might be said to be 'members of a community', with correspondingly many different kinds of community following from that. First I shall simply sketch their contours. Then, in the next section, I go on to consider how (if at all) Enlightenment models and liberal democrats might accommodate those other sorts of communities.

Communities of Generation

One of the things that the Enlightenment's model of the 'sovereign artificer' leaves out of its standard account is the simple fact of biological creation, of how we physically got here and how developmentally we came to be agents at all.

Biological facts impinge minimally on Enlightenment models. There is minimal recognition in those models of the facts that we are born and that we die, that we go through a prolonged period of tutelage and that we may go through a parallel period of incapacity in our dotage.[25] The plenipotentiary powers of the Enlightenment's sovereign artificer are clearly reserved for those in their prime and in possession of their full faculties. Those falling short of that ideal find their sovereignty— both their physical capacity and along with it their moral authority— correspondingly diminished on this Enlightenment account.

That in itself is not so bad, perhaps. Many (if not all) of us might be untroubled by a mode of analysis that denies the same standing to the mentally unformed or deranged or infirm as to those who are mentally fully formed, in full possession of their powers and their senses. The problem is not that this model treats children as children, or even that it treats infirm elders as children.[26] The principal problem is that this model gives an inadequate account of how any and all of us get from there to here—proceeding from childhood to fully formed adulthood—and it takes inadequate account of the baggage that we carry with us through that passage.

Our beings are formed in a particular culture. We are taught to think and speak and see; and we are taught from a particular perspective to do so in a particular way. We are shaped by those early experiences. Not in ways that utterly defy reshaping, to be sure: having learned to talk from our parents, most of us learn to talk with others besides our parents; most of us even manage to be more or less multilingual, finding our way around other cultures and strange milieux.[27] Still, where we started matters. It makes some things easier or more natural for us and other things harder. Even if most of us can manage to 'get there', wherever we started, where we started matters. Most things in life manifest 'path-dependence': how you got here, rather than just where you are, makes a difference to where you are inclined to go next.

All of this early childhood socialization takes place in what is recognizably a community, of sorts. It is the smallest and most intimate community of all: the family.[28] Call this a 'community of generation', to emphasize in the first instance its biological roots. But it is of course a community of generations as well, with the primary socializing unit

---

[25] Wolff 1980; Held 1987, 1989.   [26] O'Neill 1988; Goodin and Gibson 1997.

[27] Beattie 1964; Geertz 1973a.

[28] The family, of course, is a paradigmatically multifaceted community—constituting, in the terms of the discussion that follows, a community of meaning and experience and regard (and sometimes even of subsumption), at the same time as playing these biological and sociological roles in generation and socialization. My discussion of the family under this heading is, therefore, without prejudice to its multifarious other roles under those other headings.

characteristically quickly expanding to embrace grandparents and siblings, godparents and honorary aunts, as well as biological parents.[29] Such extended family-like relations are all that some unfortunates ever have. Many of the most fortunate count those as among their most important later childhood relationships.

Everyone, in this sense, has been embedded in a community. Even as we outgrow it, it leaves a mark on us and shapes our subsequent interactions with the world. Every self is encumbered by communal attachments, to at least that degree. It would be plainly crazy to pretend otherwise.

Communities of Meaning

Another related thing that the 'sovereign artificer' model leaves out of its standard account is any appreciation of the fact that some artefacts—among them many of the most central to social life—are socially shared. Far from being the province of any one sovereign artificer alone, they are created by and under the continuing control of the community at large.

The most important of such social artefacts is language itself.[30] There can be no such thing as a 'private language', spoken by one person alone. Not only would one end up talking only to oneself, using such a code. In some sense, one would end up not 'talking' at all: a language, to serve as a language at all, must be interpersonally intelligible.[31] Speakers must share conventions if they are to be able to surmise each other's meanings and to convey their own.[32]

From the simple need for a shared linguistic code to convey our meanings to one another comes much more, however. The language that serves in the first instance as a simple communication device comes to serve other social functions as well. It provides a set of coding categories for our experiences, providing a ready handle for some phenomena and only an awkward one at best for others. Experiences which are easily coded are readily recovered, figuring more centrally in our memory in turn. Language thus serves to filter and bias (or anyway

---

[29] Many of the norms into which families socialize people are themselves in some deeper sense profoundly antisocial, however; see Barrett and McIntosh 1982.

[30] Among the most vociferous advocates of communitarianism on such linguistic grounds is Charles Taylor (1985, 1989).   [31] Wittgenstein 1958: para. 243.

[32] The conventions can be rather loose and open-textured and still perform this function perfectly well. There is no need to take sides in the spat between Derrida and Austin and Searle to feel the larger force of the points being developed here. Cf. Austin 1962; Derrida 1978; Searle 1969, 1983, 1995.

differentially weight) our experiences.[33] And since the language and the coding categories implicit in it are socially shared, everyone's recalled experiences are similarly shaped by it. Selective memories are thus socially shared, shaped by socially shared mechanisms working similarly upon everyone's recollections.

Implicit in a language's coding categories is an explanatory framework. Certain explanatory frameworks are favoured and others disadvantaged by the biases built into those coding categories. The facts which the language's coding categories pick out as central—easily coded, readily recovered—are vested with special significance. No explanatory framework can explain everything. But any explanatory framework, to be minimally satisfactory within that community, must at the very least provide an adequate account of those linguistically central experiences. Other experiences, ones which are marginalized in the language's coding categories, are thereby rendered dispensable in fitting explanatory frameworks to the 'facts' which that community needs to have explained to itself.[34]

Sometimes the 'significance' that language imparts to some experiences rather than others is empirical and scientific in nature. For our basic explanatory models, the facts that 'matter' are (or are taken to be) objective facts about the empirical world. The relative ease with which we linguistically code some observations, and the relative difficulty with which we code others, shapes and biases our perceptions of those objective facts. Therein lies the explanation of how different linguistic communities come to 'see' the world differently.

Beyond all that, however, those coding categories also impart special significance of a sentimental rather than merely empirical sort to certain social experiences and aspirations. They make it easier to communicate, encode, and recall some of those sentiments and experiences and aspirations than others, and those which we can more easily recollect and communicate to one another are the ones which are more likely to come to be shared within the community as a whole.

Not only does language pick out some 'pre-existing' shared sentiments and experiences and aspirations and give them special social significance. Sometimes it actually facilitates their very existence. We could not, individually or collectively, aspire to 'greatness' or

---

[33] This is a familiar point from socio-linguistics, dating from Benjamin Lee Whorf (1956). It is encapsulated philosophically in Wittgenstein's famous phrase, 'the limits of my language mean the limits of my world' (1974: para. 5.6; 1958: paras. 90 ff.). For political applications, see Pitkin 1972; Edelman 1977; Goodin 1980: ch. 3.

[34] This is a special case of the more general analysis of how we fit analytical frameworks to empirical phenomena found in Quine (1961: 42–6).

'integrity' unless there were concepts of greatness or integrity linguist-ically available to us. We could not organize concerted, intentional action in collective pursuit of those goals without some shared notion of such goals that is linguistically accessible to all parties to the project.[35]

The linguistic community thus becomes a 'community of mean-ing', in a variety of senses.[36] Through language, we share conventions about what we 'mean' when we say something. Those shared mean-ings, in turn, help shape shared perceptions and shared intentions. By partly shaping our perceptions of what has happened, coding categories embodied in a shared language help to shape shared interpretations— a shared sense of what certain facts 'mean'. By partly shaping our perceptions of what matters, socially, and the resources available to us collectively for doing something about it, shared linguistic codes similarly help to shape a shared sense of social significance—a shared sense of the 'meaning' of life, individually and collectively. The sharing is never absolute, the shaping of perceptions by language is never more than partial.[37] But its influence is almost always present and is quite frequently strong.

Communities of Experience

There is yet another sense in which the standard interest-based com-munity of the Enlightenment 'sovereign artificer' is unlike our own. The dominant (if, as discussed above not quite correct) image of sov-ereign artificers is as not only free agents but freebooters. They form alliances, but these are typically regarded as marriages of convenience to be abandoned when they become inconvenient. Sovereign artificers are taken to be maximizing at the margin, looking to the future rather than the past. A sovereign, to be sovereign, must have no ties: no ineliminable historical encumbrances, no entangling alliances.

That is not what real people are like.[38] Real people are born, reared, and otherwise linked by shared personal histories and common exper-iences with a range of other people. We live our lives in a social setting; we live them together with other people. The social interactions which we share with them creates a bond between us. That bond may or

---

[35] Skinner 1971; Pocock 1971, 1973.   [36] Geertz 1973*b*.

[37] Goodin 1980: ch. 3.

[38] Nor is it what sovereign artificers in a community of interests are like, for reasons set out above. The qualifications to be introduced here are largely orthogonal to those, however—even though, as I hope to show in the next section, they can be incorporated into the same broader model.

may not carry any affective charge in any larger sense. But at the very least the bond gives rise to a shared personal history. To the extent we were linked with them in that joint venture, their history is ours and ours theirs. Such memories, be they fond ones or feared, are parts of us—and parts which inevitably are shared.

Of course, it is perfectly possible that we might share some history without sharing the same interpretation of it. Each one of us might have a different understanding of what it was that we were doing together. Experiences, to be experiences at all, cannot be just objective facts; to serve as experiences, there must be some subjective appreciation and interpretation of those objective phenomena.[39] By the same token, shared experiences to be fully shared must contain shared subjective frameworks for interpreting shared objective situations.

Here we skirt the deep waters of false consciousness, of reification and mystification. Nothing can be said for certain: or anyway without the certainty of its being challenged. Still, it seems likely that (except perhaps where there are strong interests in thwarting this natural tendency) most objectively shared situations will ordinarily give rise, over time, to subjectively shared appreciations and interpretations of the shared experience. In Marx's inescapable terminology, 'class in itself' almost inevitably sooner or later becomes a self-conscious 'class for itself'[40]—and likewise various other groups sharing common objective circumstances of a non-productivist sort. In so far as people are doing things together in a face-to-face fashion, a self-conscious 'community of experience' with both subjective and objective components will eventually arise, at least in the absence of the intervention of strong interests devoted to thwarting that process.

There is another sense of 'community of experience', however, which points to what might be called 'homologous' rather than literally 'shared' experiences. Here, various people operating at some distance from one another face objectively similar circumstances. But these people are not directly in touch with each other (or anyway not with all others) in objectively similar circumstances. They form 'imagined communities' in which experiences are 'shared' only in an attenuated sense.[41] Let us call this an 'extended' community of experience.[42]

Such communities of experience built upon nothing more than commonalities of objective circumstance have obvious parallels with 'communities of interest' discussed at the outset. Certainly the Marxian

---

[39] Scott 1991.   [40] Marx 1871.   [41] Anderson 1983.

[42] It is 'extended' in the spatial sense, reaching beyond one's immediate social surroundings. It is also 'extended' in the linguistic sense, representing an attenuated usage, a non-paradigmatic case of a community of experience.

analogies—to 'classes in themselves', united by common interests even if they do not, yet, know it—invite that thought. But the convergence is not complete.

Experiences are not strictly equivalent to interests. For one thing, experience is backward-looking whereas interests point forward. Having a past shared history does not necessarily portend a common fate for us far into the future. Furthermore, experiences can be significant things that happened to people (indeed, which shaped their lives) without impinging upon their interests, strictly speaking. We were trapped in an elevator together, or were together on a cruise, or raised children together: all of those are shared experiences which might matter deeply to us, without their necessarily having any effect at all on what we should now do in pursuit of what now matters to us. In this respect, what is true of shared experiences of this face-to-face sort must be all the more true of experiences which are shared only in some extended sense with others whom we have never met.

Consider, in this connection, feminist arguments about the distinctively female 'ethic of care' born of the shared experiences most women have of mothering.[43] What are shared within the 'extended community' to which these shared experiences give rise are not exactly interests, for different carers find themselves in very different positions facing others with very different needs and requiring very different resources.[44] What is shared, instead, is an attitude, an approach to the world, a mindset, a perspective, a standpoint. Those things may shape perceptions of interests. But they are not themselves strictly equivalent to interests, and however strongly they may shape interests they never fully form them.

In other cases, though, these 'extended communities of experience' will often be not all that different from standard communities of interest. Sharing the same objective circumstances often will (probably, if not necessarily) lead us to share (broadly, if not exactly) the same interests. In so far as they do, then whatever is going on in this 'extended community of experience' is perfectly well representable in terms of the more ordinary sovereign-artificer analysis of a community of interests.

As in communities of interest, so too in analogous 'extended communities of experience' there is room for false consciousness about their shared interests. Because people in such communities are not directly in touch with one another, the structural similarities in their objective circumstances might not translate into self-consciously

[43] Tronto 1987, 1993; Ruddick 1980, 1989.   [44] Thomas 1993.

shared subjective experiences at all.[45] Or they might translate into any number of differently construed 'shared experiences', as some people focus upon certain of the structural similarities and other people focus on others as central to their own understandings of the 'experience' that the group is supposed to share.

Such divergent interpretations of shared events are possible even in face-to-face society, of course. But it seems likely to the point of virtual inevitability in the absence of the constraints of face-to-face society. In a face-to-face society the process of ordinary human intercourse obliges us to make moderately stringent efforts to ensure that others' interpretations are tracked by (and track, in turn) our own. There, the constraints of a shared language map into constraints of shared meaning structures and a shared sense of social significance, more generally.

The process of mapping is far from mechanical, and the slippage is often considerable. But even where we disagree over such matters, in face-to-face society we standardly have some shared view as to what it is we disagree about: we have disputes rather than genuine misunderstandings; we talk to, even if sometimes shouting at, one another rather than merely talking past one another. None of that is nearly so necessarily true in more extended communities of a non-face-to-face sort.

Communities of Regard

There is yet another sense in which real people are all members of communities in a way only very partially known to the Enlightenment's sovereign artificer. Call these 'communities of regard', for reasons which will be explained shortly.

This sort of community grows out of the fact that we take certain other people and certain groups as our 'reference groups'. We use such reference groups in various ways. One is as benchmarks in assessing our own achievements and allotments, in determining whether we have done as well as we ought to have done and have got as much as we should have got for it.[46]

One of the reasons our standing relative to others might matter to us has simply to do with the logic of relative power. In the struggle for scarce goods which many desire but not all can obtain, relative resources are what count. What determines the allocation of scarce goods is not one's absolute quantum of resources (wealth, status, or power) but rather how much one has, and is willing to commit to that

---

[45] That is at least one way in which 'alienation' of labour was supposed to work according to the early Karl Marx (1844).   [46] Merton and Kitt 1950; Dahrendorf 1958.

quest, relative to others with whom one is competing for the scarce goods in question.[47] That, however, is something which would be well recognized by sovereign artificers of the standardly calculating sort. Reference groups, understood merely as competitors, are a kind of 'negative community' which sovereign artificers of the Enlightenment could well comprehend.

There is another side to reference groups which is not captured by this story about objective interests in competitive settings, though. Reference groups not only fix one's external standing but also shape one's internal assessments.[48] The standards of a reference group are internalized by those who take that group to be their point of reference. One supposes one should have done as well as one's peers; and if one has not, one feels shame or chagrin for that failing. All that is in addition to the dread that comes from knowing, as simple sovereign artificers might, that those disparities are subsequently bound to be multiplied in the competition of life.

Connected to that fact is a further one. Reference groups serve as sources of standards as well as of benchmarks. One internalizes not only one's group's standards of how well one ought have done but also one's group's values: its sense of what it is to have done well. One values oneself in its terms, through its eyes. Self-regard is a function of social regard, or at least of the regard that that part of the social world which one takes to be one's reference group.

Sometimes those reference groups are embraced self-consciously, in good sovereign-artificer fashion. When first joining clubs or covens, universities or unions, we knowingly and willingly submit ourselves to the judgement of others in those groups; and, if we are acting in good faith in doing so, we internalize their judgements as our own. Other times, though, we acquire our reference groups accidentally, unintentionally, sometimes even unknowingly. One's very first reference group—one's parents—is like that. So too are many of the other reference groups we acquire over the course of life. Among them are classmates, neighbours, friends, workmates. Also among them are the race or nation or church or social class into which we were born.

Ordinarily we internalize and apply their standards without thinking much about it. When challenged, we might reconsider; when reconsidering (or rather considering for the first time) those received views, we may find ourselves appalled or approving. Most of the time,

---

[47] Goodin and Dryzek 1980; Sen 1983.

[48] This is the basis for the defence of the rights of cultural membership in Kymlicka (1989: esp. ch. 8; 1995: esp. ch. 5). See similarly Tamir 1993.

though, we apply our reference groups' standards fairly unreflectively. This, obviously, is far from 'best practice' for sovereign artificers. Even if they do not assess their reference groups before joining, presumably good sovereign artificers should at least assess their groups' pronouncements before internalizing them. In so far as people ordinarily do not, to that extent they depart once again from the Enlightenment ideal.

Communities of Subsumption

Finally, there is the sort of community in which we can literally lose ourselves. People there define their own identities by reference to the group and evaluate their own accomplishments in light of it, its aspirations, and its valuations. In this stronger sort of community, people merge their own identities with—to the point of submerging it beneath—that of the group.[49]

There are some groups and institutions which demand precisely that sort of 'subsumption' of self. These are what Coser calls 'greedy institutions', what Goffman calls 'total institutions'.[50] Examples range from monastic orders to military brigades, from asylums to boarding schools. What all these sorts of institutions demand is not just loyalty in any conventional sense. They lay claim not just to their member's allegiances but to their souls, to their 'whole selves', in some sense or another. And there clearly are some sorts of individuals who want to be so subsumed, 'true believers' who happily align themselves so completely and so unquestioningly with their group or their cause as to lose any trace of their own personality in just this way.

That there are such communities and people keen to submerge themselves in them is undeniable. But these are not our standard communities. They are the communities not so much even of the commune or the kibbutz as of the cult.[51] They constitute the limiting case, well beyond the bounds of what the most dedicated communitarian would commend to us as being in any sense an ideal community.[52] Some communities undeniably take these forms, and they are undeniably communities by any reasonable definition of the term. But communities such as these clearly constitute distopias, not utopias.

There are of course certain circumstances in which such social forms may sometimes be socially necessary. Arguably that is so in the paradigm cases of armies and mental asylums, but even there their

---

[49] My objection is in the first instance to people doing so, in the second to communities which enable and encourage them to do so.

[50] Goffman 1961; Coser 1974; see also Foucault 1975.   [51] Kanter 1972.

[52] Cf. e.g. Etzinoi 1993.

necessity is disputable. And if necessary, they are even there to be counted as unfortunate necessities.

Accommodating the Communitarian Critique

How then can champions of the Enlightenment model of politics and morality respond to the communitarian challenge, thus disaggregated?

Let us begin by recalling the various ways, discussed above, in which the classic Enlightenment 'community of interests' can be extended beyond its most crassly calculating roots. Enlightened self-interest dictates far more adherence to communal norms, far more reciprocity, and far more mutual respect—even in the service of ultimately narrowly egoistic concerns—than one might intuitively suppose. Let us also recall that the self of the Enlightenment's sovereign artificer might be interested in all sorts of things (be they people or principles, causes or communities) that range well beyond narrow egoism, standardly construed. Enlightenment artificers are strictly obliged to take on board the former sorts of considerations of enlightened self-interest, and they certainly are permitted by Enlightenment logic to let their interests range far beyond narrow self-interest.

Communitarian critics of the Enlightenment model are looking for something beyond any of that, however. Their talk of communities of generation, or meaning, experience or even of regard, points to something that stands above and before any calculation of enlightened self-interest. Communitarians themselves would phrase this in terms of the social construction of identity, of the communal 'sources of the self'.[53] Whereas the Enlightenment fiction is that sovereign artificers make communities, the communitarian emphasis is upon the various ways in which communities make individuals: literally, in the case of communities of generation; figuratively, in communities of meaning, experience, and regard.

In the end, though, all those propositions turn out to be almost puns or metaphors, asked to bear more weight than mere metaphors can reasonably be expected to sustain. Biologically, each 'individual' is made by a 'community' of two others—but to seize upon that as evidence of communities 'making' individuals is akin to the facile attempt to assimilate feminism within orthodox Marxism by pointing out that reproduction is just a form of production like any other.[54] Sociologically and psychologically, individuals acquire their orientation in the

---

[53] Taylor 1989: pt. I.   [54] Barrett 1980; Hartmann 1981.

world from and in relation to other individuals, who themselves stand in some previously negotiated relation to one another—but even when those pre-existing groups are deliberately organized to shape the next generation (as are teachers or preachers), what they do in pursuit of those objectives can only in the most metaphorical way be assimilated to the activities of a group of farmers 'making' a barn together.

Most of those activities involved in communities 'making' individuals amount, more, to 'influencing' and 'imparting'. What we acquire from others, particularly as newcomers and youngsters, are a range of assets and resources, facts and values, ways of seeing and ways of thinking, habits of thought and of action, understandings and interpretations. All of this, I submit, involves 'enlightenment' of an absolutely standard Enlightenment sort. All these mechanisms are ways of finding out about the world in which we will subsequently have to take our place.

Enlightenment artificers are sovereign, but they are neither omnipotent nor omniscient. Their not being omnipotent leads them to enter into agreements, make exchanges, and form coalitions with one another: to create communities of interest. Their not being omniscient leads them to exchange information, in the broadest sense, with one another: to create what I shall call 'communities of enlightenment'.

The information exchanged in such communities has many aspects. In its broadest sense, information consists not just in facts but also in interpretations of those facts, frameworks and schemata, webs of belief, ways of 'knowing how' as well as 'knowing that', and so on.[55] In its social sense, information necessarily concerns values as well as facts, normative expectations, rules, codes of conduct, honour, and rectitude. Minimally, communities impart information to their members about what people expect from one another within such communities.[56]

Much, if not all, that communities of meaning, of experience, and even of regard are doing might be conceptualized as imparting or exchanging information of these various sorts. That is not all they are doing, perhaps; this way of looking at them may be somewhat at odds with their own self-conceptions. Upon reflection,

---

[55] Ryle 1949: ch. 2; Polanyi 1958.

[56] Whatever truth status moral propositions can themselves aspire to, in any larger sense, what moral code prevails in any particular community is itself purely a matter of fact. It is an undeniably true fact about any particular community that its members expect one another to behave according to certain well-defined rules and that they will be judged, and rewarded or punished, accordingly. Whatever our metaethics, we can none the less talk sensibly about normative 'information' of this at least minimal sort being communicated within communities.

though, it seems that most of the things that those communities are doing can be accommodated more-or-less comfortably within this framework.

It might be said, for example, that communities of meaning and experience impart a sense of *significance* to certain things that this bare information-processing model cannot capture. But significance can be easily enough translated in terms of 'centrality to one's belief system'— as something which is nearer the core of Quine's 'web' of analytic and synthetic beliefs about the world, for example.[57] Or significance can be translated in terms of 'facts that prescriptively engage people', in terms of whatever 'logic of appropriateness' conventions govern the workings of the groups within which they find themselves.[58] Talk of 'information', expanded to include interpretive frameworks and prescriptive implications as well as bare facts, thus seems sufficiently capacious to accommodate notions of 'significance' of a recognizably sociological or psychological sort.

Or, again, it might be said that communities of regard impart a sense of *affection* and *respect* which is hard to cash in terms of bare information alone. That is undeniably true. What people enjoy, when they enjoy the high regard of others, is not itself information. But how it is that they know that they enjoy that regard, and how they come to know how to get it, can indeed be talked about in terms of information flows. A community of regard consists not just of a group of people who all have certain attitudes towards one another; it consists, more importantly, of a group of people who communicate certain attitudes to one another. And it is in modelling this crucial process of communicating our regard for one another that notions of information-processing come into their own.

Finally, it might be said that this information-processing model of communal attachments does not capture the *narrow-mindedness* of closed communities in the real world. But, again, an implicit Bayesianism goes a long way towards capturing that phenomenon, too. What fits people's preconceptions—their previous experiences and their pre-existing categories for interpreting them—people can relatively easily take on board. Evidence that does not fit their preconceptions is more likely to be dismissed as misleading (fantasy, fable, fib, or fiction). That is a process familiar from all corners of social life,

---

[57] While no proposition is utterly immune to revision, on Quine's (1961: 43–4) analysis, some are clearly more central in the sense that their revision would have wider ramifications and require more extensive revisions in other propositions if they were themselves to be revised.   [58] March and Olsen 1989: esp. ch. 9; 1995: esp. ch. 2.

from the way we process reports of miracles to the way we assess the impact of educational reforms.[59]

All of that is perfectly rational, at least on the assumption that our experiences are a random sample of all possible experiences and on the assumption that our interpretive schema is the one best fitting the facts thus presented. But the inevitable consequence is that closed communities—groups of people sharing many of the same experiences and much the same framework for interpreting them—will perfectly rationally be different from one another in the way they see the world.

Therein lies much of the case for 'feminist epistemology', born of the characteristically different experiences of women.[60] Therein lies the explanation for the very different reactions of whites and blacks to O. J. Simpson's acquittal, born of the very different experiences the two races have of the probity of American police.[61] Therein lies the explanation for the very different stances of the poor and rich towards redistributive politics, born of their very different experiences of the relative workings of luck and effort in economic markets.[62]

Therein also lies the explanation of much intergroup strife. Different groups, with characteristically different experiences and different ways of interpreting them, will be more or less dismissive of one another's way of seeing the world. And not just understandably but even rationally so: for from the perspective of the facts available to each group, their own framework best fits the facts as they know them; and in so far as other groups' frameworks differ from their own, those other groups are promulgating pernicious error untrue to the facts as they know them. Narrow-mindedness within communities, and disputes among communities, can both be explained in broadly this way.[63]

There may be more, sociologically and psychologically, to communities than can be explained in these ways as rational responses to practical constraints alone. There may be a role for pure sentimentality, over and above any of these rationalistic Enlightenment rationales for group ties among sovereign artificers. Still, if most of the story can be told in these terms—if most of the undeniable facts to which communitarian critics of the Enlightenment model appeal can thus be accommodated in just that sort of model—then the question is simply how much the residual might actually matter.

It is undeniably true that people and peoples sometimes suffer a rush of blood to the head, and much blood is undeniably spilt in

---

[59] Hume 1777b: sec. 10; March 1972; see also March 1976; Schön and Rein 1994.
[60] Harding and Hintikka 1983.   [61] These are matters to which I return below.
[62] Piketty 1995.   [63] Hardin 1993, 1995; Goodin 1997.

consequence of the jingoistic excesses that ensue. But as long as we can accommodate the ordinary effects of social attachments within our universalist moral theories, few of us would be tempted to rewrite moral and political theory around outrages, exceptions, and excesses. A moral theory of the decently encumbered self should be enough. The fanatically immersed self is to be properly regarded as the subject, and object, of psychotherapy.

Contrasting Visions of the Deliberative Community

Facts and interpretations are certainly among the many things that communitarians suppose that members of the same community inevitably share. Indeed, communitarians envisage people sharing them not just passively but actively, in communication and deliberation with one another.[64] Although Enlightenment and communitarian models both provide an account of these processes, the accounts they give of them differ in important ways that set in stark contrast the fundamental differences between the two models.

For communitarians, our attachments are 'constitutive' of the persons we are, in some fairly strong sense. My 'enduring attachments and commitments', Sandel says, 'partly define the person I am'. Without some such enduring commitments and attachments, Sandel says, he would be devoid of character, incapable of friendship, incapable of genuinely reflecting upon who he really is and what he really wants.[65]

So too, for communitarians, are our collective conversations and deliberations partly constitutive of who we are and what we want.[66] Where the Enlightenment model sees conversations among independently constituted interlocutors, who by pooling information and comparing perspectives come to some shared judgements, the communitarian model sees conversations constituting and reconstituting interlocutors who are partly made and remade through them.[67] Where the Enlightenment model sees independent assessors converging on certain facts and values, premises and conclusions, the communitarian model sees interdependent agents constituted at least in part by that which they share in the course of their conversations.

Of course what we are doing when deliberating on political affairs is importantly different than what we are doing when deliberating on

---

[64] Sandel 1996.   [65] Sandel 1982: 179–81.   [66] Sandel 1982: 181.

[67] Thus, in *The Human Condition* Hannah Arendt (1958: 175–81) talks of the 'second birth' which people experience in the political forum, in discovering their true selves through the process of revealing them to one another.

the correct inference from some scientific experiment. In the latter case, we are trying to come to some intersubjective understanding of what happened among some objects external to the deliberating assembly. In the former, we are trying to come to some more deeply shared understanding of what sort of group we deliberators want to be. The subject-matter under discussion makes that sort of discussion necessarily communal in a way the other is not.[68] It necessarily evokes different 'we-oriented' aspects of people's preference functions.[69] All that simply must be conceded by Enlightenment liberals. But in so doing, they are still not conceding what communitarians centrally need for their claims to be true—which is that the communities constitute the people rather than the people constituting the communities.

The Enlightenment's sovereign artificers can, and typically do, have preferences for sociability. Certain sorts of clubs and communities they need to form to advance their own interests; others they want to form to satisfy their other cravings. They can, and typically do, have views about what characteristics they want those groups to display. But in so far as they want, for whatever reason, to form groups, their most fundamental preference in this regard is to do things in and through those groups, whatever characteristics those groups display (at least within certain broad limits). Sovereign artificers, in short, can and typically do have just the sort of 'we-oriented' preferences that are on the table in political discussions of the loftiest sorts.

The difference between the Enlightenment's sovereign artificer and the communitarian's encumbered self in this regard lies not in the capacity to express such 'we-oriented' sentiments but rather in the standpoint from which such sentiments are expressed. The sovereign artificer stands partially apart from the 'we' in question, constituting an independent locus of value and judgement to be blended with others to form the 'we' in question. The encumbered self, in so far as it is constituted by the attachments that constitute the 'we', is naturally subsumed within it.

Thus, while both Enlightenment and communitarian models provide for information transfer and value alignment among members of a group, there are important differences in what each envisages as going on in those processes of transmission and alignment. Where the Enlightenment sees sovereign artificers deliberating from a number of independent perspectives, the communitarian sees embedded selves in communion with one another. Where the Enlightenment sees the

---

[68] Beiner 1983: 138–9.   [69] Sagoff 1988, 1994.

exercise of independent judgement, the communitarian sees revelation and the incantation of shared sentiments.

Deliberative democrats similarly hope to construct or reconstruct our political community, via free public discussion.[70] This project of civic renewal is, in its dominant mode, much more an Enlightenment than communitarian one, however.[71] It starts, *ex hypothesi,* from a situation where community attachments are weak and individuals are not adequately embedded in civil society. The deliberative democratic project is to bring those unconnected individuals together, through the medium of public discussion, to form a more coherent whole. But in this process, it is the individuals who will be forming the whole rather than the other way around.

Individuals are 'transformed' in the process of deliberation, to be sure.[72] In part that is because they have to recast their arguments and appeals in ways that get a grip on others.[73] In part, it is just because of the broadening of horizons: when people start talking to one another in ways they used not to do, it is no surprise that they are exposed to new facts and new perspectives.[74] Both of those influences, however, are easily accommodated with the extended Enlightenment model of a sovereign artificer. Neither of them make interlocutors in civic republican dialogues look remotely like communitarian souls who are literally constituted by their interactions in the discursive community.

The two contrasting models of what goes on in a deliberative community—the Enlightenment model of people coming to terms with one another, contrasted with the communitarian model of people reconstituting one another—represent in miniature the larger contrast between the Enlightenment and communitarian models of social life as a whole.

In the Enlightenment model, independent agents come together to talk. What they say to one another matters. It is capable of influencing them, of changing their minds. But it is none the less a case of independent agents interacting with one another, in some meaningful way.

In the communitarian model, agents lose whatever independence they ever had when they come together to talk. They subsume themselves within a discursive community. In the process, what people do

---

[70] Manin 1987; Cohen 1989; Sunstein 1988, 1991, 1993*a,b*, 1996*b*, 2001.

[71] Some self-styled 'civic republicans', such as Sandel (1996) and Selznick (1992), prefer a more communitarian interpretation. But even among civic republicans, the dominant mode is more Enlightenment-liberal-individualist (see particularly the work of Sunstein cited in n. 70).   [72] Michelman 1986; Sunstein 1988, 1991.

[73] Lindsay 1929: 36; Elster 1986*b*; Barber 1984: 171; Goodin 1992*c*: ch. 7.

[74] Pitkin 1981: 347; Sunstein 2001.

is not simply 'influence' one another but rather 'remake' one another. Communitarian conversations end not so much in agreement or convergence as in the remaking of interlocutors in such a way as to deprive them of any independent stance from which to disagree.

That, I submit, is not what most of our conversations are like. Nor, I submit, is it what most of us would like many of our conversations to be like. In so far as I am correct in that, then most of us ought to regard communitarianism as descriptively inaccurate and prescriptively unattractive.

Conclusion: Communities of Enlightenment

Contrary to the claims of communitarian critics, the sort of 'sovereign artificer' posited by liberal Enlightenment theory does not stand wholly outside human society. On the contrary, such agents would find themselves situated in perfectly recognizable communities of various sorts.

However sovereign they may be, truly enlightened artificers would immediately see that they are far from autarkic. They need the cooperation of others to work their will on, and in, the world. To secure that cooperation on a sustained basis and in maximally efficacious ways, they would have to adopt and adhere to social norms of roughly the sorts that communitarian critics standardly claim as uniquely their own. That is the first sort of 'community of enlightenment': a community of enlightened self-interest (and, *mutatis mutandis*, of 'enlightened advocacy' for those of their interests that extend beyond themselves).

Sovereign artificers also inhabit a 'community of enlightenment', in the second sense that they enlighten themselves (they learn facts and fictions, meanings and significance, techniques and values) in and through their associations with others. However sovereign they may be, real actors in the real world are inherently limited in their time and information and understanding. What they have, they have acquired through only through their experiences; and those experiences are ones which are (hardly accidentally, but not exactly intentionally, either) shared with various others. Enlightenment, in this sense, is gained through communities.

Finally, however, enlightenment also serves as a constraint on the kinds of communities that sovereign artificers could sanction. Certain sorts of community involvements are inevitable. Others, while hardly inevitable, are undeniably useful both for finding out about the world and for working one's will on and in it. The sovereign artificers of the Enlightenment would accept the former, and welcome the latter.

What they could not accept, in the name of enlightenment, are community involvements of a sort that gratuitously constrain the sovereign will or that gratuitously constrain the artificer's actions. Sovereign artificers would baulk at participating in 'greedy institutions' (what I have called 'communities of subsumption') precisely because in so participating they would cease to be sovereign artificers at all. They would cease to be democratically self-governing citizens of the sort this book is concerned to discuss.

Thus, while participating happily in all sorts of 'communities of enlightenment', sovereign artificers should, by the same token, strictly limit themselves to 'communities of enlightenment'. Communities of darkness—all-consuming attachments, of the sort which has so powerfully seized the recent world, to one's race or nation or religion— cannot pass muster. But that fact and the reasons behind it seem to tell more powerfully against such communities than against the Enlightenment model itself.

All that seems to provide very solid foundations indeed for liberal democratic theory, predicated as it is on the free interplay of individual wills in shaping as well as being shaped by collective determinations of what we want to do and to be. This seems to me to represent roughly the right kind and degree of individualism and autonomy to characterize a properly democratic community. If the compromises it embodies constitute a departure from the bolder claims of classical liberalism, they do so only in so far as is strictly necessary to accommodate what seem to me undeniable sociological and psychological truths; and they do so only in respects that in no way compromise the deeper moral values embodied in those older traditions. They should, I submit, be seen as friendly amendments to classical liberal democratic theory.

CHAPTER 3

The Authority of Preferences

Varied though they may otherwise be, theories of liberal democracy necessarily have certain things in common. All theories of liberal democracy like mine necessarily rest on Enlightenment premises of individual autonomy, as discussed and defended in Chapter 2. Furthermore, all theories of liberal democracy like mine necessarily require systematic responsiveness to popular wishes, in ways which make them fundamentally 'preference-respecting'. That is the subject of the present chapter.

There are however many different kinds of preferences and correspondingly many different ways of respecting them. Different models of democracy will be better at providing certain sorts of respect for certain sorts of preferences than others. Which model of democracy liberal democrats want to adopt therefore depends on which sorts of preferences they want to accord which sort of respect. The central claim of this chapter is that my preferred model of 'democratic deliberation within' is preference-respecting in the right way, and it therefore deserves a key role in any larger system of democratic accountability.

Respecting Preferences, Not Just Recording Them

Some forms of democracy are purely aggregative, just adding up people's votes. Merely 'registering preferences'—which is what 'tick-the-box' forms of aggregative democracy would have us do—stops well short of genuinely 'respecting preferences'. That has us respecting the mark on the ballot, rather than the person or the reasoning for which it stands.

Liberal democracy ought to take people's preferences more seriously than that. Doing so requires us to make a genuine attempt at understanding what the other is trying to say to us: what the other is asserting, and why. Otherwise, we end up merely 'counting' rather than really 'respecting' their preferences.

Once we step back from the sheer mark on the ballot paper and start probing what might lie behind such superficial expressions of preference, however, the liberal democratic injunction to 'respect people's preferences' becomes more complicated. If the object of our respect is people's reasons rather than brute expressions of their preferences, then it is incumbent upon us to look to people's 'deeper preferences' rather than the 'superficial expressions' they give of them in everyday actions like voting.

Liberal democrats are rightly wary of going too far down that track. They demand some awfully good warrant before agreeing to override people's expressed preferences in this way. Sometimes, however, just such a warrant can be found, grounded in people's own deeper preferences. Paternalism it may still be, but of a peculiarly weak form: we are then not really substituting our judgement for the person's own; we are instead substituting more reliable indicators of the person's own true preferences for less reliable ones.[1]

Such warrants are relatively rare. That fact justifies the traditional liberal democratic prejudice in favour of 'respecting people's preference as stated, no questions asked'. But sometimes such warrants *are* available. When they are, liberal democrats should be—and they are, in the practice of public policy—prepared to override people's expressed preferences in the service of their own deeper preferences. Being prepared to do so, as appropriate, is part and parcel of what it is for liberal democrats genuinely to *respect* preferences, rather than merely tallying them.

In developing these themes, I begin by examining the actual practice of liberal democratic regimes as reflected in public policy. There are clearly some sorts of cases in which even liberal democrats are quite comfortable in practicing paternalism. Reflecting upon those cases, I then adduce some more general principles governing liberal-democratic practices in this area.

Those are principles governing public policy, in the first instance. But I then reapply those same principles, to guide our choice among alternate models of democratic rule, in the second instance. That is to say, having determined what sorts of paternalistic policies liberal democrats want to be able to practise, and why, I then ask what sorts of model of democracy they should choose in order to enable them to do so.

---

[1] Goodin 1995*b*: ch. 8.

Given what it is for liberal democrats genuinely to respect people's preferences, the model of democracy best suited to that task would be one which is reflective rather than unreflective, indirect rather than direct. Conventional models of representative democracy, of a trusteeship sort, fare well on these criteria. So too does my model of 'democratic deliberation within'. A composite model combining the two, as suggested in the final section of the chapter, would best enable us to respect preferences in the ways that liberal democracy ideally should.

Permissible Paternalism

Let us take as our starting point, here, the realization that liberal democrats do not feel invariably obliged to respect all of people's preferences in an absolutely unequivocal fashion. Devoted though they may be to principles of individual autonomy, even the staunchest liberal democrats concede that there are sometimes cases in which it is proper for others to intervene to protect people from themselves, coercively substituting their judgement of what is good for a person for that person's own judgement. Those cases of 'permissible paternalism' mark the limits of liberal democracy's preference-respecting proclivities.[2] From them, we can adduce some more general principles pertaining to what sorts of inputs liberal democrats think they ought to allow into the social decision procedure.[3]

In practice, such discussions usually focus on particular kinds of people or policies as constituting cases where people's preferences may (or must) be overridden. But those are just manifestations of a larger issue that goes to the heart of democratic theory itself, which is as follows. Democracy is standardly seen as being a matter of the being systematically responsive to people's preferences. But in practice (a practice too little theorized) liberal democrats seem to want to draw distinctions among preferences, some of which deserve more respect than others. Which, then, are the preferences responsiveness to which constitutes the standard according to which the system is to

---

[2] Elsewhere I have developed these themes, using smoking as the running example (Goodin 1991).

[3] After the fashion of my earlier arguments in Goodin (1986). There are also 'output filters' denying respect to certain sorts of collective choices. In liberal democracies, for example, decisions representing 'majority tyranny' are blocked by strong constitutional guarantees of individual (and sometimes group) rights and liberties. Such output filters serve merely as side-constraints on the operation of democracy, however: they are what makes the regime 'liberal', not what makes it 'democratic'.

be democratically assessed, and which preferences may (or must) be democratically ignored?

Examples of Permissible Paternalism

The first and clearest case of permissible (indeed, arguably obligatory) paternalism comes in the parent–child relation. Even in this era of 'children's rights' parents retain an obligation to look out for the best interests of their children. Those of tender age and unformed minds are not taken, even presumptively, to be the best judge of their own interests. It is conventionally thought to be perfectly proper for others to act on their behalf, even if (indeed, especially when) that proves to be flatly contrary to the preference, will, and proclivity of the children themselves.

Those others who are thus empowered to substitute their judgement for the children's own are, first and foremost, the children's parents or guardians. The state tolerates interference by parents or legal guardians in the liberty of their wards in ways well beyond those in which it would ever tolerate one person's interfering in another's liberty in general.[4] The liberal democratic state, however, also takes upon itself a certain residual guardianship role in protecting the best interests of the child. The state mandates compulsory education (and compulsory inoculation, typically in connection with that). The state prohibits children from working long hours or in unsafe environments. *In extremis*, the state takes children into care, removing them from the family home and placing them in state institutions or foster homes under state supervision.

It would be wrong to say that the children's own preferences in all of this count for naught. As they grow older, the children themselves are often consulted in all these matters and, within broad limits, their choices are increasingly determinative of outcomes with their advancing years. But especially as regards younger children, and even as regards older children in the making of 'big' decisions, there is virtually no doubt (among liberal democrats, or any others) as to the propriety of other people telling them what they must and must not, may and may not do. Such edicts are invariably, and rightly, justified in baldly paternalistic terms of those other decision-makers' better capacities to judge the true interests of the children in question.

It is indecently easy to justify paternalism *vis-à-vis* children. The reason is simply that they are so clearly unreliable, in so very many

---

[4] O'Neill and Ruddick 1979; Blustein 1982; Feinberg 1986: 325–32.

ways, when it comes to judging their own interests. The very young are typically uninformed, and irredeemably so: they do not appreciate causal connections (or even, when very young, the concept of causation itself), and no amount of explaining will enable them to grasp those connections. The very young are typically incontinent: they are incapable of forgoing present pleasures, however small, for future satisfactions, however large. And so on.

In all these respects, the case of the very young shades into the case of 'incompetents' more generally—the Alzheimer patient, the mentally deficient. What is common to all those cases is a deficiency of basic information-processing abilities. We might hesitate to treat such people, literally, as children. More nuanced treatment of adults who are lacking in ordinary competences might be appropriate, for all sorts of reasons.[5] Still, in so far as we do paternalistically substitute our judgement of what is good for them for their own determinations, we do indeed justify doing so by appealing to much the same grounds as with underage minors.[6]

In the first instance, the paternalistic interveners in question are 'carers', typically family and friends who take it upon themselves to look after the other. Still, adults are presumed to be competent unless courts have declared them otherwise; and no one else is allowed to substitute her judgement for mine unless the courts have awarded her legal guardianship over me. Thus, even in the standard caring relationship, carers can exercise paternalistic authority only on licence from the liberal democratic state. And where there are no family or friends willing or able to care for the person in question, she becomes a direct 'ward of the state'. In one way or the other, therefore, the liberal democratic state is deeply implicated in paternalism *vis-à-vis* the frail old or otherwise incompetent.

Those constitute the core cases of putatively justifiable paternalism. But the more peripheral cases are in many ways more interesting and illuminating. Deficiencies of cognitive capacities are taken clearly to justify paternalism. But so too are cases involving something more like mere deficiencies of the will. That is presumably what mainly underlies

---

[5] Wikler 1979; Feinberg 1986: ch. 26.

[6] Cases of 'medical paternalism' are sometimes related, sometimes not. They sometimes involve physicians substituting their judgement for that of patients who are comatose, incapable of expressing any preferences in the matter either way: that really is a case of substituting rather than overriding the patients' preferences, though; it is paternalism, perhaps, but of a simpler form. Where it is a matter of physicians' overriding their patients' expressed preferences, by treating them with procedures contrary to their religious beliefs for example, it is much more like treating an incompetent. At least this is how the case would have to be justified, if it is to be justified at all (Buchanan 1978).

laws requiring motorcyclists to wear helmets and automobile drivers to wear seat belts, for example. To some extent, of course, the justification for those policies is not paternalistic at all.[7] And to some extent paternalistic intervention in these realms is justified in terms of broadly similar cognitive failures, associated either with faulty processing of information about risks[8] or with failure to internalize those intellectual facts emotionally.[9] But to some extent the justification for seat belt and helmet laws is also couched in terms of volitional rather than cognitive defects. Even where the risks are intellectually and emotionally appreciated, people still sometimes suffer 'weakness of will': they know they should take precautions, but just cannot be bothered to do so.

The same is true in trumps with respect to narcotic drugs, alcohol, or tobacco.[10] To some extent, consumption of these substances is regulated, nonpaternalistically, on account of external effects on others of that consumption (drug-induced crime, drunk driving, passive smoking, etc.); to some extent, consumption is regulated paternalistically on account of consumers' stubborn ignorance, at some level or another, of the harmful effects those substances will have on them. To a large extent, however, consumption is once again regulated paternalistically, more on grounds to do with volitional than cognitive defects. In so far as consumption of these substances is clinically addictive or even just powerfully habit-forming, people cannot (or cannot easily) stop once they have started, and on those grounds policy-makers sometimes paternalistically take steps to prevent them from starting.[11]

Such policies are paternalistic, in the sense that the policy-maker is refusing to allow implementation of the person's own choice for reasons pertaining to that person's own good. They are weakly paternalistic, though, in so far as the policy-maker is appealing to the person's own subsequent choice. A crucial component of the argument here is that most people who start using these substances will at some subsequent point want to stop, but when they try to stop will be unable to do so (which is the World Health Organization definition

---

[7] There are also non-paternalistic arguments in favour of those policies, couched in terms of distress to others or costs to the public health service from the injuries that would otherwise be incurred.

[8] One reason people fail to buckle their seat belts voluntarily, in the absence of legal compulsion, is that they underestimate their chances of crashing by a factor of ten or more (Arnould and Grabowski 1981: 34). Kahneman *et al.* (1982) map various heuristics that wrongly bias people's risk assessments, more generally.

[9] People believe 'it can never happen to them' or underestimate what it would feel like if it did; for details see Goodin (1982*b*: ch. 8) and references therein.

[10] Goodin 1989*b*.   [11] Goodin 1989*b*: ch. 2.

of 'addiction'[12]). If so, then the 'paternalistic' intervention is justified in distinctly nonpaternalistic grounds of the person's own subsequent choices.[13]

Finally, and least familiarly among the range of paternalistic policies, consider a whole raft of 'contracts' that would be deemed legally unenforceable ('because contrary to public policy', as contract lawyers would characteristically phrase it). Primary among these legally unenforceable contracts would be 'slavery' contracts. People are not allowed to sell themselves into slavery, understood as an irrevocable commitment serving in perpetual bondage to the arbitrary will of another.[14] Nor, for much the same reason, do we think that 'suicide pacts' ought to be legally enforceable, even if suicide itself ought to be made legally permissible. Nor, again, does the law of contract generally look kindly upon 'perpetuities' of virtually any form.[15]

Some Principles of Permissible Paternalism

Those are all cases of what seem to be 'permissible paternalism', from even the most liberal democratic point of view. From that catalogue of cases, let us try to adduce some principles which seem to guide liberal democrats in justifying them in paternalistically overriding of people's preferences.

Notice that it is not just a matter of looking for cases of people who are incompetent across the board. The previous catalogue started with them, but it quickly proceeded to cases of flawed preferences found in ordinarily competent agents. When looking for general principles to unify those instances of permissible paternalism, therefore, what we ought be looking for are characteristics of preferences, not for classes of people.

Here I shall identify three broad principles. Roughly speaking, liberal democrats feel more justified in overriding people's preferences the more those preferences display certain flaws. First, they will more readily override people's own judgements of their interests the more *uninformed* those judgements are; and liberal democrats feel freer to substitute their own judgement for the person's own the more *irremediably* uninformed that person's own judgements prove to be.

---

[12] Goodin 1989*b*: 26–7.   [13] See further Goodin 1982*b*: ch. 3.

[14] Feinberg 1986: 71–81.

[15] What were obviously intended as 'irrevocable, forevermore' commitments are characteristically reinterpreted by courts as if they were merely 'indefinite but in principle terminatable' promises.

'Uninformed' here embraces a range of failings. One has to do with insufficient or otherwise defective factual content. Another has to do with inadequate appreciation of logical or causal connections. (Included here are considerations of the relevance of preferences to the actions in view: is this a good way to achieve that goal?) Yet another related failing is inadequately appreciating, emotionally, the force of purely factual information—knowing but not feeling the force of a point.

Those are the grounds on which liberal democrats readily override the preferences of the immature and the incompetent. Such people are deemed inadequate judges of their own interests precisely because their judgements are ill-considered and uninformed in all of those ways. Sometimes those defects are remediable, and in that case what is justified is at most 'provisional paternalism': substituting our judgement for theirs for only as long as it takes to teach them the error of their ways. In so far as those defects are irremediable, however, paternalism of a more ongoing sort is typically thought to be justified instead.

Secondly, liberal democrats more readily override people's own judgements of their interests the more *unsettled* those judgements are; and liberal democrats feel freer to substitute their own judgement for the person's own the more *irrevocable* the decisions concerned are likely to be. When people are of a firm mind and can say with confidence what they want, then we are more inclined to respect their wishes. When they equivocate or vacillate, then we rightly attach less credence to any one of their many varying reports of their own desires. Especially when the choices in view would fix the outcome for a very long time, over the course of which people's preferences seem likely to shift wildly, we have little reason to respect their own present-but-wavering reports as if they were authoritative statements of what those people will want over the long term.

Those are the grounds on which liberal democrats refuse to enforce contracts involving irrevocable choices, involving perpetuities, suicide pacts, slavery contracts, and the like. In various other respects, of course, liberal democrats are perfectly happy to—and in still other respects, have no choice but to—respect certain irrevocable choices that people make. Basic life choices (the choice of careers, partners, procreation) are all substantially irrevocable.[16] Even where people can change tacks late in the day, the history of their past choices cannot be rewritten nor can the continuing consequences of those choices always be evaded. We try to discourage people from taking such steps

[16] Care 1984.

prematurely.[17] But since most people of mature years are of a tolerably settled mind in such matters, we are perfectly comfortable respecting their choices. It is the combination of irrevocable decisions and unsettled preferences that provides liberal democrats a peculiarly strong warrant for paternalistic intervention.

Thirdly, liberal democrats are more comfortable in overriding people's own preferences the more *insecurely attached* they are to those preferences. 'Insecurely attached' serves to straddle several possibilities. Sometimes the preferences in view are overridden because they are not in any serious sense the person's own (having been 'implanted' by manipulative advertising or peer-group pressure, perhaps).[18] In so far as the reason we respect a person's preferences is as a token of our respect for persons themselves, we have less grounds for respecting preferences the less the extent to which those preferences are genuinely the person's own.[19] Other times the preferences in view are overridden because they are 'superficial and misleading' ones, not fully in accord with the person's own deeper preferences. Let us distinguish here between first-order preferences (for outcomes, for objects, for states of the world) and second-order 'preferences for preferences'.[20] In so far as a person has preferences that s/he would prefer not to have, policy-makers are merely respecting that person's own higher-order preferences in refusing to respect the person's lower-order ones.[21]

That is what is involved, paradigmatically, in overriding the preferences of people for addictive substances.[22] Once they have literally checked themselves into a detoxification centre, we no more respect their demands for dope than we do Ulysses' entreaties to be untied so he can go join the Sirens.[23] By extension, knowing that most people who start taking the substance eventually want to stop but find they cannot, we are just respecting people's perfectly predictable future higher-order preferences in refusing to let them start taking the substance in the first place.

---

[17] Furthermore we encourage, particularly among the young, wide experience and sampling of alternative courses for their lives—what Mill called 'experiments in living' (Anderson 1991).

[18] Some claim that all preferences are like that (at least in certain settings, e.g. capitalist economies), which amounts simply to an argument against using preference satisfaction (at least in those settings) as the proper way of evaluating social outcomes at all (Gintis 1972). It is only in so far as preferences vary in the extent to which they are genuinely a person's own that this attribute can be used to choose among them.

[19] Goodin 1982*b*: 79–81.

[20] Frankfurt 1971; or perhaps better 'evaluational' ones (Watson 1977).

[21] Goodin 1986: 82–5.   [22] Goodin 1989*b*: 25–30; 1991.   [23] Elster 1979: ch. 2.

While policies towards addictive substances offer the paradigm cases of this rationale for paternalism, other applications are found in policies designed to prevent people from being caught short by their own irrationally inconsistent patterns of time-discounting.[24] If, come the time an outcome actually occurs, a person would have preferred to have attached more weight to it than s/he did at the time the choice was made, then that might be regarded as a diachronic version of 'preference-for-preferences'; and we might 'paternalistically' refuse to respect the more immediate first-order preferences that people express by appeal to those subsequent higher-order preferences. Much of the paternalism practised towards the immature or incompetent might be justified in these terms. So too might many of our policies of refusing to respect irrevocable choices.

Some Caveats

At least a couple of caveats ought to be entered at this point. First, as regards the principles just developed, it ought be said that, of course, each actually points to a continuum. Any given individual may display any of those failings to a greater or lesser extent. Furthermore, any given public policy decision will affect (typically, it will apply uniformly to) a great many people, each of whom is slightly differently situated along each of those continua.

The upshot is that paternalism is always going to be more-or-less justifiable on each of these grounds, and where the threshold of a 'barely adequate' justification for it falls is always going to be a tricky question. Still, it is always worth clearly identifying each of the dimensions at work, and isolating their endpoints, even if most of the actual cases inevitably fall in the middle of the map rather than at its edges.

Secondly, the present exercise has a distinctive emphasis which bears reiterating. The issue under investigation here, recall, is which sorts of preferences are deserving of respect and which ones are not. Questions of when paternalism might be permissible certainly involve that issue—but more as well. We can, as we have done above, point to particular circumstances in which people are particularly poor judges of what is truly in their own best interest. But that will constitute a full-blooded justification of paternalism if and only if we can go on to identify some *other* persons who are systematically better judges of people's interests in those self-same circumstances.

---

[24] Elster 1979: ch. 2; Goodin 1982*b*: chs. 2 and 9; 1989*b*: 22.

Many of the most persuasive arguments against paternalism effect-ively concede the first point (that people are often poor judges of their own interests) and ground the case against paternalism on a denial of the second point alone (asserting, in effect, that however badly people judge their own interests there is no one else who is a better judge).[25] In the present context, though, whether or not anyone else is better able to judge people's interests is largely irrelevant. The important point, here, is merely that certain of a own person's preferences command considerably less respect than others.

Recall the use to which these findings will here be put—to guide our choice among alternative models of democracy, under-stood as essentially preference-respecting systems. In the context of that choice, the issue is not so much about substituting one person's judgements for another's. It is not about *whose* judge-ments to respect. The issue instead is more one of *which* of a person's *own* preferences liberal democrats ought to be more con-cerned to respect, and which they should be more relaxed about not respecting.

Assessing Alternative Models of Preference-Respecting Democracy

Once we know what sorts of preferences liberal democrats think ought to command what sort of respect in those more policy-specific contexts, we can choose among alternative systems of democratic rule so as to maximize the chances of the right sorts of preferences being respected in the right way. That is to say, we can reapply the principles which were adduced from more specific policy set-tings to that larger issue of choice among democratic political systems themselves.

Here I shall begin that process, first setting out a broad taxonomy of models of democracy and then commenting on how each sort might fare with regards to the criterion of 'respecting respectable preferences' set out above.

---

[25] Some arguments against paternalism assert, bravely, that each person either is or ought, on principle, to be treated as if s/he were the only ultimate judge of his/her own interests. But those arguments are ultimately unpersuasive, and what is left is merely the claim that each person is the 'best judge' of his/her own interests (Goodin 1990*a*; see more generally Kleinig 1983).

A Taxonomy of Models of Preference-Respecting Democracy

There are as many models of democracy as there are democratic theorists, or more. This is no place for an exhaustive survey of them all.
Instead, I shall merely offer a simple taxonomy of the basic ways in
which models of democracy might be preference-respecting.

Models of democracy differ, in this regard, along two principal
dimensions. They respect people's preferences either *directly* or *indirectly*. 'Direct democracy' (and to a lesser extent 'indirect democracy')
are already familiar terms in democratic discourse: much the same is
meant by them here. People's preferences are respected 'directly' if
they serve as an unmediated input into the policy-making process.
They are respected 'indirectly' if their input is somehow mediated
through some other agency. This dovetails nicely with standard distinctions between direct democracy, where people's votes directly
determine policy outcomes, and indirect democracy, where they shape
representative institutions that themselves then shape policy in turn.

Cutting across this direct/indirect distinction is a distinction
between respecting preferences *reflectively* or *unreflectively*. Models
of the former sort quickly split into several subspecies, corresponding
to the great many ways of spelling out what exactly it is that makes
preferences 'reflective' and to the several different agents who might
do the 'reflecting'.[26] It is easier to mark the contrast by focusing upon
the former 'unreflective' mode. There we find ourselves respecting
people's preferences without any qualification whatsoever regarding
their source or content or the process by which their holders came to
hold them or how they relate to any of the holder's other preferences.
In democratic theories that would have us respect people's preferences
unreflectively, an expression of brute preference counts as an automatic
diktat to policy-makers—with no further questions asked.

These dimensions cutting across one another give rise to the twofold
taxonomy depicted in Figure 3.1. A classic example of a model of democracy which is *directly* and *unreflectively* preference-respecting would

---

[26] This model thus straddles 'respecting people's reflective preferences' and 'reflectively
respecting people's preferences'. In the latter case, the reflection is being done by those
respecting the preferences, whereas in the former case the reflection is being done by the
person whose preferences they are. Institutionally it is an important difference. Morally,
it is not clear that it is all that important. Whatever reasons of moral principle democratic
theorists might have for wanting preferences to be subject to such critical scrutiny as is
entailed in 'reflection', the same reasons would surely lead them to want whoever translates
preferences into policy to ensure that those critical standards have been met. In direct
democracy, that is the people themselves; in indirect democracy, it is representatives or
other agents acting as filters.

	unreflective	reflective
direct	• populist democracy	• pluralist democracy • directly deliberative democracy
indirect	• delegate democracy	• trustee democracy • democratic deliberation within

Figure 3.1. Preference-Respecting Models of Democracy

be 'populist democracy'.[27] There, people's preferences are aggregated directly to form a social decision, with no intervening filters or sub-stantive mediation anywhere along the way. Why people want what they say they want, or whether getting it will satisfy their purposes, or whether there is some other way of satisfying them at less cost to others' similar satisfactions, are all issues which simply do not arise within this sort of model.

A model of democracy that respects preferences *directly* but *reflectively* would be 'pluralist democracy'.[28] In bargaining games of that sort, people lodge their demands directly with one another, with no intervening agents mediating between them. Their preferences serve, in that way, as 'direct' inputs into the social decision process of 'partisan mutual adjustment' of pluralist bargaining. But bargaining games involve reflection on both sides. You reflect upon what you want to demand of the other (if only by tailoring your demands to what you think the other is going to be willing and able to deliver). And others consider not only what you say you want, but also why you want it, in their search for 'win–win' solutions to what on the face of the expressed demands might look like zero-sum situations.

Another model of democracy that respects preferences directly and reflectively would be 'directly deliberative democracy'.[29] Such models involve 'face-to-face' interaction among interlocutors who are expressing their preferences and perspectives directly to one another.[30] How they cast those expressions may well differ from the way bargainers lodge their demands; how they process one another's expressed preferences and perspectives quite certainly does.[31] But the central idea

---

[27] See e.g. Dahl 1956: ch. 2; Pennock 1979: ch. 5; Riker 1983.

[28] Dahl 1961, 1982; Dahl and Lindblom 1953: chs. 12–13; Lindblom 1965.

[29] The term is borrowed from Cohen and Sabel (1997), though it is clearly what virtually all self-styled 'deliberative democrats' actually have in mind. See e.g. Cohen 1989; Miller 1992; Bohman and Rehg 1997; Elster 1998a; Dryzek 2000.

[30] After the fashion of Laslett (1956).

[31] A distinction Elster (1994) marks as one between 'arguing' and 'negotiating'.

underlying all the standard models of directly deliberative democracy is that we should listen directly to what one another has to say, and that we should then reflect both upon what others have said and upon what we have ourselves previously said in light of that. Thus, 'directly deliberative democracy' can be classed as an example of a model of democracy that is both direct and reflective.

Next consider models of democracy that respect people's preferences *indirectly* and *reflectively*. A classic example of this sort of model is representative democracy, where the representatives conceive their role to be one of 'trustees' rather than delegates.[32] There, people's preferences shape public policy; but they do so only indirectly, through the people's elected representatives. But representatives who conceive of themselves as 'trustees' rather than mere 'delegates' will reflect upon constituent preferences rather than simply 'reporting' them. In that process, they will obviously weigh more heavily those preferences which seem to represent the more 'reflective' ('considered', 'settled') will of the constituents concerned.

Another example of indirect and reflective democracy would be what I call 'democratic deliberation within'. That is a subspecies of deliberative democracy where the ordinary emphasis on interpersonal discussion is replaced by an emphasis on our internal reflections upon the perspectives of one another. In that sort of model, other people's preferences and perspectives shape policy only indirectly, through the mediating influence of one another's minds. And they do so reflectively, as each of us tries to come to grips with one another's perspective in their most coherent ('reflective') form.

The final cell in Figure 3.1 represents cases of indirect and unreflective ways of respecting people's preferences. An example of that is a model of political representation in which representatives are seen as 'delegates', acting strictly under instruction from their electorates.[33] There representatives act purely as ciphers or conduits, passing along messages from the electorate without reflecting upon their contents. Within this model, the influence of the electorate's preferences on policy would be indirect, transmitted through their representatives. But as delegates, those representatives would report those preferences unreflectively.

---

[32] Burke 1774; Pitkin 1967; Pennock 1979: ch. 8. Models of 'democratic elitism' more generally fall into this mould, in so far as they are genuinely 'democratic' at all; Schumpeter 1950; Bachrach 1967; Pennock 1979: ch. 5; Riker 1983: ch. 1.

[33] Burke 1774; Pitkin 1967; Pennock 1979: ch. 8.

Discard Unreflective Democracy: Populist and Delegate Models

With that basic taxonomy of different models of preference-respecting democracy before us, we can now begin to assess which types of democracy are best suited to respecting preferences which liberal democrats deem most worthy of respect.

The first and most striking upshot of that discussion of permissible paternalism, as I foreshadowed at the outset, is that people's preferences do not always and everywhere command complete and unqualified respect. Even the staunchest liberal democrat is sometimes suspicious of certain sorts of preferences that might be expressed, even by ordinarily competent people of mature years and sound judgement.[34]

That first finding has clear consequences for our choice among models of democracy. It serves to set us conclusively against unreflective models of democracy, be they 'populist' or 'delegate-style representative' in form. The problem is that all such 'unreflective' models would have us respecting any and all of people's preferences, utterly without discrimination. In populist-style democracy, people's preferences are aggregated directly to form a social decision, with no intervening filters or substantive mediation anywhere along the way. In delegate-style models of representative democracy, similarly, representatives act on strict instructions from their electorates, serving merely as conduits passing along messages from the electorate without reflecting on the contents.

In both of those essentially 'unreflective' models of democracy, why people want what they say they want, whether getting it will satisfy their purposes, whether there is some other way of satisfying them better or at less cost to others' similar satisfactions, are all issues which simply cannot arise. Preferences are preferences, each as worthy of respect as the next.

That is not the way liberal democrats think, however, when it comes to public policy. There, as we have seen, they are clearly of a mind that people's more informed judgements command more respect than their less informed ones, their more settled judgements more respect than their less settled ones, their preferred preferences more respect than their less preferred ones. In choosing among models of democracy, liberal democrats ought to seek political arrangements that

---

[34] They may not have any greater respect for anyone else's preferences in these matters, of course; so the case for actually practising paternalistic intervention in any given case may remain unproven. But what certainly is true is that liberal democrats respect some of a person's preferences more than others.

systematically allow them to do that, rather than just unreflectively registering whatever preferences people might happen to express, however inconsistent those may be with all the other evidence we have about their deeper desires.

Virtues of Broad Public Discussion in Direct-Reflective Models: Pluralist and Directly Deliberative Democracy

Such considerations lead us to favour models of democracy that enable us respect preferences *reflectively*—to *differentiate* among preferences, respecting some but not others. Such models of democracy provide mechanisms, of various different sorts, for sifting among people's preferences and weighting some more heavily than others (and discounting still others altogether) in reaching social decisions.

We ought not underestimate the extent to which sheer public deliberation—open discussion in a public forum—might induce people to cull their own preferences and help others to cull them, in turn. At the very least, the obligation to give a public account of yourself and your reasons for favouring some particular course of action forces you to report only those reasons that others might plausibly be expected to share.[35]

This virtue might emerge even in models of 'pluralist democracy', wherein people lodge their demands with one another and the ensuing bargaining games are resolved purely by processes of 'partisan mutual adjustment'.[36] It emerges more clearly, of course, in models of 'directly deliberative democracy', conceptualized literally as face-to-face interactions among interlocutors who express their preferences and perspectives directly to one another.[37]

Directly deliberative democracy differs importantly from pluralist bargaining in many ways. But both are the same in one crucial respect. Both would have us listening carefully and directly to what one another has to say, and then reflecting upon what each of us has previously said in light of that. In those ways, both models of 'pluralist democracy' and of 'directly deliberative democracy' count as models of democracy which are reflective in the requisite sense.

---

[35] Lindsay 1929: 36; Habermas 1973; Goodin 1986: 86–9. For divergent critical appraisals, see Pettit 1982; Elster 1986*b*; Dryzek 1990. Strictly speaking, the filter imposed by constraints of 'discursive defensibility' works on the arguments that people give rather than on the preferences that they have: but there are at least some grounds for supposing that once people start talking that way about their preferences they eventually come to think that way about them, as well (Goodin 1992*a*: ch. 7).

[36] Dahl and Lindblom 1953: chs. 12–13; Dahl 1961, 1982; Lindblom 1965.

[37] Cohen and Sabel 1997; Laslett 1956.

Discursive dynamics aside, there is another equally important way in which people might be led to a reflective culling of the preferences that they express in collective decision-making contexts. In any very large group, each person's own expressed preferences will inevitably have little impact on the overall outcome. In one way, that liberates each member of the electorate to be irresponsible, in the sense of being literally careless of the consequences. In another way, though, that selfsame fact also frees each member of the electorate to behave in a more principled fashion: the very fact that electoral outcomes are so largely independent of anyone's vote frees every voter to act on the basis of an ethical rather than self-interested stance.[38] Theory here is borne out in practice. In assessing a government's economic record, for example, people tend to vote to re-elect governments that have been good for the national economy rather than asking whether their own personal pocketbooks have benefited.[39]

Those two considerations would seem to dovetail to form an argument for making democratic decisions by way of 'broad public discussions'. In truth, however, those two considerations pull in different directions.

The 'virtuous discursive dynamics' here in view are felt with greatest force in small face-to-face discussions, where each is genuinely in a position to challenge the other, and everyone offers the arguments that they do in anticipation of such challenges. The 'virtuous release of higher motives', however, occurs only where the size of the group is sufficiently large to make each individual's contribution almost literally inconsequential.

Virtues of Indirect-Reflective Democracy: The Trustee Model and 'Democratic Deliberation Within'

It is even more obvious, of course, how people's preferences might be sorted and sifted through the cut-out mechanisms at the heart of models of indirect democracy. The whole idea of indirect democracy involves interposing between people's preferences and policy outcomes some

---

[38] See further Goodin (1986: 89–91) and Brennan and Lomasky (1993: esp. ch. 9). As I said in Ch. 1, this blindness to consequences is a morally mixed blessing, in so far as consequences morally matter. Any given voter is as powerless to determine collective consequences as personal ones. Those who internalize consequentialistic considerations in their moral codes might none the less vote for that course of action that will have the best collective consequences as a matter of high moral principle, even if there is no instrumental calculation of direct consequences that would lead them to vote in that way.

[39] Kiewiet 1983. Sagoff (1988) makes the same argument, and Rohrschneider (1988) finds evidence of the same voting patterns, with respect to environmental policy.

other intermediate agent with substantial independence to pick and choose which of the people's preferences to respect.

Elected representative play this role in trustee-style models of representative democracy.[40] That is the most familiar version of this sort of model. But in my model of 'democratic deliberation within' the same sort of thing happens. When 'democratically deliberating within', each of us plays that same 'intermediary' role *vis-à-vis* the preferences and perspectives of others which we are representing to ourselves. That intermediaries should exercise independent reflective judgement in such ways is central to indirect democracy in all its forms.[41]

The great fear with all systems of indirect democracy is the spectre of unwarranted 'substitution of judgement', people's preferences being accorded *too little* respect in the process of social decision-making. Cloistered representatives are often left imperfectly accountable owing to slack of various sorts in electoral procedures, and they often prove altogether too indifferent to citizen preferences in their legislative deliberations in consequence. Hence our ongoing attempt to construct political institutions in such a way as to make representatives genuinely accountable through all the familiar accoutrements of democratic equality: extensive suffrage, fair districting, fair electoral law and parliamentary procedure, and so on.

Assuming such devices are in place to ensure that representatives will eventually be held democratically accountable, they can frame policies in disregard of people's preferences only ultimately by the leave of those people themselves. Models relying purely on 'democratic deliberation within' lack any such automatic check.

Were people directly representing their own views to you, as in models of 'directly deliberative democracy', they would have an opportunity to correct any mistaken views of their preferences that you may have. That direct check is not available in models of 'democratic deliberation within'. Being indirect, that model must instead simply trust us to correct our own mistakes, as we discover that our attempts to make sense of what others are saying to us increasingly ill-fit their own pronouncements.

---

[40] Pitkin 1967; Pennock 1979: ch. 8; Riker 1983: ch. 10. On 'democratic elitism', more specifically, see Schumpeter 1950; Bachrach 1967.

[41] Were the people's representatives perfectly responsive to the people's will in every respect, it would be a case of 'delegate-style representation' rather than 'trustee'. Were each of us to take everyone else's professions at face value, without any reflection upon them or upon our own values or beliefs in light of them, it would be a case of 'populist democracy' rather than 'democratic deliberation within'.

Thus it is crucial for the results of any 'democratic deliberation within' to be confronted with occasional feedback through more formal electoral systems, as a check and corrective. As I said in Chapter 1, and will reiterate throughout the book, 'deliberative democracy within' should be seen as an aid to democratic deliberation, not as a substitute for voting. Full democratic legitimacy can only be conferred on the results of 'democratic deliberations within' through the ordinary political processes of voting and elections.

Such considerations militate against relying upon 'democratic deliberation within' alone. But it is perfectly possible to combine it with trustee-style representative democracy, in ways sketched in the final section of this chapter. I shall there argue that this pair of models forms a very attractive package.

The Virtues of Sporadic Assessments: Preference-Respecting Arguments for Indirect Democracy

In assessing alternative models of democracy, attention is ordinarily focused on issues of *how* people have input into the policy process. Equally important, but less often discussed, are questions of the *frequency* with which they do so.

The two issues are not unrelated. Models of direct democracy require direct democratic legitimation of each and every decision. That inevitably means that they tend to require almost continual inputs from people. Models of indirect democracy, in contrast, allow more sporadic democratic legitimation. What is needed there is not constant legitimation but occasional checks to vouchsafe the system's democratic credentials. Thus, in the classic form of indirect democracy, representative democracy, representatives are elected only every few years and left to get on with it in between times. The same might be true of indirect representation through 'deliberative democracy within': people might deliberate in that way periodically, in connection with elections, but leave things largely with their elected representatives in between.

My concern here is with the character of the preferences evoked by different modes of decision-making. There are several reasons to suppose that more sporadic democratic decision-making, and indirect forms of democracy in consequence, is more likely to be a more reflective enterprise. It is more likely to evoke preferences which are more worthy of liberal democratic respect, as a result.

One reason has to do with the 'size' of the policy packages on the table. In systems of sporadic indirect democracy, electors necessarily pass reflective judgement on the whole legislative plan of the competing parties over a whole term in office, rather than on particular policies in isolation from one another.

Of course, even in a direct democracy it is always possible to bundle together policies that strongly interrelate (combining taxing and spending measures in an omnibus money measure, for example) and to insist that people vote on the package as a whole. My point is simply that that will always and inevitably occur in indirect democracies, in a way that it may or may not in systems of direct democracy.

Another reason why sporadic indirect democracy evokes more reflective preferences has to do with people's time horizons. By their very nature, periodic elections provide an occasion for electors to reflect back across a government's whole period in office. People assessing policies one-by-one, in contrast, would ordinarily focus much more heavily on the more immediate past and more proximate future.[42]

Again, there is no necessity in this. It is perfectly possible for electors to be as myopic in assessing governments as they are in their ordinary affairs. So too is it perfectly possible for people, upon reflection, to adopt a very long-term view every time they vote directly upon specific policies. Still, it seems highly likely that bundling policies together into an all-in assessment of governments, at periodic elections, will have the effect of extending the time horizon people employ in making that assessment, as compared to assessing policies one-by-one.

This bundling of policies and of time periods as a result of the sporadic nature of electoral checks in indirect democracy has the effect of evoking preferences from people which, by the standards set out above, make them more worthy of respect.

Because of the bundling of policies, preferences over them are *better informed*—at least in the sense that causal connections and interactions between component policies within the package are better taken into account. Thus, even if you do not believe that representatives (external or internal) are necessarily better informed than their 'constituents', there is none the less reason to regard as more informed the preferences which are evoked by sporadic indirect models of representative

---

[42] The sporadic elections also have the countervailing effect of discouraging democratic representatives themselves from thinking too far beyond the next election, or anyway the one after that. Very long-term planning is therefore harder in a democracy, even an indirect democracy, than in a system where leaders enjoy more security of tenure (a stable monarchy with a young queen, perhaps). But the comparison here, remember, is merely between direct and indirect democracy. As between those two, time horizons are likely going to be longer in the indirect system.

democracy than those evoked by other models of direct democracy on a day-to-day basis.

Moreover, because of the bundling of time periods, sporadic elections within indirect democracies are more likely to evoke *preferred preferences*—at least in the sense that people are passing 'all-in' judgements, giving what upon reflection they themselves would ultimately regard as 'due' weight to payoffs in each period.[43] Again, even if you do not believe that representatives (internal or external) necessarily have longer time horizons than their 'constituents', there is none the less this reason to suppose that the preferences evoked by systems of sporadic indirect democracy would be preferred by the people themselves on this score to those evoked by any system of direct democracy.[44]

On those first two standards, then, models of sporadic indirect democracy seem to evoke preferences that are more worthy of respect than those evoked by other models. On the final criterion—that we ought favour that model of democracy which does the best job of evoking preferences to which people are most *securely attached*—the verdict is less clear-cut.

The notion of preferences to which people are relatively 'securely attached' evokes two dimensions, recall. The first refers to the extent to which those are a person's *settled* preferences. The second refers to the extent to which those are a person's *own* preferences.

Which model of democracy is better able to filter out unsettled preferences is not only unclear but also quite possibly pretty unimportant. Contrary to the claims of early survey research, people's public policy preferences might not be particularly unsettled, anyway. Recent reanalysis of survey findings over the past fifty years suggests that the electorate's policy preferences are in fact really quite stable across long periods. How best to account for that collective-level stability in the face of continuing evidence of individual-level instability is unclear. But the most plausible story seems to be in terms of each individual having an underlying policy preference which is stable in the long term, with their day-to-day preferences inevitably oscillating around that settled mean preference under the day-to-day pressure of events and new information.[45]

---

[43] This is most obviously true when people predominantly vote 'retrospectively', rewarding or punishing incumbents according to their performance (Fiorina 1981). But it would be equally true if people vote 'prospectively', assessing competing parties according to promised future action, so long as they assess the promises across the whole prospective term in office.

[44] This critique of (direct) democracy in terms of the myopic policy choices it induces was made by Tocqueville (see Elster 1988: 92–7).   [45] Page and Shapiro 1992.

Why public policy preferences should be stable, when ordinary preferences about more personal affairs are not, requires some explanation. It might have to do with some utterly mundane facts: perhaps there are fewer options on offer in that sphere, so even if people vacillate they will vacillate less wildly simply because there is less to vacillate among. Or it might have to do with the periodicity of elections in an indirect democracy: people have fewer opportunities to vacillate in how to allocate their votes than their dollars.[46] Or it might have to do with some notions of 'collective deliberation': perhaps in the great debate conducted across the community through the mass media people have reached more genuinely settled judgements on public policies than on private consumer pursuits; or perhaps it is just that (for reasons given above) collective deliberations on public policies are guided mainly by people's moral principles which do not fluctuate nearly so wildly as their first-order private preferences.

Were people's policy preferences genuinely unstable, that would be yet another reason to reject 'populist' models of unreflective, direct democracy and to favour instead one of the other models.[47] Which model we ought to choose instead would depend on the relative weighting attached to each of the possible dynamics just described—whether the collective deliberations involved in a 'directly-deliberative democracy' seem a better bet for settling people's preferences, or whether tapping them less often (as in systems of indirect democracy) seems a better bet instead. If the survey evidence is to be believed, however, it is a problem we seem not to have to face.

The second reason preferences might be deemed unworthy of respect, on grounds that the person is insecurely attached to them, is that those preferences are not genuinely the person's own. In so far as preferences have been manipulated or implanted by others, those preferences are to that extent less the person's own and command correspondingly less respect in consequence.

Of course, there are all sorts of perfectly legitimate ways in which politicians might properly try to influence opinion. There is for example a considerable body of evidence that citizen preferences change in response to inputs of additional information, particularly during political campaigns.[48] That makes preferences 'endogenous' to the political process in ways which certainly complicate formal modelling, but it does not make them 'unsettled' in any irrational way that

---

[46] More generally: one simply has fewer occasions to express a political preference, even in sample surveys or in bars, than one has to spend money.

[47] Riker 1983. The fear of demagogues manipulating mass opinion has constituted the classic case against democracy from Aristotle forward.　　　[48] Gelman and King 1993.

would deny them respect.[49] Quite the contrary, viewing the political process as a 'learning process' makes the preferences that emerge from it more worthy of respect.[50] Close investigation of the particular manipulatory techniques available, their strengths and weaknesses, suggests however that most of them are equally available to all in the community and in any case usually relatively short-lived in their effects.[51]

What is of particular concern, in the context of the present discussion, is less how much of a danger manipulation of public opinion might be and more which model of democracy might be best able to curb it. On this score, too, there seem to be no systematic grounds for thinking directly deliberative democracy is necessarily superior to other models.

Models of representative democracy are sometimes thought to be particularly susceptible to manipulation. A representative elite is created, with privileged access to relevant information and with an interest in leading (if necessary, by misleading) the public. In so far as it is representative democracy we are talking about, however, those elites are competing with one another for office. Thus they create a plurality of potential aspirant representatives with almost-as-privileged access to much the same information, and with an interest in providing countervailing advice to the public.[52]

Models of 'directly deliberative democracy', in contrast, sometimes are thought to be substantially impervious to manipulation of public opinion. There, after all, everyone is speaking and being spoken to in turn; and in such circumstances the scope for manipulation seems slight. But, as democrats have known since the days of the Athenian assembly, the risk of demagogic manipulation of opinion in such circumstances is high.

Athenian democracy institutionalized *graphe paranomon*, a mechanism whereby a person could be indicted and tried for making an 'illegal' proposal to the Assembly, even if that proposal had actually passed a previous vote of the Assembly.[53] Advocates of directly deliberative democracy in today's world will need to take the risks of demagogic manipulation of public opinion equally seriously and find some equivalent mechanisms for coping with it. Whether in the end those mechanisms are better at coping with that sort of manipulation of

---

[49] Gerber and Jackson 1993.

[50] Macpherson 1977: ch. 3; Bowles and Gintis 1986: ch. 5.   [51] Goodin 1980.

[52] It would presumably be easier for 'democratic pluralist' interest-group leaders to form a conspiracy against the public in this regard, which presumably makes that a less preferred version of indirect democracy from this perspective.   [53] Elster 1979: 88.

public opinion than the mechanism of an institutionalized opposition as in models of 'democratic elitism' remains an open question.

Combining 'Democratic Deliberation Within' and Trustee-style Representative Democracy

The bulk of the forgoing considerations militate in favour of democratic institutions which respect preferences indirectly and reflectively. Perhaps the most convenient (certainly the most familiar) way of doing so is through trustee-style representatives, sporadically accountable at periodic elections but substantially independent in between elections. Let us simply accept that that is the most realistic way, in present circumstances, of implementing democratic accountability and of underwriting democratic legitimacy.

Even accepting that, however, nothing that has been said so far serves to specify the form that democratic accountability ought to take, come election time. How ought people to go about deciding whether their representatives have done well or badly in serving them?

There are various ways of filling out the 'democratic' component of 'representative democracy'. One way—a natural extension of direct (populist or interest-group pluralist) models of democracy—would be to say that people should simply vote to re-elect representatives who seem to have been responsible for giving them what they want, and against those who have not succeeded in giving them what they want. That would have people voting on the basis of their unreflective, brute preferences. Being unreflective, however, there is every reason to suppose that those preferences would fall foul of the standards set out above of what count as preferences worthy of respect by liberal democrats.

Another alternative would be to say that people ought to vote on the basis of an assessment of a 'directly deliberative democratic' sort.[54] If that ideal could be realized, the preferences thus evoked would be reflective in all the ways described above. But in so far as actual interpersonal discussion is key, there are clear limits to the number of people with whom one can engage in face-to-face discussions. In any remotely large group, most people will inevitably have simply to 'listen' while a very few of their number do the talking.[55] That opens the 'directly

---

[54] The Ackerman and Fishkin (2002) proposal for a national 'Deliberation Day' the last weekend before national elections would be a step in that direction.

[55] Over television, for the first half of Ackerman and Fishkin's (2002) 'Deliberation Day'.

deliberative democratic' process to risks of manipulation, in ways that are all too familiar.

A third way in which people might go about deciding whether their representatives have served them well—and the way I here recommend—is through the process of 'democratic deliberation within'. That process has each of us empathetically projecting ourselves into the place of (ideally) every other. We would then conduct the 'democratic conversation' imaginarily, inside our own heads rather than in any actual discursive forum.

'Democratic deliberation within' is a subspecies of deliberative democracy, putting the emphasis less on interpersonal discussion and more on our internal reflections upon the perspectives of one another. In this model, other people's preferences and perspectives shape policy; but they do so indirectly, through the mediating influence of one another's perceptions and appreciations. They do so, furthermore, reflectively, as each of us tries to come to grips with one another's perspectives in their most coherent (and in that sense, too, 'reflective') form.

Imperfect though the implementation of that ideal will inevitably remain, in any actual implementation, it seems to me to hold out the most promise of any of the models I here consider for generating a set of preferences which pass the tests of being respectably reflective in ways set out above. Thus, the best model for ensuring that we respect the right sort of preferences in the right way seems to be a combination of two indirect and reflective forms of democracy: trustee-style representative democracy, for making day-to-day policy; and 'democratic deliberation within', for use by citizens in evaluating the performance of their representatives at the polls.

Belief Democracy

We have long been taught that politics consists in the 'authoritative allocation of values' and, more especially, in the distribution of valued objects ('who gets what, when and how').[1] From the wars of religion onward the central task of political rule in general, and democratic rule in particular, has been seen as one of articulating divergent value premises. Across the centuries, principles and practices of religious toleration, social pluralism, and multicultural accommodation—political liberalism in all its multifaceted glory—have derived from that basic imperative. Democratic theory's traditional preoccupation with the evaluative side of political life is thus well justified. Value disputes drive many of the most intractable political conflicts, and they must be somehow reconciled for democratic rule to be sustained.

Before turning directly to the more value-laden side of politics, however, it is important to notice that there is a cognitive side to political judgement and action as well—and to acknowledge both the potential contribution, and the strict limits to the contribution, that democratic politics can make there.

Differing factual beliefs drive political disputes, as much as differing value premises or differing distributional desires. Democratic politicians bargain over what factual premises they will act upon, just as they bargain over what value premises they will act upon. The propositions they put to the electorate characteristically contain a substantial factual component.

The purely aggregative aspects of democratic politics—simply adding up the votes, and in that way pooling the information possessed by multiple independent electors—can go a very long way towards rationally resolving factual disputes. But political disputes are never purely factual disputes. The remaining differences over value premises must be resolved through other means. The course of action we will collectively pursue will therefore always have to be a matter for bargaining and negotiations in which issues of facts and values are intertwined.

---

[1] Easton 1965; Laswell 1950.

CHAPTER 4

Negotiating Beliefs

The Place of Beliefs in Democratic Bargaining

Bargaining, as it is ordinarily understood within politics just as within economics, is principally over distributions.[2] Those distributions are seen as being paradigmatically of benefits and burdens, principally of a material sort. Beliefs of several sorts lie in the background of that sort of bargaining, to be sure.[3] But beliefs are not themselves the subject of democratic political bargaining, as ordinarily conceived.[4]

That constitutes a serious deficiency within models of democratic competition built on the bargaining models bequeathed us by modern economics. Much of what goes on in actual social and political bargaining does indeed concern the negotiation and renegotiation of beliefs. That is what judges and juries are supposed to be arguing about; that is what fact-finding commissions of inquiry are supposed to be arguing about; and that is at least part of what political parties are arguing about, in promoting their rival election manifestos.

---

[2] For a formalized bargaining model incorporating these considerations, see my co-author's half of the article on which this chapter is based, Goodin and Brennan (2001).

[3] We have to believe that certain things will serve our desires (otherwise we would not want them); we have to believe we presently lack those things (otherwise we would not seek them); we have to believe that there are not enough of those things to go around (otherwise we would not compete for them); we have to believe that the distribution of those things is under the control of specific others (otherwise we would not try to strike a bargain with them).

[4] Other disciplinary traditions differ fundamentally in this respect. When sociologists, social anthropologists, and philosophers of language talk of society as being a 'negotiated order', what they refer to is a system of shared beliefs and understandings. Comprehending the 'rationality' of social action is, for them, essentially a matter of elucidating the shared beliefs and understandings of the agents involved. This theme unites such otherwise diverse writers as Schutz 1943; Berger and Luckman 1966; Wilson 1970; Geertz 1973a; Taylor 1985; Walzer 1987; MacIntyre 1988; Searle 1995.

Such disputes over beliefs sometimes get resolved through persuasion. One side convinces the other of the truth of its beliefs, perhaps; or perhaps both come to see that the truth genuinely lies in some third proposition altogether. Free and open discussion among equals sometimes has this effect, even in politics.[5]

In the real world of democratic politics, however, more disputes over beliefs get 'resolved' through negotiation than through persuasion. Each still believes the truth of the proposition she was originally advocating; but each sees the need to 'get on with it'; so all agree to treat certain propositions 'as if true', for the particular purposes at hand.[6] The latter process is what I shall be calling 'bargaining over beliefs'.[7] My aim in this chapter is to show that that is a form of bargaining, on a par with any other, in ways that economists and democratic theorists inspired by them can and should take on board.

In exploring that novel form of bargaining, my strategy is to proceed through the analysis of 'most different cases'.[8] Ordinarily, many different modes of bargaining are intertwined, and the presence of the more familiar forms ('bargaining over distributions' or over 'values') blinds us to the presence of less familiar ones ('bargaining over beliefs'). To bracket out these confounding factors, I therefore focus on situations in which familiar forms of bargaining seem necessarily absent. I then show that, even there, bargaining, of a sort might still occur. The sort of 'bargaining over beliefs' thus identified in those atypical situations, however, is not confined to them alone. Having isolated the phenomenon in relation to extreme cases, we can perceive elements of it at work in more common sorts of social and political bargaining.

Bargaining: The Standard Story

Rational choice, as it is standardly understood, is the joint product of belief and desire. Desires dictate the ends. Beliefs merely inform as to which means are best for serving them.

---

[5] As Chs. 5–6 go on to argue, it ought rationally to have this effect much more often still, if pure facts are all that is at issue; Ch. 7 offers various reasons it might not, pre-eminent among them the very different dynamic governing disputes with a value component.

[6] As happens in ordinary conversations and other such circumstances requiring groups to come, however provisionally, to some 'jointly accepted views' (Gilbert 1989: 288–314). The conversational example is discussed further below.

[7] More strictly speaking: 'bargaining over what we collectively are going to treat as if it were true for purposes of our collective action' (but that phrase lacks the same alliterative appeal).   [8] Mill 1843: bk 3, ch. 8.

As with rational choice, so too with rational bargaining. Each agent is presumed to have a complete and consistent preference ranking over all the options which are potentially on the table; and that preference ordering is supposed to be unaffected by what is or is not on the table at any moment. Bargaining is supposedly a mere matter of each bargainer's deploying her skill and resources so as to induce the others to accept a joint solution which takes her as high up her preference ordering as possible.

Different mathematical models offer different 'solution concepts' defining which bargains ought rationally to be struck. But common across all those models is that central image of bargainers as coming to the table with independently given and settled preferences. Bargaining, as it is standardly conceived, is strictly over outcomes evaluated in terms of those settled preferences.[9] Bargaining is not supposed to change people's preferences, desires—or beliefs, either. All that is taken as given, as exogenous to the bargaining process itself.

Formal models, of course, abstract from the messiness of the real world. There, hard bargaining is indeed interspersed with persuasive appeals; bargainers alternatively threaten and cajole; negotiators seek agreements that everyone can live with, rather than pressing their own bargaining advantage to the hilt.[10] For present purposes, however, I shall be sticking to those formalizations, to show ways in which those models can and should be amended and extended even in their own terms.

Identical Interests, Different Perceptions: Bargaining over Beliefs

On the standard account, bargaining is driven purely by values, by people's divergent goals. Bargaining comes about because people have opposing objectives. Those opposing objectives give rise to conflicts of interests.[11] To some greater or lesser extent, one person getting more of what she wants necessarily entails the others getting less of what they want. That, on the standard account, is the sort of situation that gives rise to bargaining problems.

Following the 'most different cases' strategy, I here focus on cases as unlike that as possible—cases where everyone has literally the same goals, where everyone ranks all the alternative possible outcomes in exactly the same way. In cases such as those, the most that they could

[9] Luce and Raiffa 1957: ch. 6; Young 1975.   [10] Raiffa 1982.   [11] Axelrod 1970.

possibly suffer would be a 'coordination problem'.[12] If everyone were literally agreed as to goals and indifferent as among several equally good ways of attaining them, then the problem would simply be one of settling on one of those courses of action and communicating that choice clearly to everyone who has a part to play within that plan of action. The necessary information might not be easily conveyed; misunderstandings might arise; coordination and communication may be urgently required. But bargaining as such would have no role to play. Or so it might be supposed.

Even in that 'pure coordination game' scenario, however, we might still face an occasion for bargaining of a sort: bargaining over beliefs. Consider the following variation on the basic 'coordination game' scenario—a scenario of 'identical interests, different perceptions'. Suppose that we face a coordination problem of the familiar sort. Everyone must go the same way, if any of us are to get anywhere at all. Everyone has the same goal: everyone wants to end up at exactly the same place. Everyone recognizes that it is a coordination problem: everyone appreciates that they must all proceed in the same direction if any of them are to get there. But imagine, now, that there is disagreement within the group as to which is the 'right' way to go to get there.

Imagine, for example, a convoy which for reasons of safety must travel together, journeying across the Nullarbor desert of central Australia. Everyone in the party wants to reach Perth, but (these being the 1950s, before paved roads or reliable signposts) there is disagreement within the group as to which is the right track to take to get there. Or for another example, imagine members of the Federal Reserve arguing over the best way to control inflation without plunging the economy into a recession. Or for yet another example, imagine members of a firm's board of directors arguing over whether or not to buy out a rival firm.

Note that that is precisely what underlies standard contemporary accounts of 'deliberative democracy' and 'public reason'. Of course, those are idealizations of real-world practice[13]; and there are many varying strands to these literatures.[14] But according to what might

---

[12] Schelling 1960; Lewis 1969.

[13] Still, even if legislators are actually pursuing personal or sectoral advantage, they feel none the less obliged to couch their appeals in terms of the public interest. And even if statutes really are just the senseless product of one log-roll after another, legislators feel none the less obliged to attach to them a 'preamble' which purports to offer a single, agreed rationale for their enactment.

[14] Dryzek (2000: esp. chs. 1, 3, and 4) and Young (2000: esp. chs. 1–3) canvass various grounds for dissenting from the 'standard version' sketched below.

reasonably be regarded as the 'standard version', democratic deliberators are supposed to focus on what is in the common interest rather than what is in their particular personal or sectoral interests; public reasoning is supposed to focus on 'public reasons' which all citizens can share.[15] In so far as there is a single 'public' upon whose reasons and interests each deliberator is supposed to be focusing, the reasons and interests which each deliberator is supposed to be addressing are identical to those which each other deliberator is supposed to be addressing. Deliberation is necessary, in such circumstances, merely because each perceives those same things differently. On those accounts, what deliberation is all about is resolving those differential perceptions of what is required by public reasons and the public interest.[16]

In the ordinary course of events, we resolve factual disagreements by pooling our information or by conducting further experiments.[17] But incremental trial-and-error processes are often precluded, either by the pressures of time or by some other awkward feature of the situation (options are lumpy, or the response function is time-lagged, or whatever[18]). In the ordinary practice of democratic politics, we often have to take some joint action well before information-pooling processes have played themselves out: and in the ordinary politics of democratic politics, there are some clear cases in which we would never expect them to do so.[19] Let us call those cases of 'arrested convergence', and let us confine our attention in this chapter to situations of that sort.

Finally, let us suppose that the people involved want a 'rationally grounded decision'. Sometimes collective decisions represent just a pragmatic consensus, whereby everyone agrees on the same course of action, but each for her own very different reasons and with different

---

[15] Represented by e.g. Cohen 1989; Rawls 1993: lecture VI; 1997; and most of the contributors to Bohman and Rehg 1997.

[16] In the terms introduced below, deliberators in these processes certainly are in initial disagreement over 'means'. They may even be in initial disagreement over 'proximate ends' as well. But, at least on this 'standard version' of the public reason/deliberative democracy story, they are all agreed that there is an 'ultimate end' (details of which have yet to be determined) which they share.

[17] Modelled, variously, by Harsanyi 1967–8; Aumann 1976; Lehrer and Wagner 1981; Goldman 1994. I discuss those sorts of models more fully in Chs. 5–6, and their limits in Ch. 7.   [18] Goodin 1982*b*: ch. 2.

[19] In Waldron's (1999*b*: 107) phrase, 'we must find a way of choosing a single policy in which . . . [all] of us can participate *despite* our disagreement on the merits'. In *Political Liberalism* (1993: 58), John Rawls similarly characterizes his 'political conception of justice' as a way of proceeding in the absence of agreement on any 'comprehensive doctrine'. In so far as the comprehensive doctrines in question are substantially value-laden, Ch. 7 shows why ordinary processes of democratic information-pooling leading to convergence should be expected to fail to work in those cases.

ends in view.[20] Saying that people involved in a situation of 'identical interests, different perceptions' want a 'rationally grounded decision' is to say that they want more than that sort of bare agreement as to *what* they should do. They want their collective action itself to be based on some collectively agreed view as to *why* they are doing it, as to exactly how that action is supposed to work to produce the end in view.[21] They want this, in no small part, to ensure that any success they collectively enjoy will be sustainable, rather than the product of some unreproducible fluke.[22]

Here of course I am focusing on cases of 'identical interests, different perceptions', so *ex hypothesi* everyone has the same ends in view and they differ only in their perceptions of how best to bring about those ends. Saying that the group wants a 'rationally grounded' resolution of their quandary is, in those circumstances, therefore to say that they want collective agreement to act on the basis of one or another of those differing perceptions as to how best to achieve those shared ends.[23] The task of collective decision-making is to determine which it will be.

In the course of those deliberations, people with differing perceptions will naturally try to persuade one another of the greater accuracy of their own perspectives. But *ex hypothesi* they will have to act before they have been able to achieve full convergence of their perceptions. Wanting a 'rationally grounded decision' in such circumstances forces them to opt for one of those sets of perceptions (and its concomitant action-plan and rationale), in preference to various other perceptions, action-plans, and rationales that are still extant among some members of the group.

---

[20] MacCallum 1966; Sunstein 1995.

[21] Note that the requirement of a 'rationally grounded decision', as employed here, is a very weak constraint. All that it requires is this: for whatever course of action the group chooses, there must be some coherent story, based on the perceptions of some (perhaps just one) person, about how this course of action is supposed to lead to those results. What the constraint is designed to rule out is the phenomenon of shifting coalitions leading to a series of partial decisions which, taken together, are simply incoherent. Thus, in the Nullarbor example, what we want to rule out is this: Suppose the track forks in three at three separate places. Jack thinks the convoy should go straight, then left, then right. Jill thinks it should go left, then straight, then right. James thinks it should go left at all forks. If they decided their route one step at a time, through majority voting, the convoy would go left, then left, then right. But *nobody* thinks that that is what they should do: that sequence of choices corresponds to no one's mental map of how to get out of the desert (see Brennan 2001).

[22] Wanting arrangements which are stable over time is one of the reasons Rawls (1993: 148–9) gives against settling for a mere *modus vivendi*.

[23] In Margaret Gilbert's (1989: 301–4) terms, they want to come to a 'jointly accepted view', one which is accepted for purposes of what the group should do but from which any given member of the group might still dissent 'in her personal capacity'.

But Is It Bargaining?

Spirited discussions inevitably ensue. Views diverge as to which way the group ought collectively to proceed, with some people championing one way and some another. Such discussions are naturally characterized by arguments and counterarguments. All of that is broadly reminiscent of negotiation and bargaining behaviour. But is it bargaining, strictly speaking?

There are two obvious (but opposing) respects in which such discussions might seem radically unlike bargaining of the ordinary sort. Both are rooted in the observation that bargaining games are, paradigmatically, 'mixed-motive games'. In any bargaining situation, there must be 'gains from trade': there must be both motives for cooperation and motives for competition. Absent either—absent either elements of cooperation or elements of conflict—a situation could not involve bargaining, as it is ordinarily understood.

Objections to seeing cases of 'identical interests, different perceptions' as cases of bargaining might focus on the absence of one or the other of those essential elements of a mixed-motive game. The first objection is that such situations of 'identical interests, different perceptions' do not contain enough conflict for them to quality as a case of a mixed-motive or hence bargaining game. The second objection is that there is not enough scope for cooperation. Both objections, I argue, are in error.

No Conflict of Interest?

In ordinary bargaining over the distribution of spoils, each player is trying to secure some narrow advantage for herself at the expense of someone else. Situations of 'identical interests, different perceptions' are 'most different' in that respect. There, what each person is trying to do is simply to promote interests which she shares with each and every other party to the discussions. In terms of the structure of the ultimate payoffs in view, the discussion must be classed as purely cooperative rather than competitive or even a mixed-motive one. And that being so, it seems not strictly speaking to be a situation that can give rise to 'bargaining' at all. Or so the first objection would go.

The lived experience of such situations is, of course, otherwise. Those discussions are, first and foremost, *arguments*. In them, each is trying to 'get her own way'. In them, each is trying to prevail over others who are advocating a position opposed to her own. True, the what they are arguing about is what is best for all and for each. But what they have in common (a shared concern for the interests of all and each) is eclipsed in their actual behaviour by that about which they disagree (how best to promote that shared concern).

While there clearly is conflict, a persistent objector might reply, there is still no conflict of interest. No one stands to gain at anyone else's expense. (Indeed, *ex hypothesi*, in the situation in view, everyone will at the end of the day receive exactly the same identical payoff.) Game theorists standardly take the 'division of spoils' to lie at the core of bargaining games; and for them, the very fact that everyone's fortunes rise or fall together means that this is not a game of dividing anything up, and hence not a bargaining game.

That objection seems to us to rest on a misunderstanding of what is going on even in the most standard of bargaining games, however. Consider this. Even when we pirates are bargaining over the division of spoils—gold for you, gems for me—what we are talking about is the extent to which each of us *gets what we want*. What *ultimate* payoff each of us might get from getting what we want is a separate issue, which is (rightly) left wholly to one side in any formal characterization of the bargaining game. Upon further inspection the gold may well turn out to be fool's gold and the gems to be cut glass, both worthless. As it eventually happens, then, we actually had no conflict of interest after all: there was nothing of any real value to any of us on the bargaining table, to start with. But we did not know that at the time we were carving up the booty. We each (however erroneously) valued everything that was on the table, and we each bargained hard with one another over the distribution of those (ultimately worthless) things.

In retrospect, we were (in this case, both) mistaken. But that retrospective re-evaluation of our mistaken positions does not flow backwards in time, forcing a reassessment of what we had been previously doing as 'not really bargaining at all'. With the benefit of hindsight we can say we *should not* have been bargaining over that. But that does nothing to change the fact that we *were*.

The same is true in the case of 'identical interests, different perceptions'. We each *want* our group to adopt whatever course of action we perceive as being best for promoting our shared interests.[24] And since we perceive things differently, we want the group to adopt different courses of action. In so far as those are incompatible courses of action,

[24] Strictly speaking, what we each want is the group to adopt whatever course of action *is* best for promoting our shared interests. But, *ex hypothesi*, we are in a situation of 'arrested convergence'. We have no further time to discuss, debate, or discover further facts. We are thus forced to act partly in ignorance, on the basis of the facts *as we presently perceive them* rather than on the basis of the facts as they 'really are'.

my getting what I want precludes you from getting what you want. There is a 'conflict of wants'.

Furthermore, that 'conflict of wants' gives rise to a genuine 'conflict of interests' in the relevant game-theoretic sense of the term. In situations of 'identical interests, different perceptions', different people perceive things differently. Because of our differing perceptions, each of us *expects* different outcomes from various courses of action. And our choice behaviour must inevitably be governed by our *ex ante* expectations. Thus, even if *eventually* we will all get the same payoff, *ex ante* I might expect that that payoff to each of us will be $2000 from our doing X and $1000 from our doing Y, and your expectations might be just the opposite.

At the end of the day, of course, each of us will actually receive exactly the same payoff, be it large or small. In bargaining based on our differential perceptions and different expected payoffs based on them, what we are haggling over is simply which course of action is the right one for maximizing the payoff that will accrue identically to both of us. But that still leaves us plenty to argue over, at the time.

Looking at the payoffs from the perspective of some omniscient observer who knows how things will eventually turn out is, in short, simply the wrong perspective. We ought instead to be looking at the situation from the point of view of the people who have to make the choice at the time. And in those terms, differing perceptions yield different expectations, which give rise in turn to differing 'expected utilities' and hence to a genuine 'conflict of interest' of the ordinary game-theoretic sort.

Whether that conflict is amenable to resolution by bargaining remains an open question. (I turn to that next.) The point, for the moment, is simply that the first objection is in error. Contrary to superficial appearances, a situation of 'identical interests, different perceptions' does indeed contain elements of conflict of the standard game-theoretic sort. It is not disqualified from being a mixed-motive (and hence bargaining) game on that score.

No Possibility of Compromise?

A case of 'identical interests, different perceptions' might seem not to involve 'bargaining', strictly speaking, for a second reason opposite to the first. The first objection was that there was not enough conflict in the situation to ground a bargaining game. The second objection claims, conversely, that there is not enough scope for cooperation in them. Something in the nature of such situations, it may be objected, precludes compromise solutions of the sort which are essential in ordinary bargaining.[25]

Of course, even in ordinary bargaining games of 'dividing the spoils', each person is keen on getting her own way. But those ordinary bargaining games are also characterized by a certain amount of 'give and take'. In the final analysis, each of us is prepared to settle for something less than she was initially seeking. That willingness to compromise is precisely what allows bargaining solutions to emerge.

Unless there is some scope, however limited, for each getting 'more or less' of what she wants, there would be no scope for bargaining among them over a division of the spoils. Suppose that the item at issue were utterly indivisible, and therefore has to be given entirely to one party or entirely to the other. Then they clearly have something to *argue* over, but they have nothing to *bargain* over—nothing to *divide* among themselves.[26]

Now, that may seem to be precisely the situation with respect to bargaining over beliefs as to 'what is best' in games of 'identical interests, different perceptions'. In the case of the travellers in the Nullarbor, the road to Perth is *either* the track going to the north-west *or* the one going to the south-west: it makes no sense to split the difference, going due west over the rocky plain where there is obviously no track at all. In the case of the quarrelling members of the Federal Reserve, one group has a model of the economy that recommends an increase of 0.5 per cent in interest rates, while the other has a model which recommends an increase of 2 per cent. But it makes no sense simply to split the difference, rising it 1.25 per cent: there is simply no credible model of the economy presently on offer which can justify a move such as that. In the case of the quarrelling members of a firm's board of directors, one group has reasons for thinking it would maximize their profits to buy out their rival while another group has reasons for thinking that that would do grievous damage to their own firm's bottom line. But it makes no sense simply to split the difference, buying a 25 per cent stake in the other firm: neither group has any reason for thinking that that would maximize their own firm's profits.[27]

[25] The 'no scope for compromise' (or 'autocratic dictator') worry has been developed, in much more formal fashion and using models different from this one. See e.g. Hyllund and Zeckhauser 1979; Seidenfeld *et al.* 1989.

[26] Supposing also that it is temporally indivisible (so they cannot 'take turns' having it for fixed periods of time), that there is nothing else that these two people want from one another (so they cannot make side payments to one another in some other currency), and so on.

[27] Of course, splitting the difference in such ways might lead to moves which, fortuitously, prove to have been 'just right'. But if so, that would have been purely fortuitous. We have been given reasons for believing that each of the opposing recommendations might be

In the fullness of time, more discussion or more experience might lead our perceptions to converge. But suppose circumstances require a decision before our perceptions have had a chance to converge. Then if we want a collective decision backed by a coherent rationale, we have no alternative but to opt for one or another of the contending perspectives on offer. In such a resolution, one side gets things all its own way—and other people's perspectives get ignored altogether. And all-or-nothing choices like that seem to leave us with no differences which can be split. In winner-take-all games, there seems to be no scope for compromise and hence nothing over which to bargain. That, anyway, is the essence of the second objection to viewing these sorts of situations as ones involving bargaining.

Once again, however, that seems to mischaracterize the situation. In the sort of scenario I have been sketching, it is certainly true that one of the contending sets of perceptions (and the concomitant action-plan and rationale underlying it) will have to be adopted as the one on which the group will act, and all others set aside. In that sense, it may well be that one side will 'get things all its way', and other sides will get ignored altogether. But the point remains that the action being taken, while based on one particular perspective, might to some greater or lesser extent be 'in accord' with other perspectives which are being set aside in the group's choice of how to proceed.[28]

That is simply to say that the choice of perspectives upon which we will collectively act may not be an 'all or nothing' matter, after all. It is not necessarily a game which you either win completely or lose completely. Even once it has been decided that your own perspective will not be the one upon which we will collectively act, you might none the less have preferences among the other perspectives, based on their affinities with your own. In so far as you do, those 'preferences over perspectives not your own' create some middle ground of the sort required for a genuine compromise, a genuinely bargained solution.

The fact that people's perceptions have greater or lesser affinities with one another's creates the scope for people cooperatively

---

the right thing to do, but we have been given no reasons for believing that splitting the difference between two incompatible models might yield the right results. Splitting the difference in such circumstances literally 'makes no sense'. There is no coherent model explaining why that might be the correct course for achieving our shared goals. And that course of action would therefore be rejected by a group which is seeking a 'reasoned decision', agreement not only on what they are going to do but also on why.

[28] The practical upshot—the action-plan—may be more or less similar. Even the rationale that the acted-upon perspective gives for those actions might itself be to some greater or lesser extent in accord with the rationales that would be given for similar actions by some of the other perspectives.

coalescing behind some alternative or another. From the perspective of many of them, the alternative being pursued may be merely second- or third-best. But what even those people can agree is that the alternative being pursued is much better than some of the other alternatives not being pursued. It is not at the top of their preference ranking, but it is not at the bottom either. It is, in short, a 'compromise' solution of just the sort which (according to the objection set out at the beginning of this subsection) initially seemed unavailable in cases of 'bargaining over beliefs'.

The Nature of the 'Bargain'

The burden of my argument so far has been that situations of 'bargaining over beliefs' might contain both enough conflict and enough cooperation to qualify as 'mixed-motive games'. That is a necessary condition of 'bargaining over beliefs' qualifying as bargaining at all. But it is not a sufficient condition. Bargaining games are a subspecies of mixed-motive games, but not all mixed-motive games involve what we ordinarily think of as bargaining.

Agreed Joint Action

The sequence of moves and countermoves in an ordinary mixed-motive game just involves each player doing the best she can for herself, given what the other has done or is expected to do. Bargaining, in contrast, involves give-and-take aiming, ultimately, at an agreed joint action. Bargaining, when successful, ends in an agreement, whereas the most we get with ordinary mixed-motive games is an equilibrium.

To show that bargaining is indeed involved in cases of 'bargaining over beliefs', we therefore also need evidence that an agreement of some sort has been reached. Of course, this cannot be an agreement as to 'who is right'. *Ex hypothesi,* people cannot agree on that. Instead, the agreement is on 'what we will do, and why'.

The upshot of bargaining over beliefs is thus not any change in people's beliefs.[29] Nor is it simply an 'agreement to disagree'.[30] The upshot of bargaining over beliefs is instead that bargainers settle on

---

[29] Supposing belief is not something we can conjure up through any act of will, we cannot bargain over what we will 'will ourselves to believe', either. Cf. Williams 1973.

[30] Literally, that makes no sense (as argued by Aumann 1976). And simply agreeing to leave certain matters unresolved—which is what that phrase ordinarily actually involves, as shown in Sunstein (1996)—is not what we actually do in the cases at hand.

some course of action, together with some rationale as to how it is supposed to work to produce the desired results. In the course of that, they agree to treat certain beliefs 'as if they were true'. But they definitely do so in the subjunctive case—in the tentative and hypothetical way in which propositions being tested are treated in scientific experiments.

That is very different from the upshot of ordinary mixed-motive games, in which we do not make any decisions at all on what we collectively will do. Each merely has views as to what she will do, given what the others have done or are expected to do. Bargaining over beliefs, in contrast, leads us to treat certain beliefs 'as if true', for purposes of our collective endeavours—which is to say, it results in a collective agreement as to what we will collectively do and why. The presence of such a collective agreement, rather than merely an equilibrium outcome, is what elevates the situation into that special class of mixed-motive games which we call 'bargaining games'.

A Conversational Analogy

There is nothing mysterious about this business of 'treating a proposition as if it is true, for the purposes at hand'. It is just what we do in ordinary conversations all the time. In trying to make sense of others' utterances, we apply a 'principle of charity'. We assume they are trying to talk sense; we assume that they are asserting propositions which they believe are true and relevant for the purposes at hand; and so on. As part of that process, we implicitly agree to 'treat as true, for the purposes of the present conversation' that set of background conditions which would render most coherent the propositions which our interlocutors seem to be asserting.[31]

Of course what propositions we find ourselves provisionally 'treating as if true' in this way vary from conversation to conversation. In agreeing provisionally to treat them as if true in one context, we are not thereby committing ourselves to believing they are true, or even to acting as if we believe they are true in any other context.[32]

The same is true with parties in a 'identical interests, different perceptions' collective action situation. They, too, have to treat as if true one or another of the contending perspectives, in order to mount any collective action at all in pursuit of their shared interests. Members of the group do so, in their public capacities, without in any way

---

[31] Davidson 1984; Grice 1989; Sperber and Wilson 1986; Lewis 1979.
[32] Gilbert 1989: 294–8.

committing themselves to those beliefs in their private capacities and without necessarily committing themselves to those beliefs in any other collective-action contexts.

Bringing Politics Back In: Credit, Blame and Mixed Cases

Social institutions of credit and blame are standardly imposed to encourage people trying to influence the group's actions to get it right and discourage them from getting it wrong. Nowhere is that more true than in incentive structures facing politicians seeking re-election on the basis of their past performances. Those constitute the payoffs (rewards and penalties) accruing to those responsible for taking the lead in guiding the group down one path rather than another.[33]

Those who 'take the lead' in advocating a particular course of action get a relatively larger share of the credit or blame, satisfaction or shame, for what happens as a result of the group's following their lead. But while the lion's share of credit or blame goes to the leaders, a certain measure of credit or blame goes to their 'junior partners' in the coalition advocating that course of action.

To isolate 'bargaining over beliefs' as a distinct category of bargaining behaviour, I have here been deliberately focusing on cases 'most different' from the cases of conflicts of interest which give rise to most ordinary bargaining. But as I said at the outset, most real-world bargaining games involve elements of both 'partially conflicting interests' and 'differing perceptions'. People are bargaining, at one and the same time, both over distributions and over beliefs.

In a literally zero-sum game, any error that your opponent makes in pursuing her interests inevitably rebounds to your own advantage: there is no advantage to you, there, in helping correct any false beliefs that others might be harbouring. But most games in the real world are no more pure-conflict games of that sort than they are purely cooperative ones of the sort I have here been discussing.

Many real-world bargaining games can be aptly characterized as 'unequal coordination games', the classical instance of which is the Battle of the Sexes. This is a coordination game, in the sense that each

---

[33] In so far as people cannot change their beliefs through any act of will, it would be odd to hold people responsible for what beliefs they have (cf. Stocker 1982). Notice, however, that what we are holding people responsible for is not what beliefs they hold but, rather, for encouraging others of us who do not share those beliefs to permit them to undertake actions on our collective behalf which are predicated on the assumption that their beliefs are correct.

of us prefers that we do something together rather than go our separate ways. But it is an unequal coordination game, in the sense that each of us has our own preferences as to what that should be. You want to go to the wrestling, I to the opera; but you would prefer to go to the opera with me than to the wrestling by yourself, and I would prefer to go to the wrestling with you than to the opera by myself.[34]

In situations like that, we do not have literally 'identical interests' any more. But diverge though our interests may at the margin, everyone's overriding interest in such situations coincides. Attracted though each of us may be by our own preferred activities, most of all each of us wants to do something together. There is in such situations a dominant interest in cooperation which overrides any subordinate interests we have which conflict.

Now, suppose in such situations we have 'different perceptions' as well. Suppose I think that this opera is one you would really enjoy, and that that wrestling match is one I would find particularly silly; and you have just the opposite perceptions. Given our shared interests in doing something or another together, each of us has a reason to try persuading the other of the accuracy of our own perceptions in that regard. But given those shared interests in doing something or another together, each has a reason to yield—acting on the other's perceptions as well as on the other's preferences—if that is the only way for us to do what we both want to do, which is to go somewhere together.

That looks very much like a case of 'bargaining over beliefs', as discussed above. We jointly agree to 'treat as true' the perceptions of one or the other of the parties. The party who won is held responsible for being right, and if things turn out otherwise that party is the one to blame; and someone else's perceptions will be the ones we act upon in future.

Because it is not a purely cooperative game, that is not quite all there is to the story. In 'unequal coordination games', just as in zero-sum games, there are conflicting interests which might tempt us to mislead one another, professing beliefs we do not in fact hold about how attractive the other would actually find our preferred activity. But in repeated games of unequal coordination, such temptations are minimized by the realization that those whose perceptions are acted upon will be held responsible for the accuracy of those perceptions. If we have been intentionally misleading (or even just simply mistaken),

---

[34] Luce and Raiffa 1957: 90. For more politicized application, see Hardin's discussion of Pax Romana solutions to nuclear deterrence games (1983) and of constitution-writing (1999).

we are likely to pay the price in future rounds of the game by having our perceptions not be the ones upon which collective action is based.

Conclusion

In all these ways, beliefs and disagreements over beliefs are absolutely central to democratic politics. Electoral contests inevitably evoke high-minded rhetoric and principled posturing. To some (perhaps large) extent the value differences are genuine; and when they are, that makes a big difference to how we have to go about resolving the disputes (as I shall show in Chapter 7). But intermixed with, and perhaps occasionally underlying, the value-laden rhetoric are often factual disputes of a very ordinary sort. In so far as that is all that is actually at stake, a simple democratic aggregation of votes can be a powerful device for resolving the dispute, as I shall now show.

CHAPTER 5

Democracy as a Condorcet Truth-Tracker

It is a long-standing debate within political philosophy generally whether we want our political outcomes to be *right* or whether we want them to be *fair*. While democratic theory has traditionally taken the latter focus, democracy can be defended in the former way as well. How that can be done is the subject of this chapter and the next.[1]

For epistemic democrats, the aim of democracy is to 'track the truth'.[2] They see democracy as being more desirable than alternative forms of decision-making because, and in so far as, it does that. And one democratic 'decision rule'—one way of aggregating votes—is more desirable than another according to that same standard, so far as epistemic democrats are concerned.[3]

For procedural democrats, the aim of democracy is instead to embody certain procedural virtues.[4] Procedural democrats are divided

[1] This chapter is an 'informal restatement' of an earlier paper co-authored with Christian List (List and Goodin 2001), which should still be regarded as the more precise and hence authoritative version of these arguments. The proofs and calculations reported in this chapter are drawn from that earlier paper and are based on the work of my co-author there, Christian List.

[2] Estlund 1990, 1993, 1997, 1998. Rousseau arguably recommended democracy on the grounds that it tracks truths about the 'general will' and 'common good' (Rousseau 1762: bk 4, ch. 2; Barry 1964: 9–14; Grofman and Feld 1988; Coleman 1989: 204–5; cf. Estlund *et al*. 1989; Miller 1992: 56). Nineteenth-century utilitarians advocated democracy on the grounds it tracked truths about 'the greatest good for the greatest number' (Mill 1823).

[3] As characterized in Cohen's (1986: 34) article, which is primarily responsible for introducing the term into the literature, 'An epistemic interpretation of voting has three main elements: (1) an *independent standard* of correct decisions—that is, an account of justice or of the common good that is *independent* of current consensus and the outcome of votes; (2) a *cognitive* account of voting—that is, the view that voting expresses beliefs about what the correct policies are according to the independent standard, not personal preferences for policies; and (3) an account of *decision making* as a process of the adjustment of beliefs, adjustments that are undertaken in part in light of the evidence about the correct answer that is provided by the beliefs of others.'

[4] The modern *locus classicus* is Dahl 1979. See similarly Schumpeter 1950: pt 4.

among themselves over what those virtues might be, as well as over which procedures best embody them. But one central point that marks off all procedural democrats from epistemic democrats is this. Democracy, for them, is not about tracking any 'independent truth of the matter'. Instead, they see the goodness or rightness of an outcome as being wholly constituted by the fact of its having emerged in some procedurally correct manner.[5]

When voters are choosing between only two options, both epistemic and procedural standards point in the same direction. In that case, Condorcet's jury theorem—set out in the next section—reassures epistemic democrats that the correct outcome is most likely to win a majority of votes. In the two-option case, procedural democrats agree, on procedural rather than truth-tracking grounds. Different procedural democrats advocate various different decision rules.[6] But different though their recommendations might be in many-option cases, in the merely two-option case all those different decision rules converge on the majority winner.[7]

This happy coincidence is confined to the two-option case, however. Where there are three or more options on the table, recommendations of the different strands of democratic theory diverge. As Borda says in the opening sentences of his 1784 paper which fathered the modern literature on social choice:

There is a widespread feeling, which I have never heard disputed, that in a ballot vote, the plurality of votes always shows the will of the voters. That is, that the candidate who obtains this plurality is necessarily preferred by the voters to his opponents. But I shall demonstrate that this feeling, while correct when the election is between just two candidates, can lead to error in all other cases.[8]

Much modern writing on both social choice and electoral reform is dedicated to exploring the merits of alternate ways of aggregating people's

---

[5] Coleman and Ferejohn 1986: 7.

[6] Condorcet pairwise comparisons, the Borda count, the Hare or Coombs systems, etc. See the key to Table 5.1 for definitions. For further discussion of these and other decision rules, together with analyses of the extent to which they select the same outcomes, see Levin and Nalebuff 1995; Merrill 1984. For a discussion of their formal properties from a social-choice theoretic perspective, see Riker 1983: ch. 4.

[7] Even in the many-option case, there is convergence between the recommendations of those other procedurally favoured rules and rule by super-majorities of a requisite size. As Borda (1784: 88–9) shows, the majority winner will also be the Condorcet and Borda winners whenever $m > (k - 1)/k$, where m is the proportion of votes the majority winner receives and k is the number of options over which they are voting. A suitably large super-majority winner will therefore also be the Condorcet and Borda winner, provided it achieves two-thirds majority in a three-option contest, a three-fourths majority in a four option contest, *et seq*. [8] Borda 1784: 83.

votes into an overall social decision in those many-option cases.[9] Heretofore, however, those disputes have been conducted almost purely as intramural arguments within the proceduralist camp. Different social decision rules (different ways of aggregating votes into a collective decision) display different procedural virtues, and it is on that basis that we are typically invited to choose among them.[10]

There is an epistemic dimension to that choice as well, however. It is a mistake to suppose—as philosophers writing about epistemic democracy sometimes seem to do[11]—that the epistemic case for democracy based on the Condorcet jury theorem is at risk of collapse where there are more than two options on the table.

Anathema though it may be to some procedural democrats, plurality voting is arguably the simplest and possibly the most frequently used voting rule in many-option cases.[12] It is shown below that the Condorcet jury theorem can indeed be generalized from majority voting over two options to plurality voting over many options.

All that proves, however, is that the plurality rule is an 'epistemically eligible' decision rule, not that it is epistemically uniquely preferred. Two other decision rules, Condorcet pairwise criteria and Borda count procedures, have also been shown to have considerable truth-seeking powers.[13] Among all these alternative possible democratic decision rules, which is the most reliable truth-tracker in the more general 'many-option' case?

That question is addressed below. The sample calculations reported suggest that the differences are not great. Even the simplest democratic decision rule—the plurality rule—performs epistemically almost as well as any of the others, where the number of voters is at all

[9] Surveyed, respectively, in Mueller 1989 and Dummett 1985, 1997.

[10] Most especially, 'decisiveness': their capacity to yield transitive orderings and hence determinate choices, without cycling (Arrow 1963). In List and Goodin (2001: appendix 3) we show that cycling is not a problem, just so long as voters are even just slightly more likely to vote for one option rather than another (thus violating the so-called 'impartial culture' assumption, i.e., that they are as likely to vote for one as any other). See similarly Grofman 1993: 1554–7.

[11] Referring to previous versions of the Condorcet jury theorem, Estlund (1997: 189), for example, notes that 'the Jury Theorem assumes there are only two alternatives'. He goes on to say, 'For these and other reasons, the Jury Theorem approach to the epistemic value of democratic procedures is less than trustworthy.'

[12] Levin and Nalebuff 1995: 19. Condorcet (1792 in McLean and Hewitt 1994: 218; McLean and Urben 1995: 145) acknowledges the impracticality of his exhaustive pairwise comparison procedure; indeed, it has since been shown that some voting procedures, including ones following from Condorcet's and Lewis Carroll's proposals, are not computationally feasible (Bartholdi *et al.* 1989).

[13] As proven by Young (1988, 1995), building on Condorcet (1785)—though the assumptions built into that proof are problematic, in ways suggested in n. 20 below.

large (fifty or more, say). The conclusion, therefore, is just this: so long as the number of voters is reasonably large, virtually any of the social decision rules commonly employed (or recommended on democratic-proceduralist grounds) seem to perform reasonably well—and to perform nearly as well as each other—on epistemic-democratic grounds.

Condorcet's Jury Theorem

The Condorcet jury theorem, in its standard form, says this. Suppose each member of a jury is more likely to be right than wrong. Then the majority of the jury, too, is more likely to be right than wrong. Furthermore, the probability that the right outcome is supported by a majority of the jury is a rapidly increasing function of the size of the jury, converging to one as the size of the jury tends to infinity.[14]

Extrapolating from juries to electorates more generally, that result constitutes the jewel in the crown of epistemic democrats, many of whom offer it as powerful evidence of the truth-tracking merits of majority rule. The following passage from Brian Barry's famous article on 'The Public Interest' serves as a good illustration:

If we have a voting body of a thousand, each member of which is right on average fifty-one percent of the time, what is the probability in any particular instance that a fifty-one percent majority has the right answer? The answer, rather surprisingly perhaps, is: better than two to one (69%). Moreover, if the required majority is kept at fifty-one per cent and the number of voters raised to ten thousand... the probability that the majority... has the right answer rises virtually to unity (99.97%).[15]

The Theorem

What drives the Condorcet jury theorem is just the 'law of large numbers'. Think about tossing a fair coin. By definition, it has a 50:50 chance of landing heads or tails. In a small number of tosses (100, say), the actual numbers of heads and tails might well be 58:42, which is a considerable deviation from the expected proportions of 50 per cent and 50 per cent. But in a larger number of tosses (1,000, say), the actual

---

[14] Condorcet 1785: 279 ff.; Black 1958: 163–5.
[15] Barry 1964: 9. See similarly Barry 1965: appendix A, pp. 292–3; Kuflik 1977: 305–8; Spitz 1984: 206; Cohen 1986: 35; Grofman and Feld 1988; Estlund *et al.* 1989; Martin 1993: 142–4, 370–1; Gaus 1997: 149–50; Estlund 1993: 92–4; Waldron 1999*a*: ch. 5; 1999*b*: 134–6.

numbers might be 520 : 480—which is of course much closer to the expected proportions of 50 per cent and 50 per cent.[16]

So too with juries and electorates. As the number of voters increases, the actual proportion of the vote won by the correct option comes increasingly to approximate the antecedent probability of each individual's voting for the correct option. Suppose, for example, each voter has a 51 per cent probability of voting correctly. Among a small group (of 100, say), the actual distribution of votes might turn out to be 48 : 52, and the correct option might therefore lose. But the larger the group, the more likely it will be that the proportion of people voting correctly approximates the same 51 per cent as the probability of each individual voter's voting correctly. And that of course is just to say that it is more likely among a large number of voters that the correct option will win the election (and indeed, will do so by the same majority as represented by the individual's probability of voting correctly in the first place). Hence, if each individual is more likely to be right than wrong, then majority of such individuals is more likely to be right than wrong—and increasingly so, thanks to the law of large numbers, as the number of voters increases.

Here are the mathematics underlying the Condorcet jury theorem. Suppose there are N members of the jury, and let m be the number of jurors required for a majority. Suppose that all jurors have the same probability, p, of accurately assessing guilt or innocence. Suppose, finally, that jurors' assessments are statistically independent of one another's. Then the probability, P_N, that the jury collectively will reach a correct decision is given by the equation:

$$P_N = \sum_{i=m}^{N} (N!/[N-i]!i!)\,(p)^i\,(1-p)^{N-i}$$

Assuming each juror is more likely to be right than wrong in her own independent judgement (that is, $p > 0.5$), the majority of jurors are even more likely to be right than is any individual juror (that is $P_N > p$). Furthermore, the probability of the majority being correct increases rapidly as the size of the jury increases (N) increases, approaching certainty (1.0) in the limiting case.

A sample calculation might be useful. Suppose we have a jury of 3 people, each of whom is twice as likely to be right than wrong

---

[16] The point of the law of large numbers is that, although *absolute* deviations from the expected numbers still increase as the number of trials increases, those absolute deviations are a decreasing *proportion* of the total as the number of trials increases.

($p = 0.67$). Suppose the right result is to convict the accused. There are four ways a majority of jurors can reach that conclusion. All three jurors might vote to convict. There is exactly one way that might happen (that is, all three voting to convict). The probability of its happening is just the probability of Juror 1 voting correctly to convict ($p = 0.67$), multiplied by the probability of Juror 2 voting correctly to convict ($p = 0.67$), multiplied by the probability of Juror 3 voting correctly to convict ($p = 0.67$). The product of multiplying all those probabilities is 0.301. Alternatively, the 'correct' result might be achieved by a two-to-one vote: two out of three jurors might vote to convict. There are exactly three ways that might happen, corresponding to the cases in which Juror 1 or Juror 2 or Juror 3 votes erroneously to acquit, while the other two vote correctly to convict. The probability of each of those eventualities is just the probability of the two jurors voting correctly (0.67 times 0.67, again) multiplied by the probability of the other juror voting incorrectly ($1 - p = 0.33$). The product of those probabilities is 0.148. And, as I said, there are three different cases in which that outcome might occur.

The overall probability of the jury, by majority vote, coming to the correct decision to convict is then just the sum of the probabilities associated with each of the four ways it might come to that correct decision: 0.301 for the case of a unanimous vote to convict, and 3 times 0.148 for the three different ways in which they might vote by two to one to convict. That sum adds up to 0.745. In other words, the majority of the jury is in this case almost *thrice* as likely to be right than wrong, even though each juror individually is only *twice* as likely to be right than wrong.

Perceived Limitations

Much has been done—by statisticians, economists, political scientists, and others—to extend that result in many ways. It has been shown, for example, that a jury theorem still holds if not every member of the jury has exactly the same probability of choosing the correct outcome: all that is required is that the mean probability of being right across the jury be above one-half.[17] It is also known, for another example, that a jury theorem still holds even if there are (certain sorts of) interdependencies among the judgements of different electors.[18] The effects

---

[17] And the distribution to be symmetric: Grofman and Feld 1983: 268 ff.; Borland 1989: 183.

[18] Grofman and Feld 1983: 273–4; Borland 1989: 185–6; Ladha 1992; Estlund 1994.

of strategic voting in a Condorcet jury context have also been studied extensively, showing mixed results.[19] And so on.

What extensions and elaborations of the Condorcet jury theorem have almost invariably preserved, however, is the binary-choice form. The choice is thus typically between two options, or a series of options taken two-at-a-time.[20] And in choosing between each of those pairs the average competence of voters is required to be over one-half.[21]

Democratic theorists suppose that those constitute real limits on any epistemic case for democracy built on these foundations. As Estlund says, there is no reason to think that most important decisions in a democracy are going to boil down to two options[22]; neither, we might join Riker in adding, is there any reason to think that they can be innocuously decomposed into a series of such two-option decisions.[23] As Gaus says, there is no reason to think that people are generally more than half-likely to be right (particularly, we might add, where there are more than two options)—and the standard Condorcet jury theorem result works equally dramatically in reverse where they are more likely to be wrong than right, the probability of the collective choice being wrong quickly approaches certainty with growth in the size of the electorate.[24]

---

[19] Austen-Smith and Banks 1996; Feddersen and Pesendorfer 1998; Wit 1998; Coughlan 2000; Gerardi 2000; Guarnaschelli *et al.* 2000.

[20] Young (1988, 1995), following Condorcet's (1785) own lead, extends the theorem to cases of more than two options, but does so through a series of *pairwise* votes between them. Like Condorcet before him, Young assumes that each voter has the same probability of making the correct choice in each pairwise comparison as each other voter and as in each other pairwise comparison. On the face of it, this seems problematic in so far as it seems to treat probabilities in each of a voter's pairwise choices as independent of those in each of the same voter's other pairwise choices, when the probabilities in the one case may seem to constrain and be constrained by the probabilities in all the others (especially if people's preferences satisfy certain consistency conditions).

[21] Or almost always so: as Grofman and Feld (1983: 271) show, the majority might be more likely to be right than wrong even if the average competence of voters drops to $p_{mean} > 0.471$, although the value goes that low only when there are just three voters.

[22] Estlund 1997: 189.

[23] Shapley and Grofman (1984: 337) suggest that, 'The theorems discussed in this essay concern dichotomous choice, but this restriction may not be as serious as it might at first seem. If a group must choose from a set of alternatives ($k \geq 2$), then it may do so by using any one of a number of binary choice procedures that decompose into sequences of pairwise (right fork or left fork) choices.' But as Riker (1983: 60) says, 'Unfortunately, there is no fair way to ensure that there will be exactly two alternatives. Usually the political world offers many options, which, for simple majority decision, must be reduced to two. But usually . . . the *way* the reduction occurs determines *which* two will be decided between. There are many methods to reduce the many to two; but, as has long been obvious to politicians, *none* of these methods is particularly fair . . . because *all* methods can be rigged.'

[24] Gaus 1997: 150.

Thus, there is a lingering wariness in many quarters about just how general the Condorcet jury theorem might be, and whether it is really able to provide epistemic warrant for democratic procedures in any remotely realistic political situations. It seems unrealistic to suppose that there only two options on the table. It seems unrealistic to suppose that voters—individually, or even on average—are more than half-likely to be right in their assessments, especially where there are more than two options on the table. And where there are more than two options, it seems unrealistic to suppose that any one of them will necessarily command a clear majority. Any theorem that is limited to a two-option world is unlikely to be of any very general applicability to the social world as we know it.

Extending the Theorem

The Condorcet jury theorem can actually provide much more comfort to epistemic democrats than previously imagined. Contrary to what democratic theorists conventionally suppose, that theorem can be extended to plurality voting among many options. In those many-option cases, furthermore, voter competences can drop well below 50 per cent and the plurality winner remain most likely the correct choice.[25]

Plurality Voting Over Many Options

Condorcet's jury theorem can be extended to the case of plurality voting over k options, where one option (option i) is the epistemically 'correct' outcome. Specifically, the following can be shown to be true:

Proposition 1   (List and Goodin 2001)   Suppose there are k options and that each voter/juror has independent probabilities $p_1, p_2, \ldots, p_k$ of voting for options $1, 2, \ldots, k$, respectively, where the probability, p_i, of voting for the 'correct' outcome, i, exceeds each of the probabilities, p_j, of voting for any of the 'wrong' outcomes, $j \neq i$. Then the 'correct' option is more likely than any other option to be the plurality winner.

[25] How can that be? After all, if the probability of each voter being right is less than half, is not the probability of each being wrong more than half? And in that case, does not the 'reverse Condorcet' result set in, with a vengeance? The answer, of course, is simple. Under plurality rules the winner does not have to beat *all* the other options taken together. It has only to beat *each* of its rivals taken separately, where the opposition is divided $k - 1$ ways.

Proposition 2   (List and Goodin 2001)   As the number of voters/
jurors tends to infinity, the probability of the 'correct'
option being the plurality winner converges to 1.

The formal proof of those two propositions is provided elsewhere.[26]
But informally, what drives that result—just as the traditional version
of the Condorcet jury theorem—is the law of large numbers once again.

Among voters who are $p_1 = 0.40$ likely to vote for option 1 and
$p_2 = p_3 = 0.30$ likely to vote for options 2 and 3 respectively, the
statistically expected distribution of votes would be 40 per cent for
option 1 and 30 per cent each for options 2 and 3. Where the number of
voters is small, there might be sufficient deviation from those patterns
to tip the balance away from option 1 and towards one of the other
options. But that is less likely to happen as the number of voters grows
larger, since the actual proportions will approximate the expected ones
more and more closely with an increasing number of voters.

Thus, if each individual is individually more likely to vote for the
'correct' option than any other, then it is likely that more individuals
will vote for that 'correct' option than any other—and that likelihood grows nearer and nearer to certainty as the size of the electorate
increases.

Implications

There are endless refinements, extensions, and further challenges to be
investigated.[27] For the present purposes, however, it is more important to concentrate on the philosophical implications of this extended
Condorcet jury theorem in its simplest form for democratic theory
more generally.

The major consequences of the result, as it bears on theories of epistemic democracy, would seem to be the following. So long as each
voter is more likely to choose the correct outcome than any other,
each of the following implications are true.

---

[26] List and Goodin 2001: appendix 1. Fung (1995) sketched a similar result in an
unpublished paper that came to our attention subsequently.

[27] For example, we here assume that all voters have identical competence, that is,
identical probabilities of voting correctly. The standard (majority voting, two option) Condorcet jury theorem has been generalized to cases of unequal levels of competence across
voters/jurors; it is sufficient that their heterogeneous competences be symmetrically distributed around a mean which is itself greater than 0.5 (Grofman *et al.* 1983: 268–9). Similar
generalizations might be made in the k-option case. Among the further challenges that jury
theorems, in all their forms, must eventually confront is the issue of strategic voting.

Implication 1   The epistemically correct option is always more likely than any other option to be the plurality winner, and its probability of being the plurality winner increases with the number of voters.

This is just the analogue, for plurality voting over many options, to the standard Condorcet jury theorem's conclusions about majority voting over two options. Note however this difference between plurality and majority voting: in the case of plurality voting, the epistemically correct option only has to beat *each* alternative (unlike majority voting, where it would have to beat all alternatives taken together, scoring more than half the votes however many options there were). Whether or not the probability of the epistemically correct option being the chosen is greater than half ($P_N > 0.5$), making it a majority as well as plurality winner, at least the epistemically correct option is always more likely to be the plurality winner than is any *other* option—which is all it takes for it to win under the plurality rule.

Implication 2   Where there are several options on the table, the plurality jury theorem can work even where each voter is substantially less than one-half likely to be correct, as required in Condorcet's original two-option formulation.

The epistemically correct choice is the most probable among k options to be the plurality winner, just so long as each voter's probability of voting for the correct outcome exceeds each of that voter's probabilities of voting for any of the wrong outcomes. This implies that (if error is distributed perfectly equally) a better than $1/k$ chance of being correct is sufficient for the epistemically correct option to be most likely to be the plurality winner among k options.

Implication 3   The correct option is more likely than any other option to be the plurality winner, regardless of how likely each voter is to choose any other option.

That is to say, even if each voter is more than $1/k$ likely to choose each of several outcomes, the correct one is more likely to be the plurality winner than any other, just so long as the voter is more likely to vote for the correct outcome than that other outcome.

The Speed of Convergence

While the result just described shows that the probability of the correct option being the plurality winner converges to certainty as the number of voters tends to infinity, it says nothing about how quickly that probability increases with increases in the size of the electorate. So far as epistemic democrats are concerned, how the function behaves at the limit—where the number of voters approaches infinity—is of less practical significance than how it behaves when presented with plausible-sized electorates.

The great boast of the Condorcet jury theorem in its traditional form is that the probability of the correct option being the majority winner grows quite quickly with increases in the size of the electorate. To what extent can the extended plurality jury theorem make the same boast?

To address that question, consider some illustrative calculations.[28] First, notice that where each voter has a probability of more than 0.5 of choosing the correct option, the probability of the correct option being the plurality winner not only increases quickly with the size of the electorate: it increases *more* quickly in the k-option case than it does in the two-option case.[29] Take the case of a fifty-one-voter electorate, where each voter has a probability of $p = 0.51$ to choose the correct option. If there are just two options on the table (the $k = 2$ case), the correct option has a probability of only 0.557 of being the plurality (there, the majority) winner. If there are three options on the table (the $k = 3$ case), the probability of the correct option being the plurality winner in that same electorate jumps to 0.937.

Secondly, consider what happens in the multi-option case where voters are less than 50 per cent likely to choose the correct option, but where they are still substantially more likely to choose the correct option than incorrect ones. Suppose for example there are 3 options ($k = 3$), and suppose that the probability of each individual choosing the correct one is $p = 0.40$ while the probability of each choosing the two incorrect ones are $p = 0.35$ and 0.25 respectively. The probability that the correct option will then be the plurality winner in an electorate of fifty-one voters is 0.605; in an electorate of 301 voters it rises to 0.834; and in an electorate of 1,001 it rises to 0.965. The same happens in the four-option ($k = 4$) case all the more dramatically. Suppose the probability of each voter choosing the correct option is $p = 0.40$ and

---

[28] This discussion draws on the fuller set of such calculations reported in List and Goodin (2001: table 1, p. 287).

[29] That should not surprise us, given that choosing the correct option with a probability of more than 0.5 is a more stringent demand in the k-option case than in the 2-option case.

of choosing each of the three incorrect ones is $p = 0.3$, 0.2, and 0.1 respectively. Then the probability that the correct option will be the plurality winner in an electorate of fifty-one voters is 0.770, and in an electorate of 301 is 0.980.

Finally, consider the case where voters are only *slightly* more likely to choose the correct option than incorrect ones. Where each voter's probability of choosing the correct option from among k options is just over $1/k$ and the probability of choosing incorrect ones just under that, the probability of the correct option being the plurality winner increases much more slowly with increases in the size of the electorate. That is true with majority voting in the two-option case: where each voter is only $p = 0.51$ likely to choose the correct option, it takes over a thousand voters before the probability of the correct option being chosen rises to 0.737. Similarly with the many-option case. Take the $k = 3$ option case, where each voter is $p = 0.34$ likely to choose the correct option and $p = 0.33$ likely to choose each of the two incorrect ones; then a thousand voters raise the probability of the plurality winner being the correct option to 0.480 per cent. Or, again, take the $k = 4$ case, where each voter is $p = 0.26$ likely to choose the correct option and $p = 0.25, 0.25$, and 0.24 likely to choose each of the incorrect ones; then a thousand voters raise the probability of the plurality winner being the correct option to 0.476 per cent.

Even in these 'worst-case' scenarios, where voters are only a little more likely to be right than wrong, the movement of the probability figures is clearly in the desired direction. In the two-option case, with each voter only $p = 0.51$ likely to choose correctly, the probability that the majority winner will be the correct option rises from 0.580 where there are 101 voters to 0.737 where there are 1,001. In the three-option case just described, with each voter 34 per cent likely to choose correctly, the probability that the plurality winner will be the correct option rises from 0.358 with 101 voters to 0.489 with 1,001 voters. And in the four-option case, just described, with each voter 26 per cent likely to choose correctly, the corresponding rise is from 0.296 with 101 voters to 0.476 with 1,001. Clearly, as the size of the electorate increases the probability of the correct option being the plurality winner will eventually approach certainty.

Alternative Democratic Procedures and Their Epistemic Power

The plurality rule is not the unique truth-tracker in the k-option case. Condorcet himself pointed to others, in passages in his

Essai immediately following his development of the jury theorem itself.[30]

Among the several decision rules that might have considerable epistemic merit in the k-option case is the plurality rule (as shown above), pairwise comparisons, and the Borda count (as shown by Condorcet himself[31]). The informational requirements of the latter sorts of rules are, of course, much greater: they need to know complete rankings of all options from all voters, whereas plurality rules need only to know each voter's first choice among all the options. But given that extra information, those other rules track the truth too—in fact, better than plurality rule.

The actual numbers matter, though. In the discussion of the last section, it would have been cold comfort to epistemic democrats that the plurality rule is a good truth-tracker, provided the electorate is sufficiently large—if 'sufficiently large' had turned out to be some preposterously large number (billions of billions, say). In the present discussion, it would be similarly cold comfort to epistemic democrats that some particular decision rules track the truth better than others, if even the best truth-tracker turns out to track the truth abysmally badly, by any objective standards.

The computational exercise that follows employs one particularly plausible procedure for calculating the probabilities that each of the standardly discussed decision rules will pick the epistemically correct outcome, under varying assumptions about the probabilities that each voter has of choosing the correct (and each incorrect) option and about the number of voters. These calculations of course represent only a small sample of all possible combinations; as such, they strictly speaking 'prove' nothing. Still, they are illustrative—and the general outlines of the picture they sketch soon enough become tolerably clear.

To generate these probability calculations for each decision rule in the k-option case, we require some way of moving from (*a*) assumptions about the probability that each voter will choose each option, as in the plurality jury theorem, to (*b*) inferences about the frequencies with which voters can be expected to harbour particular 'complete orderings' of preferences over all options.

Details of the heuristic are set out elsewhere,[32] but here is the basic idea. The heuristic starts with a set of probabilities of each individual choosing each option. Those probabilities are taken to dictate the

---

[30] 1785: 122 ff.; Black 1958: 168–71; McLean and Hewitt 1994: 38–40.

[31] And others following him, especially Young (1988, 1995); see similarly Risse 2001: 719 ff.   [32] List and Goodin 2001: appendix 2, pp. 297–8.

probability with which each of those respective options will appear as the *first-choice option* in each person's preference ordering. For each possible first-choice option, the relative probabilities associated with each of the remaining options then dictate the probability of each of these options' appearing as the *second-choice option* in the same preference ordering; and so on until all places in the preference ordering have been allocated. In this way the probability of any given preference ordering is adduced from the product of the probabilities of filling each of the places with the relevant options in this fashion.

This is not the only possible way of proceeding from individuals' probability profiles to probabilities of overall preference rankings, I hasten to add. So in that sense, too, the results of the computations in Table 5.1 are merely illustrative: no more. But that heuristic does have a certain surface plausibility about it.[33]

Using this heuristic, we can generate (or perhaps I should say 'stipulate') probabilities of each voter holding each of various full preference orderings, from information about probabilities of each voter supporting each of various options. Given that information, we can then calculate the probabilities with which each option would win under each of various social decision rules—not just the plurality rule, but also the Borda count, the Condorcet pairwise comparison criterion, and the Hare and Coombs systems. The probability that particularly interests us, in the present context, is of course the probability that the outcome stipulated to be the 'epistemically correct' one will emerge under each of those decision procedures.

Table 5.1 reports, for the case of fifty-one voters, the probability that the correct outcome emerges from various social decision rules, under various scenarios (different numbers of options, different probabilities of each voter supporting each).[34] That table compares the performance of five social decision rules: the plurality rule, the pairwise Condorcet rule, the Borda count, the Hare system, and the Coombs system.

Before proceeding to any more detailed commentary on Table 5.1, one important thing must be said about all the calculations within it.

---

[33] True, this procedure does not allow for the possibility of incomplete, intransitive, or inconsistent preference orderings at the individual level. But in this respect, our procedure maps a central feature of how electoral systems themselves actually work, when they demand full preference orderings from people. There, just as in our procedure, voters are typically required to rank options by assigning exactly one rank to each option. Otherwise, under typical election laws, their votes will be deemed 'invalid' and not count.

[34] List and Goodin (2001: appendix table 4, p. 299) report the probabilities of the correct option (and each of the incorrect ones) emerging as the winner under those various decision rules for a few examples involving electorates of different sizes (11, 31, 51, and 71) and a few selected probabilities of each voter choosing correct and incorrect outcomes.

Table 5.1. *Probability that the 'correct' option is the unique winner for* N = 51

No. of options k=	Probabilities $p_1, p_2, \ldots, p_k$	Probability that option 1 (the 'correct' option) is the unique winner among N = 51 voters under the following decision rules:				
		plurality	pairwise Condorcet	Borda	Hare	Coombs
Scenario 1	2	0.51, 0.49	0.557	0.557	0.557	0.557	0.557
Scenario 2	3	0.60, 0.30, 0.10	0.988	0.993	0.995	0.993	0.993
Scenario 3	3	0.51, 0.25, 0.24	0.972	0.991	0.994	0.989	0.993
Scenario 4	3	0.40, 0.30, 0.30	0.666	0.740	0.760	0.737	0.775
Scenario 5	3	0.34, 0.33, 0.33	0.333	0.348	0.360	0.369	0.372
Scenario 6	3	0.335, 0.3325, 0.3325	0.311	0.315	0.326	0.338	0.339

Sources: All definitions are from Mueller 1989: 112–13. The table is reproduced from List and Goodin 2001: 292.

Definitions

Plurality rule: 'Choose the candidate who is ranked first by the largest number of voters.'

Condorcet pairwise criterion: 'Choose the candidate [if unique] who defeats [or at least ties with] all others in pairwise elections using majority rule.'

Borda count: 'Give each of the m candidates a score of 1 to m based on the candidate's ranking in a voter's preference ordering; that is, the candidate ranked first receives m points, the second one $m - l$, ..., the lowest-ranked candidate one point. The candidate [if unique] with the highest number of points is declared the winner.'

Hare system: 'Each voter indicates the candidate he ranks *highest* of the k candidates. Remove from the list of candidates the one [or in case of ties, ones] ranked highest by the fewest voters. Repeat the procedure for the remaining $k - 1$ candidates. Continue until only [at most] one candidate remains. Declare this candidate [if any] the winner.'

Coombs system: 'Each voter indicates the candidate he ranks *lowest* of the k candidates. Remove from the list of candidates the one [or in case of ties, ones] ranked lowest by the most voters. Repeat the procedure for the remaining $k - 1$ candidates. Continue until only [at most] one candidate remains. Declare this candidate [if any] the winner.'

The probabilities reported in the cells of that table represent the probability with which the correct outcome will be uniquely chosen by each decision rule. Decision rules can fail to do so in either of two ways. One is by choosing the wrong outcome. Another is by choosing *no* outcome, or anyway *none uniquely*. Sometimes, for example, there simply is no Condorcet winner; where there is not, Table 5.1 counts that as a failure. And sometimes decision rules produce no unique winner; Table 5.1 counts indecisiveness, in cases of 'ties', as a failure as well. The probability statistics in Table 5.1 thus reflect decisiveness as well as correctness *per se*.[35]

As I have remarked, all these decision rules are extensionally equivalent to one another in the two-option case. That is shown in Table 5.1, Scenario 1. That scenario represents the 'standard' Condorcet jury theorem finding, in its classical $k = 2$ form. It serves as a benchmark against which the epistemic performance of other decision rules in $k > 2$ cases can be compared.

Where the probability of each voter choosing the correct option remains at 0.51, but the number of options increases from $k = 2$ to $k = 3$, the probability of the correct outcome being chosen is greatly increased over that of the correct outcome being chosen in the two-option case. That has already been noted in connection with plurality voting. What is seen from Table 5.1, when comparing Scenarios 1 and 3, is that that is true (indeed, even more true) of all of the other standard social decision rules as well.

Where the probability of each voter choosing the correction option drops to just over $1/k$, and the probabilities of choosing each of the wrong ones to just below $1/k$, all of these decision rules will require large electorates (larger than the computing power available on any personal computer is able to analyse) in order to achieve any very high degree of epistemic strength. That is seen clearly from Scenario 5 and especially Scenario 6 in Table 5.1. But what is clear from the computations that are reported there is that the epistemic

---

[35] That is why the probability of the 'correct' option being chosen by the group is sometimes lower (in Scenario 6, especially) than the probability of each individual voting for the 'correct' option: those are cases in which the decision rule in question yielded either no winner or none uniquely. Casual inspection of sample calculations in List and Goodin (2001: appendix 2, table 4) suggest that this might also be why the Borda rule overtakes the Condorcet pairwise rule, where n is large. It is clearly the reason why the Hare and Coombs rules seem to become 'less reliable' for $n = 51$ than for $n = 31$. Those rules can be indecisive (that is, result in ties) in the $k = 3$ case only when n is a multiple of 2 or 3; that affects the case of $n = 51$ uniquely among the values of n for which probability calculations are there reported.

strength of each of the decision rules increases with the size of the electorate.[36]

There are many odd and interesting small differences among decision rules revealed in Table 5.1. Some of them might be quirks or artefacts of the particular methodology here used for calculating the probabilities.[37] Others might reflect deeper facts about the decision rules in question.

The principal things to be pointed out about Table 5.1, however, are not the differences but rather the broad similarities among all these decision rules. Particularly where the size of the electorate is at all large (fifty-one voters, say), each of these decision rules is pretty nearly as good a truth-tracker as any other. Even in the worst case, in Scenario 6, the epistemic strength of the worst decision rule (plurality) is only a few percentage points worse than the best (Hare or Coombs).

That is the first 'big' conclusion I would draw from Table 5.1. Any of these standard decision rules is pretty much as good as any other, on epistemic grounds. We are at liberty to choose among them, according to their varying proceduralist merits, pretty much without fear of any epistemic consequences.[38]

The second 'big' conclusion to be drawn from Table 5.1 is this. All of these standard decision rules have great epistemic merits, at least whenever the electorate is reasonably large. These merits are greatest where the probability of each voter choosing the correct outcome is substantially larger than $1/k$ (Scenarios 2 and 3). But these merits are still great, at least where the electorate is at all large (over fifty-one, say), even where the probability of each voter choosing the correct outcome is much nearer the probabilities of each voter choosing incorrect ones (Scenario 4). It is only where the probability of each voter choosing correctly is just barely over $1/k$, and of choosing each incorrect option is just under that, that very large electorates will be required to yield really reliable results (Scenarios 5 and 6). But even there, with a realistically large electorate (the size of a city, say), epistemic strength

---

[36] The exception in Table 5.1 is with the Hare and Coombs rules, in Scenario 6. The explanation for that exception is provided in n. 35. If Young's result (based though it is on rather different assumptions) can be applied, then there is every reason to believe that the epistemic strength of the Condorcet or Borda rules, anyway, will even exceed that of the plurality rule reported above.

[37] Such as the apparent 'reversal' with Hare and Coombs rules, discussed in n. 36.

[38] Estlund (1997: 174) supposes that 'democratic legitimacy requires that the procedure is procedurally fair and can be held, in terms acceptable to all reasonable citizens, to be epistemically the best among those that are better than random'. The upshot of the findings reported here is that the second half of that standard is largely superfluous: in large electorates, pretty much any procedure is epistemically as good as any other.

will grow high. And all of that seems broadly speaking true of all the standard decision rules ordinarily canvassed.

Conclusions

Social choice theorists and electoral reformers debate endlessly over what is the 'best' democratic decision rule from a procedural point of view. The present results show that we can afford to be relatively relaxed about that choice from an epistemic point of view. Some social decision rules might seem marginally better truth-trackers than others. But when the electorate is even remotely large, all of the standardly discussed decision rules (including even the plurality rule) are almost equally good truth-trackers. There is little to choose among them, on epistemic grounds.

Furthermore, all of them are *good* truth-trackers—in so far, of course, as there are any 'truths' for politics to track at all.[39] Just how good they all are depends on the size of the electorate and the reliability of electors. But even in the worst-case scenarios, it takes only city-sized electorates to allow us to be highly confident that the epistemically correct outcome emerges under any of the standard democratic decision rules (just so long as we can be minimally confident in the reliability of individual voters). In short, democracy in any of its standard forms is potentially a *good* truth-tracker: it can always hope to claim that *epistemic* merit, whatever other procedural merits any particular version of it might also manifest.

Thus, the present chapter has not so much settled these standing controversies in democratic theory as circumvented them. Proceduralists of the social-choice sort who are enamoured of the axiomatic merits of the Condorcet pairwise rule, for example, may feel free to recommend that rule on democratic-proceduralist grounds, without fear of any great epistemic costs. Old-fashioned democratic proceduralists who are anxious that people be governed by rules that they can understand, and who are thus attracted to the plurality rule by reasons of its sheer simplicity and minimal informational requirements, may feel almost equally free to recommend that rule without any great epistemic costs. Democracy has great epistemic merits, in any of its many forms.[40]

---

[39] Cf. Black 1958: 163; Miller 1992: 56.

[40] Assuming, of course, there are truths to be found, in the first place: cf. Ch. 7 below.

CHAPTER 6

Democracy as a Bayesian Persuader

Shift the analogy, now, from the jury room to the science laboratory. Scientists standardly conduct a series of experiments in their attempts to discover truths about the world. No one experiment is particularly conclusive, in its own right. Individually inconclusive though they may be, however, a *series* of such experiments can indeed constitute conclusive evidence. Bayes's formula provides a mathematical expression for specifying exactly how we ought rationally to update our a priori beliefs in light of subsequent evidence, in this way.

My proposal in this chapter is that we model voters in like fashion.[1] Votes, let us suppose, constitute (among other things[2]) 'reports' of the voter's experiences and perceptions. Further suppose that voters accord 'evidentiary value' to the reports they receive from one another through those votes.[3] Further suppose that voters are rational;[4] and part and parcel of their being rational is being prepared to revise their opinions in light of further evidence (including evidence emanating from one another's votes-cum-reports) following Bayes's formula.

In that process, each of us treats our own experiences and perceptions as one source of evidence, among others. We regard our own report as 'right, so far as it goes'.[5] In that sense, we are perfectly sincere when we vote (and thereby assert) ø. But we also acknowledge that our own

---

[1] Lindsay (1929: 37) e.g. likewise treats 'democratic discussion' as an important method of discovering truths, and emphasizes 'its likeness to the discovery of truth in other spheres', science in particular.   [2] Some of those 'other things' are discussed in Ch. 7.

[3] After the fashion of Popper (1945: ii. 225). 'Evidence of what?' I leave open for now, returning to that issue too in Ch. 7.

[4] Or perhaps are 'presumed' (or, stronger still, 'expected') to be rational—after all, democratic theory arguably provides no warrant for respecting the collective will of wilfully irrational electors.

[5] In much the same way that, in another of the solutions to Wollheim's paradox, we are construed as casting provisional votes ('ø, if the majority agrees').

experiences and perspectives are particular and peculiar, and hence our own perceptions are themselves as inconclusive as is any one isolated scientific experiment.

Because of that, voters striving to behave rationally should sincerely want to adjust their a priori beliefs in light of all other experiences and perceptions that are reported at the election. Bayesian updating of that sort may well lead people who started out believing (and voting) ø to end up believing (and genuinely wanting implemented) not-ø, just so long as sufficiently many votes-cum-reports point in that different direction.[6] Bayesian reasoning can, and in politically typical cases ought to, provide people with a compelling reason to accede to the majority's not-ø verdict, even though they themselves voted ø.[7] In this way, Bayesianism 'rationalizes' majority rule in some pretty strong sense.[8]

If anything, Bayesianism underwrites majoritarianism *too strongly*. As I shall go on to discuss in Chapter 7, it looks as if Bayesian rationality requires minorities to cave in too completely, too quickly. It deprives them of any rational grounds for persisting doubts, or hence persisting opposition, in the face of even modest majorities. And *that* does not seem right, either. Anyway it hardly seems consonant with our ordinary democratic theory and practice. What we would like to find are ways to rationalize majority rule without reducing continuing opposition to the status of utter irrationality, under virtually any and all circumstances. But that is the subject of the next chapter. In this chapter I shall first show how Bayesian thinking should make democratic outcomes so rationally compelling.

Why Bayes Bites

The broad pattern of Bayesian results I shall be presenting in this chapter will be familiar from my discussion of the implications of the Condorcet jury theorem in Chapter 5. Although the results do indeed parallel one another, the Bayesian formulation actually packs a slightly different and rather more powerful punch. Here is why.

[6] Therein lies the core of the 'rational consensus' model developed by Lehrer (1976*a,b*; 2001*a,b*; Lehrer and Wagner 1981). Disagree though I do with particulars of his modelling (Goodin 2001), Lehrer's work none the less served as the inspiration for my work in this chapter.

[7] I show below that Bayesianism tracks majoritianism closely in what I take to be typical sorts of cases, deviating from it only in unusual sorts of cases (see n. 28).

[8] There are of course lots of other weaker senses in which we might legitimate or justify majority rule. I shall save the phrase 'rationalizing majority rule' for rationalization in this strong Bayesian sense, however.

The Condorcet theorem shows that majority rule can have strong 'truth-tracking' merits. In Chapter 5, I rehearsed the standard results and indicated that one of the most restrictive assumptions traditionally thought to be required to make that theorem work can be substantially relaxed. Furthermore, Condorcet-style conclusions can be generalized to democratic rule of any of its many different forms, as Chapter 5 has shown.

The Bayesian results I shall be presenting in this chapter are close cousins to those Condorcet calculations.[9] The questions to which they are answers are slightly different. (Bayes tells us 'what is the probability that outcome K is right, given the fact that the majority has chosen K'; Condorcet tells us 'what is the probability that the majority will choose outcome K, given the fact that K is the right outcome'.) And Bayesian calculations of course turn on conditional probabilities that are absent from the Condorcet formulation.[10] Still, the general tendency of the two derivations is much the same. In both, the majority verdict proves to be increasingly convincing the larger the group; and in any remotely large group (of a few hundred or more, say) it becomes utterly compelling.

Similar though the derivations are, however, there is a compelling reason to run the present argument through Bayes rather than Condorcet. The Condorcet procedures start with subjective beliefs, and from those derive propositions about what probably is true, objectively. But what Condorcet's model is missing is any feedback loop: something that obliges people to revise their own subjective beliefs, in light of the probable objective truths thus revealed. That leaves Condorcet jury theorem results open to the riposte, anticipated by Simmel: 'my beliefs are *mine*; why on earth should my beliefs track *theirs*?'[11]

---

[9] As various others have noticed before me: see e.g. Young 1988; Austen-Smith and Banks 1996; Hawthorne 2001: 26 ff.

[10] The contribution of my presentation lies not in that basic idea but rather in demonstrating the robustness of the results across a range of different assumptions—and, of course, in seeing the need none the less to rationalize 'persisting opposition'. In standard applications in statistics and science, of course, it is ordinarily regarded as a great virtue of Bayesian inference that it is relatively insensitive to differences among people in their 'prior' beliefs, since updating in light of subsequent input will quickly produce 'rational consensus' even among people who started out with very different priors (as Keith Lehrer emphasizes, in the works cited in n. 6 above). But comforting though that may be in statistics and science, it is truly disconcerting for politics. Among writers on the Condorcet jury theorem, Estlund (1997: 186) seems to be alone in worrying about this implication of the theorem.

[11] Simmel 1908: 248. Estlund's (1997: 187) card-cutting thought experiment could be adopted in this direction, though it is not the use he actually makes of it: suppose there are 1,000 cards, 999 of which contain statements which are true and 1 false; what *reason*

Of course there is an obvious reply—which is that all of us are trying to track the truth, and the Condorcet result shows beliefs shared by the majority are more likely to do so. But that, in turn, is open to the equally obvious and standardly deployed rejoinder that political opinion is not (always: perhaps not even often) trying to track the truth. Remarking on the applicability of the Condorcet jury theorem to larger issues of political decision-making, Duncan Black scoffs:

Now whether there be much or little to said in favour of a theory of juries arrived at in this way there seems to be nothing in favour of a theory of elections that adopts this approach. When a judge ... declares an accused person to be either guilty or innocent, it would be possible to conceive of a test which, in principle at least, would be capable of telling us whether his judgement had been right or wrong. But in the case of elections no such test is conceivable; and the phrase 'the probability of the correctness of a voter's opinion' seems to be without definite meaning.[12]

Bayesian-style derivations are on stronger ground in these respects. Bayes operates on subjective beliefs, all the way through. People are presumed to have a set of beliefs—initial beliefs, together with conditional ones—expressed as subjective probability judgements.[13] Anyone who has such a constellation of beliefs is obliged by those beliefs to update her initial beliefs in light of the occurrence of the contingencies specified in her conditional beliefs. A person can refuse to do so only on pain of inconsistency. In that sense, the Bayesian canons impose a veritable 'obligation of Rationality' upon people to revise their beliefs in accordance with Bayes's rule.

The Bayesian argument developed here thus provides a more pointed formulation for democratic theorists, precisely because it operates directly at the level of the rationality of subjective individual belief rather than via the objective correctness of the collective choice. It is

does it give me to believe a proposition, just because I cut the deck to a card that contains a proposition which I antecedently believed to be false?

[12] Black 1958: 163. David Miller (1992: 56) remarks similarly: 'Although occasionally a political community may have to decide on some question to which it is plausible to suppose a correct answer exists (say some scientific question in circumstances where there is complete consensus on the ends which the decision should serve), it is much more likely that the issue will concern competing claims which cannot all be met simultaneously in circumstances where no resolution of the competition can be deemed objectively right.' On whether the 'truth' has any legitimate role in democratic politics, more generally, cf. Copp 1993; Estlund 1993, 1997, 1998. I return to these issues at the end of Ch. 7.

[13] Those probabilities are also presumed to be neither 0 (in which case you could never be persuaded of something, however strong the emerging evidence) nor 1 (in which case you could never be dissuaded). Thus, for Bayesians, nothing is ever literally impossible ($p = 0$) or certain ($p = 1$), just more-or-less likely. (Cf. the proposals in Lehrer 2001b.)

literally *irrational* for individuals to refuse to update their probabilities as Bayes's formula requires, whereas they might find some more or less disingenuous way to wiggle out of internalizing the verdict of an almost-certainly-right majority of a Condorcet-style jury.[14]

The trouble, as I go on to discuss in Chapter 7, is that Bayes's rule leads them to overdo it. Bayes's rule would have minorities caving in to the will of the majority much too completely and much too quickly, to democratic theorists' ordinary ways of thinking. That is the problem to which Chapter 7 addressed. For now, let me merely emphasize that that problem is a very real one on the Bayesian formulation, even more compellingly so than on the Condorcetian one.

Bayesian Updating

Basics

According to Bayes's formula, rationality requires that any given individual update her beliefs as follows:

$$p_{\o|x} = [(p_{x|\o})(p_{\o})]/[(p_{x|\o})(p_{\o}) + (p_{x|\text{not-}\o})(p_{\text{not-}\o})] \qquad \text{(Eq. 1)}$$

where:

- $p_{\o}$ is the 'prior probability' which she originally assigned to the proposition $\o$ (and $p_{\text{not-}\o} = 1 - p_{\o}$ is the prior probability which she originally assigned to its converse, not-$\o$);
- $p_{x|\o}$ is the 'conditional probability' which she assigns to event x occurring given that $\o$ is true (and $p_{x|\text{not-}\o}$ the corresponding conditional probability that she assigns to event x occurring given that not-$\o$ is true); and
- $p_{\o|x}$ is the 'updated' (revised or 'posterior') probability which she assigns to $\o$ being true, given that x has occurred.

Suppose now that she conducts an experiment several different times, each of which is independent of each other.[15] The canons of Bayesian updating assume that her conditional probabilities themselves ($p_{x|\o}$ and $p_{x|\text{not-}\o}$) remain unaltered across all those iterations. The only thing

---

[14] For this reason, Hawthorne 2001: 28 dubs his Theorem 3, reporting Condorcet through Bayes, the 'Convincing Majorities Theorem'.

[15] It is traditionally assumed that in order to apply Bayesian procedures we need to assume that all the experiments are 'independent' of one another, just as in traditional Condorcet jury theorem proofs we need to assume that jurors are. But that assumption can be relaxed in both cases, as discussed in Ch. 7.

that changes each time is her updated, revised probability, $p_{\emptyset|x}$. In a series of experiments, the probability as revised in light of previous set of experiments assumes the role of the 'prior probability' ($p_\emptyset$ in Equation 1 above) for the next round.

Thus, suppose we conduct an experiment twice, representing the updated probability after the first experiment as $p_{\emptyset|x}$ and that after the second as $p_{\emptyset|2x}$. Letting her probability estimate as updated on the basis of the first experiment ($p_{\emptyset|x}$) take the place of prior probability $p_\emptyset$ in the original equation,

$$p_{\emptyset|2x} = [(p_{x|\emptyset})(p_{\emptyset|x})]/[(p_{x|\emptyset})(p_{\emptyset|x}) + (p_{x|\text{not-}\emptyset})(1 - p_{\emptyset|x})]$$

Substituting the value of $p_{\emptyset|x}$ from Equation 1 and simplifying[16] yields:

$$p_{\emptyset|2x} = [(p_{x|\emptyset})^2(p_\emptyset)]/[(p_{x|\emptyset})^2(p_\emptyset) + (p_{x|\text{not-}\emptyset})^2(p_{\text{not-}\emptyset})]$$

Repeating the process n times, the revised probability after n rounds of updating (which I write $p_{\emptyset|nx}$) is

$$p_{\emptyset|nx} = [(p_{x|\emptyset})^n(p_\emptyset)]/[(p_{x|\emptyset})^n(p_\emptyset) + (p_{x|\text{not-}\emptyset})^n(p_{\text{not-}\emptyset})] \qquad \text{(Eq. 2)}$$

So far, that is just the standard Bayesian story. Now let me offer an interpretation of those equations to fit the case of interpersonal learning to which I want to apply them. Instead of 'conducting experiments', we are here imagining ourselves to be taking one another's votes-cum-reports as constituting evidence, which we feed into Bayesian updating equations in the ordinary way. In this context, the expression ($p_{x|\emptyset}$), can be interpreted as 'the probability that people will vote x, if $\emptyset$ is true'— and similarly, *mutatis mutandis*, for all the other similar expressions involved in Bayes's formula.[17] (Strictly speaking, x and not-x refer to the way people vote and $\emptyset$ and not-$\emptyset$ to the beliefs underlying them; in what follows, the more colloquial expression 'votes for $\emptyset$' ought be understood as shorthand for that.)

A Further Assumption: Common Credibility

Next let us assume, mainly for convenience of modelling and exposition, that the credibility which people attach to reports of each sort is the same for everyone across the community.[18] That is just to

---

[16] The mathematics are detailed in Goodin 2002: n. 20.

[17] Thus, ($p_{x|\text{not-}\emptyset}$) will be understood to be 'the probability that people will vote x if $\emptyset$ is not true'; ($p_{\text{not-}x|\text{not-}\emptyset}$) as 'the probability that people will vote not-x if not-$\emptyset$ is true'; and ($p_{\text{not-}x|\emptyset}$) as 'the probability that people will vote not-x if $\emptyset$ is true.'

[18] I suggest how we can move beyond this assumption in Ch. 7 below.

say, assume each person's conditional probability $p_{x|\phi}$ is identical to other person's $p_{x|\phi}$ throughout the group; and so on for all the other conditional probabilities involved in Bayes's formula.[19]

Those conditional probabilities may themselves be identical to one another, or they may be different from one another. In the analyses that follow, I shall consider cases of both sorts.[20] The assumption of 'common credibility' simply stipulates that each person in the group perceives those conditional probabilities the same way as each other person perceives them. The only way in which individuals differ from one another is in their 'prior probabilities', that is to say, the values they initially assign to the probability of ϕ being true, p_ϕ (and of course its converse, $p_{\text{not-}\phi} = 1 - p_\phi$).

What it Takes to Change People's Minds

Suppose there are A individuals who vote-cum-report x (which is to suggest that ϕ is true) and B individuals who vote-cum-report not-x (suggesting that not-ϕ is true). What we now want to know is how any given individual ought rationally to revise her prior probability estimate, given the fact of A reports of x and B of not-x.

That is to say, we want to know $p_{\phi|Ax\&B\text{not-}x}$. Analogously to Equation 2, we can say that for each individual:

$$p_{\phi|Ax\&B\text{not-}x} = [(p_{x|\phi})^A (p_{\text{not-}x|\phi})^B (p_\phi)]/[(p_{x|\phi})^A (p_{\text{not-}x|\phi})^B (p_\phi)$$
$$+ (p_{x|\text{not-}\phi})^A (p_{\text{not-}x|\text{not-}\phi})^B (p_{\text{not-}\phi})] \qquad \text{(Eq. 3)}$$

Now, let us ask under what conditions Bayesian updating will lead a person to the conclusion that not-ϕ is relatively more likely than ϕ (that is, $0.5 > p_{\phi|Ax\&B\text{not-}x}$). From Equation 3, we find[21] that that will be true if and only if:

$$(p_{\text{not-}x|\text{not-}\phi}/p_{\text{not-}x|\phi})^B (p_{\text{not-}\phi}) > (p_{x|\phi}/p_{x|\text{not-}\phi})^A (p_\phi) \qquad \text{(Eq. 4)}$$

Equation 4 tells us to adjust our prior probabilities (of ϕ and not-ϕ, respectively) in light of the relative reliability of reports from others that seem to support each proposition. By 'relative reliability' I mean just the relative likelihood that reports in favour of each proposition are right rather than wrong. And the adjustment in each case takes the form

---

[19] i.e. $p_{x|\text{not-}\phi}, p_{\text{not-}x|\text{not-}\phi}$ and $p_{\text{not-}x|\phi}$.
[20] The section with Equations 7 and 8 considers the case where $p_{x|\phi} = p_{\text{not-}x|\text{not-}\phi}$ and $p_{x|\text{not-}\phi} = p_{\text{not-}x|\phi}$ while other sections operate of this chapter and the next without any such restrictions. [21] Substituting and simplifying, as in Goodin 2002: n. 29.

of multiplying those likelihood ratios by themselves, as many times as there are people reporting in that direction (raising them to the powers of B and A respectively). Equation 4 says that you ought rationally to believe not-ø if your prior probability of $p_{not-ø}$, thus adjusted, is greater than your probability of $p_ø$, similarly adjusted.[22]

Democratic Learning, Bayesian Style

Equation 4 shows that people's coming around to the view that not-ø through Bayesian learning is a function of three things:

- One is 'prior probability' assessments, $p_ø$ and $p_{not-ø}$: the less likely you thought not-ø was to start with, the more persuading you are going to require to come to believe that that is the case, after all.
- A second factor is the 'weight of opinion', A and B: the more people there are who initially thought not-ø, the more credence that view ought to rationally have.[23]
- A third is the 'relative reliability' of reports that x (arguing for ø); and that not-x (arguing for not-ø): the more relatively reliable reports are that not-ø ($p_{not-x|not-ø}/p_{not-x|ø}$), compared to those reporting that ø ($p_{x|ø}/p_{x|not-ø}$), the more confident we ought rationally be that not-ø is the case.

As a first stab at trying to get some sense of what drives Equation 4, I will bracket out the latter two factors one at a time; then I will return to modelling all three factors simultaneously in play.

Note that I shall be confining myself to cases where people think that one another's reports in either direction are more likely to be right than wrong. That is to say, I shall confine my attention to cases where $p_{not-x|not-ø} > p_{not-x|ø}$ and $p_{x|ø} > p_{x|not-ø}$. If the converse is the case, and reports are seen as being more likely wrong than right, then the more reports there are asserting ø the *less* probable we will think it to be that ø is actually the case. In Bayesian arguments, just as in the Condorcet jury theorem, majorities are persuasive only if people are thought to be more likely to be right than wrong.[24]

---

[22] Strictly speaking, 'you ought rationally believe not-ø is *more likely to be true* than ø': the likelihood of either proposition being true might still fall below the threshold you require for 'believing' a proposition to be true.

[23] Assuming, that is, that both sides are more likely to be right than wrong (for reasons given in the next paragraph of the main text).

[24] On the corresponding Condorcet result, see e.g. Waldron 1989: 1322–3; 1999b: 135; Estlund 1993: 93.

Bracketing Out the 'Weight of Opinion'

To bracket out the effects of the 'weight of opinion', let us assume that the numbers of people reporting for and against the proposition are equal. That allows us to see how far differential relative reliability and the sheer size of the group go towards changing people's minds. This reveals the conditions under which sheer Bayesian updating can convince people, even without there being a decisive majority on either side of the issue.

Ex hypothesi in the case under discussion there are equal numbers of reports on each side of the proposition $(A = B)$. Substituting that into Equation 4 and rearranging terms yields:

$$[(p_{\text{not-}x|\text{not-}\emptyset}/p_{\text{not-}x|\emptyset})/(p_{x|\emptyset}/p_{x|\text{not-}\emptyset})]^B > p_\emptyset/p_{\text{not-}\emptyset} \qquad \text{(Eq. 5)}$$

For convenience, let us use the symbol R to indicate the 'differential relative reliability' of those reporting in support of and in opposition to $\emptyset$, $R = (p_{\text{not-}x|\text{not-}\emptyset}/p_{\text{not-}x|\emptyset})/(p_{x|\emptyset}/p_{x|\text{not-}\emptyset})$. Substituting that into Equation 5 and manipulating terms yields:

$$R^B/(1 + R^B) > p_\emptyset \qquad \text{(Eq. 6)}$$

The interesting question to ask of Equation 6 is how quickly people who previously thought that $\emptyset$ was the case $(p_\emptyset > 0.5 > p_{\text{not-}\emptyset})$ will be brought around to the view that not-$\emptyset$ $(p_{\text{not-}\emptyset|Ax\&Bnot-x} > p_{\emptyset|Ax\&Bnot-x})$. In Equation 6, that is a function of two things: first, the 'differential relative reliability' of reports favouring each conclusion; and second, the absolute number of people reporting (remembering that, in the case at hand, we assume *equal* numbers on each side of the question).

Consider now some sample calculations of various conditions under which Equation 6 would be satisfied—which is to say, conditions under which Bayesian updating would have convinced people who originally thought that $\emptyset$ is true to change their mind.[25] Suppose for example that we have four voters split equally on an issue (so $A = B = 2$); and suppose we think that the reports against $\emptyset$ are three times more reliable than reports in favour of $\emptyset$ $(R = 3.00)$. Feeding those values into Equation 6 we find that anyone who initially thought $\emptyset$ to be less than 90 per cent certain $(p_\emptyset < 0.900)$ would then be convinced by that conjunction of size and relative reliabilities that it is more likely than not that the opposite is instead true (that is, $p_{\text{not-}\emptyset} > 0.5$).

---

[25] Others are presented in Goodin 2002: appendix.

These two factors—group size or differential relative reliability—can induce dramatic changes in updated Bayesian opinions, acting either alone or together. Consider some of the conjunctions of circumstances which would lead someone who was initially 90 per cent or more certain of ø to come to believe that not-ø is more likely instead, on assessments updated in the lights of other people's reports. That would be true, for example, if there were eight voters equally split on the issue ($A = B = 4$) and reports against ø were three-quarters more reliable than ones in favour ($R = 1.75$). It would be true, again, if there were twelve voters equally split on the issue ($A = B = 6$) and reports against ø were half again more reliable ($R = 1.5$). It would be true, still again, if there were sixty-four voters ($A = B = 32$) and reports against ø were one-tenth more reliable ($R = 1.10$). It would be true if there were 512 voters ($A = B = 256$) and reports against ø were one-hundredth more reliable ($R = 1.01$). In all those cases someone who was antecedently up to 90 per cent certain that ø was the case ($p_ø < 0.900$) would, after Bayesian updating, have to conclude that not-ø is actually more likely than ø (that is to say, conclude that $p_{\text{not-ø}} > 0.5 > p_ø$).

The general message is that convergence occurs really quite quickly, with increases in either the size of the group or in the relative reliability of one side's reports compared to the other's. Take the smallest possible equally divided group (with one person on each side of the question): if both parties agree that one person's reports are three times more reliable than the other's then the less reliable party ought rationally to be persuaded of the other's view, even if she was initially up to 75 per cent confident of her prior opinion. In an equally divided jury of twelve people (with, thus, six people on each side of the issue), the other side's reports need be only half again more reliable than their own to compel the rational assent of anyone who was initially up to 91.9 per cent confident of her prior opinion. With larger numbers of people on each side of the issue, even tiny differentials in the relative reliability of one side's reports over the other's will make that side's reports utterly convincing even to someone who was initially utterly convinced of the opposite (a one-hundredth differential in relative reliability proving convincing to people who were up to 92.7 per cent confident of the opposite opinion, in equally divided groups with 256 people on each side of the issue, for example).

Bracketing Out Differential 'Relative Reliability'

Next let us bracket out the effects of differential relative reliability of reports in each direction. To do that, we can assume that the conditional probability of people's 'getting it right' in either direction is the same ($p_{x|\emptyset} = p_{\text{not-}x|\text{not-}\emptyset} = p_c$) and that the conditional probability of their 'getting it wrong' in either direction is the same ($p_{x|\text{not-}\emptyset} = p_{\text{not-}x|\emptyset} = p_e$).[26]

Using that notation, Equation 4 can be rewritten:

$$(p_c/p_e)^B(p_{\text{not-}\emptyset}) > (p_c/p_e)^A(p_\emptyset)$$

which, rearranging terms and reducing, can be rewritten,

$$[p_c/p_e]^{(B-A)} > p_\emptyset/p_{\text{not-}\emptyset} \qquad \text{(Eq. 7)}$$

For ease of expression, again, let $Q = (p_c/p_e)$ and rewrite Equation 7 as

$$Q^{B-A}/(1 + Q^{B-A}) > p_\emptyset \qquad \text{(Eq. 8)}$$

Equation 8, notice, is structurally identical to Equation 6, with Q taking the place of R and $(B - A)$ taking the place of B in that previous equation. Thus, the calculations performed in the previous section also chart the consequences of Equation 8 as well, with just a couple of amendments: the size of the majority thinking that not-$\emptyset$ $(B - A)$ substituting for the absolute numbers thinking both not-$\emptyset$ and $\emptyset$ ($B = A$), which was assumed to be the same in that previous section but not here; and substituting the 'absolute reliability' of people's reports (p_c/p_e) for 'relative reliability' (R) in the previous section.

Once again, we are searching for conditions such that someone who was initially 90 per cent certain that $\emptyset$ was true would become convinced that not-$\emptyset$ was the case, instead. On the present assumptions, the convergence story is slightly different but no less strong. If there are just four more votes-cum-reports on one side of the question than the other, for example, those reports need to be only three-quarters more likely to be true in order to convince anyone who was initially 90 per cent confident that not-$\emptyset$. With a majority of thirty-two, reports need be only a tenth more likely to be true to prove similarly convincing. With a majority of 256, reports need be only a hundredth more likely to be true to prove similarly convincing. On the present assumptions, just as on the previous ones, increases in either of the two factors—here, absolute reliability or the size of the majority—alone or together can produce those results.[27]

---

[26] Politically, this might be regarded as one way of showing everyone 'equal respect', treating everyone's reports as equally reliable as everyone else's.

[27] Notice that Equation 8, and the discussion below based on it, deals strictly in terms of the *absolute size* of the majority, with no regard whatsoever for the *relative proportion*

Putting All the Factors into Play

Finally, let us see if the Bayesian model's proclivity for convergence persists even taking account of all three key factors simultaneously. The last section assumed that the conditional probabilities of being right in both directions were the same ($p_{x|\emptyset} = p_{\text{not-}x|\text{not-}\emptyset} = p_c$) and that the conditional probabilities of being wrong in both directions were the same ($p_{x|\text{not-}\emptyset} = p_{\text{not-}x|\emptyset} = p_e$). Let us now relax that assumption, to allow for the possibility of differential error rates in each direction. We will still be looking at the ratio of the probability that reports are right to the probability of that they are wrong, but we now allow that that ratio might be different for reports arguing in favour of $\emptyset$ and for ones arguing against $\emptyset$, with the former written $r_+ = p_{x|\emptyset}/p_{x|\text{not-}\emptyset}$ and the latter $r_- = p_{\text{not-}x|\text{not-}\emptyset}/p_{\text{not-}x|\emptyset}$.

Substituting those expressions, Equation 4 then becomes

$$r_-^B/r_+^A > p_\emptyset/p_{\text{not-}\emptyset}$$

or, equivalently,

$$r_-^B/(r_+^A + r_-^B) > p_\emptyset \qquad \text{(Eq. 9)}$$

Once again, let us explore combinations of votes-cum-reports in favour of $\emptyset$ (numbering A) and opposing it (numbering B) which would be required to persuade by Bayesian logic someone who was initially very confident of $\emptyset$ that not-$\emptyset$ instead. We can do that by stipulating different suites of reliability ratios (r_+ and r_-), and then asking for what values of A and B Equation 9 would hold for the case of someone who initially was 90 per cent certain of $\emptyset$ ($p_\emptyset = 0.90$).

Rather than describing in detail lots of different scenarios, let me simply describe what happens in what is presumably the most typical and therefore the most interesting case. This is the case where reports for and against $\emptyset$ are both pretty reliable and pretty nearly each as reliable as the other; that is to say, values of r_- and r_+ are both reasonably high (over 2.0, say) and close together (within 10 per cent of one another, say). In that case, someone who started out 90 per cent certain of $\emptyset$ ought rationally to change her mind whenever there are more votes against $\emptyset$ (B) than for it (A), just so long as those votes-cum-reports

of people reporting one way rather than the other. Equation 8 asserts that a majority of 6 ought rationally to produce the same effects, in terms of Bayesian updating of people's probabilities, whether the vote is 7 to 1 or 1,000,000,007 to 1,000,000,001. Intuitively, that seems crazy. A vote of 7 to 1 represents a landslide—an overwhelming majority of almost 88%. A vote of 1,000,000,007 to 1,000,000,001 represents as slender a majority as one can possibly imagine. Yet, on the Bayesian logic sketched above, both should rationally prove equally compelling in forcing the losers to change their minds.

against ø are even just slightly more reliable than those in favour of ø $(r_- > r_+)$.[28]

Conclusion

Thus, in what we might reasonably regard as the most typical case of democratic rule—the case of reasonably large electorates, where both sides' reports are reasonably reliable and where neither's is too much more credible than the other's—Bayesianism converges towards majoritarianism.[29] In those circumstances, Bayesians ought rationally to be convinced of a proposition, basically whenever a majority reports itself in favour of it, whatever their own previous views of the matter.

---

[28] Here is what happens in other sorts of scenarios. (1) Where votes-cum-reports against ø are much more reliable than votes-cum-reports in favour of ø, then just a handful of votes-cum-reports against ø might suffice to change the of mind of someone who was initially 90% certain of ø, even if there is a substantial majority voting-cum-reporting in favour of ø. Suppose e.g. $r_- = 2.02$ and $r_+ = 1.01$; then it will take four anti-ø votes (i.e. for not-*x*) to change the mind of someone who was initially 90% certain of ø; but those mere 4 votes for not-*x* ought to suffice to persuade her, even if the pro-ø vote *A* is up to about 60. (2) Where the reliability of votes-cum-reports for and against ø are close to one another but both low (just over 1.0), then it takes quite a few votes against ø before someone who was initially 90% certain of ø to change her mind; but once that number of *B* votes has been passed, each further anti-ø vote proves more convincing than each pro-ø one; and there is some further number of not-*x* votes *B* such that she ought rationally to abandon her initial belief in ø, even if pro-ø *A* voters are actually still in the majority. Suppose, for example, $r_- = 1.12$ and $r_+ = 1.008$; then someone who was initially 90% certain of ø will be persuaded to change her mind only once $B = 20$ people have cast anti-ø votes compared to her sole pro-ø vote ($A = 1$); but where there are over $B = 21$ anti-ø votes, she might be persuaded to change her mind even under many circumstances where $A > B$ (she ought rationally to change her mind e.g. if not-ø has $B = 25$ votes to ø's whopping majority of $A = 85$).

[29] And all the more so, as I have shown, where both sides' reports are equally reliable.

CHAPTER 7

Rationalizing Persisting Opposition

It is an old, familiar puzzle in the theory of democracy why, simply because you were outvoted, you should suddenly accept proposals which you had vigorously opposed at the election itself. In discussing 'The Phenomenon of Outvoting', sociologist Simmel says, 'It appears nonsensical that a man subjects himself to an opinion which he holds to be false, only because others hold it to be true.'[1] This is formalized for political philosophers as Wollheim's paradox: how can you vote for ø, but then immediately accept the majority's verdict of not-ø, when voting for ø is seen as asserting 'ø is true' and acceding to the majority verdict is seen as accepting 'not-ø is true'?[2] On its face, that seems to be a flat-out contradiction.

Many ways out of Wollheim's paradox already exist.[3] The Bayesian argument sketched in Chapter 6 offers yet another. As I have there shown, Bayesian reasoning can provide people with a compelling reason to accede to the majority's not-ø verdict, even though they themselves voted for ø.[4] In that way, Bayesian updating offers one more mechanism for overcoming Wollheim's paradox. It explains how people who initially thought ø ought perfectly rationally to come around to the view not-ø, just because the majority has voted that way.

The trouble is that Bayes's procedures seem to drive everyone toward the majority view *too strongly* in large electorates. In those typical sorts of cases, Bayesian considerations make it utterly irrational

---

[1] Simmel 1908: 248.

[2] Wollheim 1962. His talk in terms of what 'ought be done' allows for equivocation among different sense of 'ought'. Talking instead in terms of what is 'true'—or, as suggested by Estlund (1989*b*), what one 'believes' (implicitly: 'to be true')—avoids those evasions.

[3] Weiss (1973) claims that none of them work. I share Barry's (1973) sense that all of them would. Many of these moves were anticipated in Simmel (1908).

[4] Ch. 6 has shown that Bayesianism tracks majoritianism closely in what I take to be typical sorts of cases, deviating from it only in unusual sorts of cases (see Ch. 6 n. 28).

for anyone ever to continue disagreeing, once everyone has voted. By Bayesian reasoning, even rather small majorities ought rationally to be utterly conclusive, even for people who were initially pretty (for example, 90 per cent) certain that the opposite was the case.[5]

Paradoxical though Wollheim's result might have been in one direction, this conclusion seems to be every bit as puzzling in the other. Certainly it does not track how we ordinarily think about the give-and-take of ordinary political life. Frustrated though we might often feel by others' recalcitrance, nevertheless we are rarely tempted to consign persistent advocates of opposing perspectives to the loony-bin. Acceptance of both the fact and the legitimacy of persisting disagreement, not only over deep 'comprehensive doctrines' but also over mundane 'policy choices', is a (and arguably the) defining feature of liberal democracy.[6]

Thus the 'paradox of persisting opposition'. How can we rationalize persisting opposition, in the face of the Bayesian results presented in the previous chapter (and, more broadly, of the Condorcet-style results in the chapter before that)?

Evading the Paradox by Extending Bayes

Challenged to rationalize majoritarianism without derationalizing ongoing opposition, we might begin by asking what resources might remain within a broadly Bayesian framework for doing both of those things simultaneously? As we shall see, none of the easy and obvious modifications seem likely to produce that desired result.

Increasing Confidence in Prior Beliefs

Simply increasing still further the confidence with which people held their prior beliefs is decreasingly plausible. Few of us feel much more than 90 per cent sure of much of anything, certainly not prior to acquiring any evidence on the subject. In any case, that provides no real solution.[7]

---

[5] Estlund 1997: 188 expresses similar concerns with the Condorcet jury theorem, which likewise 'seems to imply that, in groups of much size ... [the majority] is ... virtually infallible. ... [T]he minority voter would have no basis for thinking the procedure tends to be correct which was not an equally good basis for thinking it is almost correct every time. To accept this is to surrender one's judgment to the process.' Earlier, Estlund (1993) had coined the phrase 'epistemic authoritarianism' for such phenomena.

[6] Rawls 1993: 56 ff. Waldron 1999b.

[7] Short of setting $p_\theta = 1.0$, in which case no amount of evidence could (according to Bayes's formula) ever change your mind. That is not only irrational but also, in the present

Suppose we were to ask what it would take to convince people who were initially 99 or 99.9 per cent confident of the opposite. Certainly it takes more people voting-cum-reporting not-ø to change the mind of someone who was initially *that* certain of ø. But in reasonably large electorates—ones numbering in the thousands, much less millions— we could easily come up with those numbers, and the basic pattern of results would be broadly the same as before.

Thus, in any very large electorate even people who were initially very, very confident of the opposite would rationally be forced to change their minds, in the face of even relatively modest majorities and/or modest differentials in relative reliabilities.

Dropping the Assumption of Common Credibility

Another way to modify the above model is by dropping the assumption of common credibility introduced in Chapter 6. That is to say, some people might think that certain sorts of reports constitute more telling evidence than do other people; and in consequence the value that one person assigns to the conditional probability $p_{x|ø}$ or $p_{\text{not-}x|\text{not-}ø}$ or whatever might be higher than the value that some other person assigns to the same conditional probabilities.

But that is unlikely to change greatly the broad pattern of results reported in Chapter 6. The equations can all simply be rewritten. Instead of being expressed in terms of conditional probabilities which are the same for everyone, we can talk instead in terms of the *average* (mean) value for each of those conditional probabilities for everyone across the entire population. Just so long as the distribution of conditional probabilities is symmetric around the mean, the same results would presumably obtain.[8]

Dropping the Assumption of Uniform Reliability

The previous derivations assume uniform reliability across all people, which is implausible in the real world. Strictly speaking, though, there is no need for that assumption, either. We can admit that some individuals are more reliable in their reports than others, and the same broad pattern of results will none the less emerge (perhaps, on one scenario, even more strongly).

context, strikingly undemocratic, amounting as it does to saying that you are never prepared to yield no matter how many others say you are wrong.

[8] In ways analogous to Grofman *et al.* (1983: 268–9) or Hawthorne (2001). This is a speculation, to be sure: but it is beyond the scope of this chapter to attempt a proof.

The Condorcet jury has been reproven for voters with varying competences, assuming just that the distribution of individual competences is symmetrical around the mean (and, of course, the mean is above 0.50).[9] So too, presumably, in the Bayesian case as well. Just so long as the reliability of reports is symmetrical around the mean, we can presumably just rewrite all the above equations in terms of the average (mean) reliability of reports, and the same results would emerge.[10]

Even the assumption of symmetry may not be strictly necessary. Suppose the reliability of reports is skewed, and furthermore it is skewed in such a way that the more frequent reports are also the more reliable ones. The reliability of reports being skewed in *that* manner would mean that the majority's views should be all the *more* rationally persuasive than they would have been, had all reports been equally reliable or had reliability been normally or symmetrically distributed.[11]

Dropping the Assumption of Independence

The most common way of repudiating the Condorcet/Bayes conclusions is to say that those models assume that voters act 'independently' of one another, in ways untrue to the real political world.[12]

Some point to the way that the course of a democratic discussion will affect everyone at once, thus undermining their independence in ways they imagine to be fatal to the Condorcet jury theorem (and Chapter 6's Bayesian derivations by extension). Others point to the effects of restrictions on the number of different channels of mass communication or of restrictions on the number of different options to choose among at the election. Still others point to the way that parties and factions undermine the independence of each person's vote from every other's.

The first factor does not in fact undermine 'independence' in any respect relevant to these derivations, though. Hawthorne's insightful remarks merit quotation at length, in this regard:

The kind of independence that is relevant to Jury Theorems [and Bayesian extensions of them] is not at all the kind of restriction on voter communication that some have taken it to be. Rather, in this context *probabilistic independence*

---

[9] Grofman *et al.* 1983: 268–9.

[10] 'Presumably': but again, it is beyond the scope of this chapter to attempt a proof of that, either.   [11] Hawthorne 2001: 13 ff.

[12] Rawls (1971: 358) e.g. dismisses the relevance of the Condorcet jury theorem in two lines, saying that 'it is clear that the votes of different persons are not independent. Since their views will be influenced by the course of the discussion, the simpler sorts of probabilistic reasoning do not apply'.

means that after the public debate each voter assesses the merits and votes his or her own best judgment. Thus, *probabilistically independent voting* means *independent voting* as the term is commonly understood—*voting one's conscience* rather than as part of a block or faction.[13]

And much the same thing can be said about having few channels of communication or few electoral options to choose among: as long as people exercise independent judgement in choosing among those options or channels, their independence is preserved in all the ways that matter to the Bayes/Condorcet derivations.

It is, therefore, only intentional factional or 'party-line' voting that will really unsettle the arguments of Chapter 6. Take the worst-case scenario, from the point of view of those derivations. Imagine a one-party state, in which everyone votes exactly the same way as the leader of that party. However many voters fall in behind their leader, the number of 'independent' points of view there is effectively only one; and in terms of the models developed above, the N of (independent) voters is one. In a two-party setting, where everyone is inextricably bound to one party or another and everyone votes exactly the same way as their party's leader, the N of (independent) voters is two. And so on.

One thing to notice straightaway is this: even with complete interdependence of this sort among voters, the Bayesian model none the less applies. All that happens is that the effective number N of (independent) voters is reduced to the number of independent parties or factions there are in the political community. Now, in any large and moderately diverse political community, the number of independent parties and factions is likely to be non-trivial: not as large as the number of voters, to be sure, but maybe plenty large enough to make the Bayesian case for acceding to the opinion of the majority (here, of parties/factions) rationally compelling.

To make it politically realistic, however, that worst-case scenario needs to be modified two ways, both of which enhance the relevance of the Bayesian arguments in Chapter 6. First, in a multi-party state, people are usually not inextricably bound to any particular party. Instead, they exercise a certain amount of independent judgement in deciding which of the parties to support. In so far as they do, Hawthorne's argument applies *mutatis mutandis* there as well.

Secondly, parties are rarely so monolithic as the strong follow-the-leader stipulation of the worst-case scenario. More typically, people's votes are interrelated with one another's to some greater or lesser

---

[13] Hawthorne 2001: 4; for further explication of reasons behind this conclusion, ibid. 15–16. See similarly Waldron 1989: 1327–8; Estlund 1994.

degree. The greater the covariance among people's votes, the larger the number of voters or the larger the majority it takes to produce changes of any given magnitude in the posterior probability that the view backed by the majority is correct. But in electorates of thousands or millions, electors' votes can covary substantially without overturning the basic Bayesian results. The majority there is almost certainly right, and persisting opposition to its edicts is almost certainly irrational.

Moving Beyond Bayes

The upshot of the last section is that modifications within the Bayesian framework seem unlikely to overcome this paradox of persisting opposition. That being so, we might next consider ways of moving beyond the Bayesian framework. There are various ways in which this might be done.

Repudiating Bayesian Reasoning Altogether

The most dramatic, of course, would be to repudiate Bayesian rationality altogether. We might simply say that people do not update their beliefs systematically in the ways that Bayes's model prescribes. That might be why we find opposition persisting. And that may be why we find ourselves feeling comfortable with that fact: maybe we are as irrational as they.

Certainly there is psychometric evidence aplenty that people are not good Bayesians, at the margins.[14] But the phenomena here in view go well beyond those margins. The psychometric experiments used to trip up people's ordinary reasoning in all those ways really ought to be seen as the artful contrivances that they are (as anyone who has ever tried designing one will immediately appreciate). What are here in view, in contrast, are cases of a perfectly ordinary sort where rationality is less prone to go astray.

In any case, the issue here is not whether people are good Bayesians but rather whether democratic theorists are prepared to insist that they *ought* to be. Arguably, at least, democratic theory prescribes rationality, among its many other prescriptions—and it does so, whether or not, in practice, citizens always do (or perhaps even always can) adhere faithfully to its edicts.

---

[14] Bell *et al.* 1988.

Who to Believe?

Voters trying to decide which side of the argument is more likely to be right than wrong, we might suppose, typically comes down to trying to decide whom they believe. They do not simply count the number of people on each side, as Bayesian procedures would have them do. They may not even just weigh the arguments, regardless of their source. A report of not-ø coming from someone we would ordinarily expect to be telling us ø is simply a lot more persuasive than a similar report coming from a notoriously not-ø sort of reporter.[15]

All of these judgemental elements are clearly crucial to political decision-making. But none of them necessarily overturn the conclusions developed in Chapter 6. Here is one way to look at it.[16] We can have all the discussion we want; and that discussion can genuinely change minds, in all the various ways the richest notions of 'judgement' might suggest. But at the end of the day—after all the discussion and debate, pondering and judging, is over—we have to decide whom we believe and what we will do. In so doing, we are acting 'as if' we are assigning conditional probabilities like r_+ and r_- (from Chapter 6) in a way that reflects our assessment of the relative probabilities that reports for and against the proposition are more likely to be right than wrong.

A message from Chapter 6 was that—certainly for any values of r_+ and r_- that are reasonably high (>2) and close together (within 10 per cent of one another)—the barest of majorities will prove altogether too convincing, in Bayesian terms. Vary conditional probabilities as we will, there is simply nowhere within the range over which they might reasonably vary that will produce any very different outcome.

Assume Disagreement Betokens Unreliability

Suppose we have a set of highly reliable informants. The conditional probability of their saying ø is true if indeed it is true is high; and conversely with the probability of their saying not-ø if that is indeed the case. But suppose now that, when asked whether ø is true, these highly and equally reliable informants split almost equally on the question.

Now, the Bayesian approach sketched above would simply be to ask which proposition—ø or not-ø—has the larger number of those equally reliable informants supporting it. It would then enjoin everyone to revise their prior beliefs accordingly. A more natural reaction, however, might be to query just how it could be that informants, who

---

[15] Goodin 1983.   [16] Following Waldron 1989: 1327–8.

were supposed to be highly and equally reliable, could possibly end up disagreeing so much on the question. After all, if they really were all *that* reliable, any large group of them should surely be expected to converge on the same conclusion. If they do not, then we surely have reason to doubt whether the informants really were all that reliable, after all.[17]

That seems to me the right reaction in the scenario just described. But it will not help to escape the problem here in view. Think back to the end of Chapter 6. There it was shown that, given moderately large numbers of voters, majority opinion ought rationally to prove compellingly persuasive, virtually no matter how individually unreliable individual electors may be and virtually no matter how differentially reliable their reports may be.[18]

Thus, we can accept the proposition that disagreement among a large group of ostensibly highly and equally reliable informants should lead us to downgrade our estimates of their reliability. Still, downgrade those conditional probabilities as we may, persisting opposition to the verdict of the majority will remain ordinarily paradoxical. Bare majorities among large numbers even of relatively unreliable informants should, in Bayesian terms, prove none the less rationally compelling; and persisting opposition in the face of such majorities seems, in purely Bayesian terms, rationally indefensible.

Assume Smaller Groups are Inherently More Reliable

Yet another approach might be to introduce a sociological-cum-psychological assumption, saying that (perversely enough) reports are relatively more reliable the *smaller* the group making them. Various stories could be told about how competence ought be expected to decline with group size. Perhaps, for example, small groups are more selective or more attentive or more responsible.[19]

In terms of Equation 4 in Chapter 6, that would be to say that the relative reliability of reports of not-ø ($p_{\text{not-}x|\text{not-}ø}/p_{\text{not-}x|ø}$, there termed r_-) would be lower the larger the number of people (B) making them. But of course the very same discount function would also apply to the relative reliability of reports of ø ($p_{x|ø}/p_{x|\text{not-}ø}$, there termed r_+); that would also be lower the larger number of people (A) making those sorts of reports. On this model, the relative reliability of the majority and of the minority would both decline, the more numerous they are.

[17] I am grateful to Luc Bovens and Dan Hausman for suggesting this line of argument.

[18] 'Virtually', just in the sense that the reliability of each is assumed to be above zero.

[19] Waldron 1989: 1324; 1999*b*: 51–3, 135.

Hence the basic flaw in this strategy. It just fiddles with conditional probabilities, leaving the rest of the broad structure of Bayesian reasoning intact. That reasoning is powerfully responsive, as we have seen, to even slightly greater numbers on one side of the question than the other. Hence, for any minority position to remain remotely credible in light of that tendency, it would have to have almost as many people in its favour as the majority position has in its favour. But since the discounting here in view would apply to each side and would depend just upon their absolute numbers, any minority that is 'almost as large' as the majority would be discounted by almost as much.

Thus, while small minorities might benefit from having their reports discounted substantially less than the majority's, small majorities can have no realistic chance of catching up large majorities, on ordinary Bayesian calculations. Conversely, large minorities might have some hope of catching up marginally larger majorities; but they cannot hope for much help from differential discounting to do so, since the absolute numbers of people on both sides of the issue are much the same.[20]

Assume Each Election is Different

A final way of evading the Bayesian conclusion about the irrationality of persisting opposition would be to claim that each election is *sui generis*. To foreshadow, the conclusion this argument most naturally suggests is not that it is rational for opposition to persist past the election, but rather that it is perfectly rational for opposition to reappear or 'recur' at each election.

Consider this analogy.[21] Suppose we are a group of a dozen birdwatchers. We see something suddenly disappearing into the bush. Three of us think it looked to us like a Speckled Warbler; the other nine think it looked more like an Inland Thornbill. We consult our *Field Guide*: we find both birds are about the same size; both have the same habitat; both fit equally well with everything we saw and heard. So it is only rational to go with the majority and record it, in our birdwatching

[20] How exactly that all works out depends, of course, on precise details of the discounting function. It is perfectly possible to write the equations in such a way that the discounting is very steep—so steep, indeed, that the more credible position is always the one with fewer adherents. But to do that would not be to rationalize a democratic opposition: it would be to make truth-seeking contra-democratic. By the same token, it is perfectly possible to write the equations in such a way that the discounting is very flat—so flat that the more credible position is always broadly speaking whichever one has the majority of adherents. Sample calculations suggest, however, that the space in between those extreme options is very small. The scope is very small indeed for writing a discount function that will make persisting opposition rationally permissible without flipping over and making it rationally compulsory.   [21] I am grateful to David Miller for this suggestion.

records, as an Inland Thornbill. Then suddenly a bird flies up from the scrub into which we saw the first disappear. Even accepting that it is almost certainly the same bird as before, surely we have no reason to feel constrained in saying what we think the bird is the second time by what the majority thought it was the first time.

The extension to the political case is this. The minority might have a good reason to accede to the views of the majority after the first election. But it has no reason not to oppose that previous majority winner come the next election. While this might not provide an argument for *persisting* opposition, exactly, at least it provides a rationale for *recurring* opposition, come every new election.

Or does it? Certainly in reporting what the bird seems to be—or what the best candidate seems to be, either—one ought not feel constrained by what other people said (or indeed say) that it seems to be. It is a firm tenet of Bayesian logic that each reporter should always act independently of all others: one should always 'call it as one sees it', saying x when one thinks one observes x. Bayesian logic does not constrain the *reports* of scientific experiments, or the sort of reporting which I here treat as their social and political analogues. But while the reports are themselves immune to Bayes's Rule, what everyone (including the reporter herself) makes of those reports is indeed subject to that Rule. If it looked like a Warbler to me, but me alone, then I do not change my report; I still say that, 'It looked like a Warbler to me'. I just infer from the size of the majority against me (together with the conditional probabilities that I attach to those reports being right), 'But it must have been a Thornbill after all'.

How much bearing prior evidence should have on present conclusions—about birds or candidates—depends on whether we think the prior evidence has continuing relevance. If we really are pretty sure there was only one bird in the bush, then when we see it fly up the second time we ought indeed pool the information from our second sighting of it with the information from our first. Each individual should 'call it as she sees it' each time, of course; one should not revise one's first report in light of what the majority said, nor should anyone let her second report be influenced by what the majority said last time. But all those independent reports from both sightings should indeed be pooled, in Bayesian fashion, in each person's estimate of what the bird most probably is.

So too politically. We ought to each vote on the basis of who we think the best candidate is; and that report ought to reflect our own independent judgement, uninfluenced by what others think now or thought at the last election. Having seen how everyone voted this time, we ought to adjust our own prior beliefs about who really is the best candidate, accordingly. But what Bayes's Rule does is to blend our reports with those of everyone else in reaching that revised judgement: it does not change our own initial reports (votes), as such.

The political consequence of that is indeed 'recurring opposition', in this sense. Every new election is a new 'observational moment'. At each such observational moment, Bayesian voters are supposed to 'call it as they see it', entering anti-$\emptyset$ votes (that is, not-x) if that reflects their own perceptions: at this stage of voting-cum-reporting, everyone is supposed to act independently of everyone else. In the election itself, therefore, oppositional voices legitimately reappear, uninfluenced (and rightly so, Bayesians say) by the majority views in previous elections.

Once all of those independent votes are counted, however, Bayesian updating ought rationally to take place. People's prior assessments ought rationally to be revised, according to Bayes's Rule, in light of the votes-cum-reports recorded in the election. That is the point at which the phenomena described above occurs: persisting opposition to the views of the majority becomes ordinarily irrational, in light of those updated probabilities.[22]

The Political Rationality of Opposition

On the preceding arguments, no good rationalization for ongoing opposition can be found either in Bayes's theorem or its environs. Let us now turn to more explicitly political arguments to see if they might be able to rationalize, after their own peculiar fashion, what Bayesian logic cannot.

---

[22] There is one set of circumstances in which persisting opposition might be rational even in terms of those updated probabilities. Suppose we think that the past is pretty well continuous with the present, and evidence from past cases truly is relevant to the present one. Then we should pool past and present reports together, in reaching our present updated judgements about what is right. Then it would be quite right for smaller or less reliable present majorities in effect to bow to the judgement of larger or more reliable *past* majorities. If past and present reports are equally relevant and equally reliable, then pooling last election's results ($A = 1000, B = 700$) with this election's results ($A = 950, B = 1050$) leaves the loser of the present election in an overall majority (of $A = 1950$ to $B = 1750$). Assuming that electors are about as reliable at one election as any other, this argument principally just rationalizes the heirs of an electoral landslide in the last election persisting in their opposition to the opposing candidate who won only a narrow victory in the next election. A landslide winner in one election being defeated by a narrow margin in the next is not an unknown scenario, to be sure. None the less, it is a moderately uncommon one.

The Oppositional Role

One argument might turn on the crucial role of opposition in democratic politics.[23] Democracy necessarily involves a 'competition for people's votes'.[24] Competition, in turn, necessarily involves a plurality of competitors. Genuine democracy requires a formal, institutionalized 'opposition' (or set of parties in opposition), offering both alternative sets of policies and alternative sets of personnel (a 'government in waiting').

That explains why democratic theory accords legitimacy to both regimes and oppositions. But legitimacy is one thing, rationality another. It may be perfectly legitimate—indeed, socially and politically useful—for opposition parties to exist. An institutionalized opposition is useful for purposes of accountability, 'keeping officials on their toes' and so on. An institutionalized opposition is useful for defusing extralegal challenges, in no small part simply by mirroring how the balance of forces might play out in any such contest.[25]

Useful and legitimate though oppositions may thus be, the Bayesian doubts remain concerning their epistemic rationality. In what seem to be the standard sorts of cases, there would be no rational reason for anyone to *believe* the minority positions it is the opposition's role to espouse.

What we would be left with is less a 'democratic opposition' than a 'daft opposition'. It would be an opposition without any *rational* claim to our consideration at all. It would be an opposition which is simply 'going through the motions', without any rational credibility. And surely *that* cannot be what democratic competition is all about.

Proceduralism

A second, related approach to legitimating both majority rule and democratic opposition is broadly 'proceduralist' in character. Bolder forms of proceduralism renounce any epistemic claims about the probable truth of propositions backed by a majority, saying simply that they deserve to become policy just because they have been adopted through fair democratic procedures.[26] Since part and parcel of what is

---

[23] Dahl 1966, 1973; Ionescu and Madariaga 1968.   [24] Schumpeter 1950.

[25] Simmel 1908.

[26] As discussed at the outset of Ch. 5 above. Weaker versions—e.g. 'epistemic proceduralism' of the sort advocated by Estlund (1997)—would relegate proceduralism to the role of a tie-breaker, assigned merely the task of choosing among epistemically equally eligible options.

involved in a 'fair democratic procedure' is giving opposing perspectives a 'fair hearing', that serves to legitimate opposing points of view as well.

If we are going to justify democratic procedures in terms of 'fairness', however, we have to assume that everyone operating within them is 'playing fair', as well. Surely part of what that means is that they are espousing propositions which they actually believe, rather than strategically advancing propositions which they do not believe, purely with a view to manipulating electoral outcomes to their partisan advantage.

I shall say more about strategic voting shortly. What we ought to notice, for now, is simply this. In so far as 'fair proceduralism' presupposes that people actually believe the propositions that they are espousing, and in so far as fair proceduralism obliges everyone to take some (positive) notice of one another's beliefs, then 'fair proceduralism' tends (unwittingly) towards the same Bayesian conclusions as outlined in Chapter 6.[27]

Proceduralists themselves would of course want to downplay those epistemic consequences, wanting as they do to differentiate their theories from those of epistemic democrats.[28] Still, what proceduralists presuppose—that voters are asserting beliefs in propositions, and that others ought to give some positive credence to those assertions—would by Bayesian logic give those others not only procedural but also epistemic reasons for accepting the verdict of the majority.

However, since the same Bayesian logic is at work in both proceduralist accounts (thus interpreted) and epistemic ones, the same problem then emerges. Majority verdicts ought, by that Bayesian logic, rationally to persuade minorities much too soon and much too strongly, to our ordinary democratic ways of thinking. Even if we are 'officially' running a purely proceduralist argument for democracy, the epistemic subtext of what is involved in participating in good faith in those procedures (when combined with the Bayesian reasoning sketched above) would undermine the rationality of persisting opposition in the face of even a relatively modest majority.

---

[27] At least in so far as people's votes have any 'factual' component at all. As I argue below, votes are typically based on a combination of factual beliefs and evaluative beliefs, with Bayesian arguments applying to the former but not the latter. While evaluative components may sometimes loom very large, it is hard to imagine how political judgements could ever be evaluative 'all the way down', having literally no factual content.

[28] e.g., in the exchange between Cohen 1986 and Coleman and Ferejohn 1986.

Denying Propositional Content

Democratic proceduralists might try to avoid that result by deflating the propositional content of votes.

To generate my Bayesian results, I had to assume that votes had some specific propositional content: specifically, that people will vote x if and only if they believe $\varnothing$ to be true. But in the real world, of course, there is rarely any such one-to-one mapping of votes and beliefs. Different people vote the same way for different reasons.[29] Indeed, any given person may have many different reasons for voting the way she does; and as long as all of them would lead her to vote in the same way, she has no pragmatic reason to decide the relative weights she assigns to each.[30]

One reaction to those familiar facts might be to say that people's votes, individually and all the more so collectively, cannot be taken to be asserting *anything* beyond the simple fact that they think that the option they vote for should be put into effect. And since each individual's vote was devoid of any determinate propositional content beyond that, so too is the collective outcome. The fact that there is a majority—perhaps even a very large majority—voting for x would not then give anyone any greater reason than she had before the vote for believing or disbelieving any particular proposition $\varnothing$.[31]

Emptying votes of any determinate propositional content in that way would certainly avoid the Bayesian paradox of persisting opposition. But it would do so by emptying the democratic result of much of its legitimacy, as well. Democracy as ordinarily understood involves citizens giving one another *reasons* for voting one way rather than another—partly with a view to persuading them to share those reasons and vote the way you are going to vote, of course, but partly too simply with a view to explaining your vote to others.[32]

To say that we should do what others dictate 'for no reason' is simply to say that the minority should pragmatically bow to the majority's *force majeure*, that the minority should accede to the dictates of the majority because there are more of them.[33] That is not democratic

---

[29] Thus making it difficult ever to infer the 'legislative intent' behind any particular statute enacted by a multiplicity of legislators: see MacCallum 1966. [30] Goodin 1989*a*.

[31] This line of argument was suggested to me by Jerry Gaus.

[32] Here I side with Mill (1861: ch. 10) against Rousseau (1762: bk 2, ch. 3)—though for my money a decently long election campaign in which citizens are actively involved would be quite sufficient to satisfy this requirement, without repealing the secret ballot and requiring electors to announce and explain their vote in public on election day itself. Compare Brennan and Pettit 1990, following Mill on this point.

[33] And of course it is quite useful to know how many people are lined up against you, before squaring off for a fight: revealing that is one useful function of democratic votes, as Simmel (1908) says.

rule: it is arbitrary rule. And it is none the less arbitrary for its being a majority who is refusing to give reasons.[34]

My aim here, remember, is to 'rationalize majority rule without reducing continuing opposition to the status of utter irrationality'. To suggest that people's votes, individually and collectively, are substantially devoid of propositional content succeeds in the second by failing miserably in the first of those goals—not just in narrowly Bayesian terms, but in any other. There is indeed nothing irrational about refusing to accept something as true just because the majority has voted for it, if votes are devoid of propositional content. But votes backed by no reasons defy rationalization.[35]

Biased Perception

Yet another explanation of persisting opposition might be found in psychological-cum-political phenomena of biased and selective perception. There is a tendency to attach more credence to evidence confirming rather than disconfirming our existing beliefs. And, in a way, that is only natural. Suppose you are trying to assess the relative reliability of various other people's reports of facts about the world; and suppose that you, yourself, believe ø to be true. Then it is only natural that you will think that people who report ø are more reliable informants than are people who report not-ø.

Notice, though, how that process feeds on itself, as you return to assessing the truth of ø itself. In that assessment, you naturally attach more weight to reports coming from people whom you deem to be 'reliable' informants. But they have been chosen, in turn, precisely for their tendency to confirm your view that ø is true. Those who started out believing ø is true thus find their beliefs reinforced—and conversely, of course, for those who started out believing not-ø. That

---

[34] Democratic proceduralists might of course simply bite the bullet and insist that all that democracy requires is that one side won in a 'fair fight' with the other. And perhaps a scrap of democratic legitimacy might still be extracted from the thought that it was a fight that both entered willingly and that either could in principle have won. But reducing political obligation sheer to 'good sportsmanship' is surely to take the gamesmanship of Rawls's (1967) 'duty of fair play' way too far. That may be a subsidiary reason for according legitimacy to democratic outcomes, but surely the main reason must be something better than *that*.

[35] The issue here, note, is not whether the reasons in question are factual or evaluative in nature. Those who hope to avoid the Bayesian conclusion by denying that votes have any propositional content empty the vote of propositional content of both factual and evaluative forms.

or something like it provides the 'rational' underpinning for blinkered ideological thinking in politics.[36]

Certainly this is a phenomenon much discussed among democratic theorists. The tendency of leftists to read only left-wing newspapers, and vice versa, is much bemoaned. The need to force people to encounter and confront perspectives different from their own is much emphasized.[37] And so on.

But that is precisely the problem with this model, understood as a rationalization of persisting opposition: there is no way within that model for such exhortations ever to succeed. Someone who filters her evidence to fit her prior beliefs will never attach sufficient credence to evidence contradicting them ever to change those prior beliefs. Hence there is no way within this model for minorities ever to turn into majorities—which is to say, there is no room within that model for democracy at all, if by that we mean (at least in part) 'democratic alternation in power'.

Consider what it would take, in terms of the Bayesian model developed above, for biased perceptions actually to rationalize intransigence in your belief that ϕ in the face of a majority reporting that not-ϕ. However strong your prior belief might be that ϕ is true, and however little credibility you attach to others' reports of not-ϕ, the Bayesian argument sketched above suggests that anyone who attaches positive credibility at all to others' reports of not-ϕ will fairly soon be won over (by the Bayesian power of majorities) to the conclusion that not-ϕ is indeed the case. The only way you can avoid doing so—the only way you can sustain your opposition to the proposition not-ϕ in the face of even just modest majorities reporting that not-ϕ—is for you to attach either no or indeed negative credibility to others' reports of not-ϕ.[38]

Neither posture would seem to be particularly attractive. Assigning others' reports no credibility would mean that you are prepared stubbornly to stick with your conclusion that ϕ is true, however many others say otherwise—be they hundreds or millions or billions. Assigning others' reports of not-ϕ negative credibility would mean that you think, perversely enough, that ϕ is more likely to be true the more other people there are who deny it. If there are millions of people telling you that you are wrong, you would be more inclined to stick to your guns

---

[36] Elster 1983; Goodin 1980: ch. 2. Indeed, this is one of the principal counters I offer to Lehrer's (2001*a*) 'rational consensus' model (Goodin 2001).

[37] Most recently, in Sunstein's (2001) *Republic.com*. Similar fears about the 'balkanization of science' are raised by the modelling of Van Alstyne and Brynjolfsson (1996, 1997).

[38] By 'negative credibility', I mean she believes that $p_{\text{not-}x|\text{not-}\phi} \leq p_{x|\text{not-}\phi}$.

than if there were only a dozen telling you that you were wrong. That seems crazy: or anyway, not the right response in what we suppose to be *very* much the more standard sort of situation.

Not only are those postures unattractive ones. They are also profoundly undemocratic ones, in the sense that anyone who adopts them can never be rationally induced to change her mind. That way of 'rationalizing' persisting opposition in a democratic polity would succeed only at the cost of undermining the democracy, rendering the opposition impervious to argument and debate.

Strategic Voting

Reflect next on the fact that political actors are strategic players trying to manipulate outcomes, rather than agents who sincerely report the facts as they see them, which is what Bayesian models seem to presuppose. Many think that strategic voting might unsettle proofs of the Condorcet jury theorem.[39] Perhaps the same might be true of the Bayesian derivation as well.

Of course, 'sincerity' is not strictly presupposed in the Bayesian model. For Bayesian purposes, it does not strictly speaking matter whether or not you actually *believe* the propositions that you are asserting. All that matter are the conditional probabilities that other people assign to the prospect of ø being true, given that you say it is. That is to say, what Bayesian calculations presuppose is merely the reliability of the people's reports, not their sincerity or honesty as such. Still, pragmatically those are usually closely related. As a bald empirical generalization, it seems undeniable that other people's reports are more likely to be reliable indicators of true states of affairs when those people are *trying* to tell the truth than when they are not.

Let us accept that people's reports are less reliable indicators of the truth when they sometimes lie for strategic purposes, rather than always trying to tell the truth. Still, their reports might still be *reliable enough* for the Bayesian arguments outlined in Chapter 6 still to work. That would be the case, just so long as people's reports are seen as being on average more likely to be right than wrong. In other words, the Bayesian derivations above do not require us to *maximize* (through conscientious truth-telling) the conditional probabilities $p_{x|ø}$ and $p_{\text{not-}x|\text{not-}ø}$. All that is required is that $p_{x|ø} > p_{x|\text{not-}ø}$ and $p_{\text{not-}x|\text{not-}ø} > p_{\text{not-}x|ø}$.

---

[39] Although it remains unclear quite how badly unsettle. Cf. Austen-Smith and Banks 1996; Feddersen and Pesendorfer 1998; Wit 1998; Coughlan 2000; Gerardi 2000; Guarnaschelli *et al.* 2000.

Strategic voting could therefore provide rational grounds for persisting opposition to majority perspectives, only if it makes other people *such* unreliable informants as to make their assertions more likely to be false than true. Then and only then would Bayesian reasoning lead us to think that the propositions which they assert are less likely to be true, for their having asserted them—and indeed, less likely to be true the more people who contra-reliably assert them in that way.

That, however, would seem to underwrite political nihilism *tout court*—doubting everything that anyone says, politically. Nothing that has been said so far supports oppositional politics as we actually know it, organized around parties, sects, and factions. The reason is just this. Assuming the situation of all voters is symmetrical, and everyone would be strategically lying as often as everyone else, everyone would be as unreliable an informant as everyone else. Hence there is no reason for minority voters to trust one group of people ('the opposition') any more than any other ('the governing party').

Thus, for the spectre of strategic voting really to underwrite oppositional politics of an organized sort, we have to assume that strategic voting is seen by minority voters as differentially affecting the reliability of different groups of voters. Specifically, minority voters would have to suppose that strategic voting renders the majority's reports strongly unreliable (so that the truth is always more likely than not to be the opposite of what they say), while leaving the minority's reports reliable enough (the truth is always more likely than not to be as they say). Then and only then can Bayesians persist in backing a minority view.

But then the same trouble arises as reported earlier. Where members of the minority group think that the majority is so unreliable that its assertions are more likely false than true, then the more people there are in that majority group the *less* credence we attach to the views that they espouse. That may be an accurate account of a deeply divided society, but it is no kind of model of ordinary democratic politics.

Segmented Information Pools

The central insight underlying both Condorcet and Bayes's derivations is the value of information-pooling in discovering truths about the world we share. In cases where everyone has more-or-less accurate information on the same overall situation, the right way for them to find out what is true is to examine what they agree upon about that situation. The truth is then contained in the intersection—the overlap—of their reports.

Where people have only very different and very partial views on the overall situation, however, the truth is sometimes better found instead in the union—the conjunction—of their reports. In the old proverb, when blind men have a hold of different parts of the elephant, they surmise the overall shape of the beast not by considering the intersection of their reports (which is *ex hypothesi* the null set: they have a hold of different parts of the animal) but rather by considering the union of their reports (each is true, so far as it goes).

Political life might sometimes be similar to that. Information might sometimes be radically segmented. Different people in different situations might experience and hence perceive things very differently. All of those reports might be right, so far as they go. But where information is segmented in that way, the right way to pool it is not to look for what is broadly common across all reports (in effect, letting disparate reports cancel one another out). Instead, the right way to pool information in a segmented setting is to blend in the differences, not just abstract out the commonalities.

Confronted with the problem of partial perspectives of this peculiar sort, the radically homogenizing tendencies of Bayes's formula ought to be put into abeyance. I may well have good Bayesian grounds for deferring to the majority view among people broadly like myself. But I also have every reason for according a very different sort of respect to groups of people with perspectives and experiences very unlike my own.

For a pointed example, consider a community which is 10 per cent black and 90 per cent white, where the police regularly beat every black but never beat any white. On the basis of their own personal experiences, that community would reject the proposition that 'the police beat people' by a whopping 90 per cent majority. But the strength of that majority gives blacks no reason for denying the reality of the scars on their backs, whatever the good Reverend Bayes may say.[40] In informationally segmented communities, majorities are never completely compelling, and persisting opposition is not necessarily irrational.

---

[40] If the proposition were properly formulated, of course, it is not clear Bayes would disagree. Consider the analogous case of any low-probability event: a drug that causes cancer in one-thousandth of its users. If we simply polled a thousand users, asking whether they got cancer, the vote would be 999 to 1 in the negative. But far from proving compelling grounds for rejecting the hypothesis that the drug causes cancer, that is wholly in line with the hypothesis that the drug causes cancer in one-in-a-thousand cases. If we run the same experiment on a billion people and find the same ratio holding up, Bayes would have us confirm that hypothesis.

That model might have more empirical applicability than we might imagine. Consider the relationships political scientists report between 'social locations' (in terms of race, religion, class, age, gender, and so on) and political attitudes. In a systematic assay of sixteen Western democracies, Franklin and his collaborators find that there are usually around a half dozen 'social structural' variables (different ones in different countries) which make an appreciable difference to electoral outcomes.[41] In the present context, we might take that evidence as indicating that there are perhaps a half-dozen different groups in any given country having systematically different social experiences.

After the fashion of the stylized account of differential black and white experiences with the police offered above, we might regard each of those groups as if they were observing and reporting on separate and distinct patterns of social experiences. Think of it as a case of each group's observing and reporting on a different scientific experiment.

When pooling my observations with those of a large number of other people in the same group as me (who are observing the same experiment as me), I have good reason to be very confident in the majority's report of the results of 'our' experiment. That is the implication of the Bayesian logic elaborated above.

But that Bayesian logic only says that, where the numbers are large, it is highly likely that the majority *within* each group is correct in its representation of its own experiment-cum-experience. That logic provides members of different groups with no reason to defer to the judgement of majorities in *other* groups (or of majorities across *all* groups), in so far as different groups are observing different experiments.[42]

This argument, notice, rationalizes oppositional politics only in circumstances of fairly radical social segmentation, and only across those informationally distinct social segments. The first limitation may be less restrictive than it initially appears: on the empirical evidence cited above, most countries might have half a dozen such radically distinct social segments. But the second limitation would still seem to have real force.

Persisting opposition can be rationalized in this way only among parties representing informationally distinct social segments. The party of Ulster Catholics thus has no reason for caving in to the party of Ulster Protestants, just because they have been outvoted, for example. But this sort of argument provides no rational grounds for persisting

---

[41] Franklin *et al*. 1992.

[42] Apposite here (as well as, more directly, below) is the reworking of the Condorcet jury theorem by Miller (1986).

opposition on the part of 'catch-all' parties representing interests, groups, and perspectives that cut across those informationally distinct social segments.[43] Thus, American Democrats ought to cave in, as Bayesian logic would seem to require, to Republicans (and most European Christian Democrats to Social Democrats, given the broadly 'catch-all' nature of those parties today) whenever they have been outvoted. So the 'segmented information pool' argument does provide a limited—but apparently strictly limited—rationale for persisting opposition, even in the face of Bayes.

Those limitations may be more apparent than real, however. It is a familiar claim in the philosophy of science that all observations are necessarily theory-laden; and if anything, that is even more likely to be true in social and political affairs than scientific ones. In so far as that is true, then to that extent adherents of different theories will 'perceive' things differently. In the limiting case, that might make for 'segmented information pools' of just the same sort as among informationally distinct social groups.[44]

Different Interests

A crucial assumption underlying virtually every model of the democratic process is that voters are all voting on the same fundamental question. 'Adding up votes' can credibly yield a collective determination of some sort or another only if we are all voting on the same proposition: x or not-x. If your ballot paper says something subtly different from mine, then your vote cannot legitimately be aggregated with mine. Your 'yea' and my 'yea' do not add up to two 'yeas', unless they are 'yeas' to the same question.[45] Formal mathematical models building on Bayes and Condorcet make that assumption explicit. But, explicitly or implicitly, that assumption lies at the centre of any procedure involving the democratic aggregation of votes.[46]

That insight has typically been taken to provide the key leverage for those wanting to reject the strong Condorcet–Bayes conclusion that the majority is almost certainly correct. Maybe it is, if (as epistemic theorists suppose) what everyone is voting on is the truth of objective, external verities which are necessarily the same for everyone.[47] But if

---

[43] Kirchheimer 1969.   [44] I am grateful to Debra Satz for this suggestion.
[45] Literally the same, with no indexicals that vary across different voters: 'what is in our common interest?' or 'what ought we collectively ought do?' (those two questions are importantly different: Little 1952) rather than 'what is in *my* interest?' or 'what *I* want us to do?' (Estlund 1993: 411–16).   [46] Estlund 1993: 403.
[47] A point made clear by the 'epistemic' label and discussions surrounding it. See e.g. Cohen 1986; Estlund 1997.

they are voting on the basis of something else that is not the same for them all (personal preferences or interests, for example, rather than shared truths), then there is no reason to think that the majority is more likely to be right rather than wrong—because there is no one thing, now, for it to be 'right' or 'wrong' about.[48]

If voters are truth-seekers and those truths are the same for everyone, then majorities are almost certainly right. But if people are voting their interests rather than their perceptions of shared truths, there is no particular reason (of an epistemic sort, anyway) to defer to the will of the majority. Reasoning along these lines, all we would need to do to evade the Bayesian conclusion that persisting opposition is irrational in the face of a clear majority vote would merely be to impugn the motives of voters, insisting that (many of) them are voting their personal or sectional interests rather than their perceptions of the common good.

Certainly that would suffice to avoid the Bayesian conclusion of the irrationality of persisting opposition. And almost as certainly that is sometimes true, as a characterization of how many voters vote. But rationalizing oppositional politics on the ground that the majority is simply pursuing narrow sectoral interest rationalizes oppositional politics at the cost of derationalizing democratic politics. The paradox of persisting oppositions is solved, but Wollheim's initial paradox re-emerges.

If politics is purely the pursuit of sectoral interest, then majority factions' winning gives minority factions no reason (certainly no *epistemic* reason, anyway[49]) to accept the result. The force of greater numbers would no longer tell us 'what is right (true, good) for all of us'—it would just tell us 'what is in the interests of the majority'.[50]

As a matter of pure power politics, it may well be prudent for minorities to succumb to the force of greater numbers. But pragmatic acquiescence is very different from principled acceptance. Simply losing a power struggle does not give the minority any principled reason for acceding to the propositions supported by the majority. Quite the contrary: if all that was involved was a power struggle among groups

[48] Thus, in Rousseauian applications of the Condorcet jury theorem it is standardly said that the Condorcet result emerges if and only if everyone is voting on the basis of their perceptions of the 'common good' rather than the basis of their particular interests. See e.g. Cohen 1986; Grofman and Feld 1988; Waldron 1989; Estlund 1993, 1997; Gaus 1997. That is of course just a special case of this point.

[49] There are, as I said at the outset, plenty of other ways of evading Wollheim's paradox, of course.   [50] Miller 1986; Przeworski 1999: 29–31.

with diverging interests, the fact that they prevailed over us would give us reason only for regret[51]—never for reconsideration.

Votes versus Reasons

The most promising overall response to the Bayes–Condorcet style proofs would seem to me to go along the following lines:

- Political positions—people's votes, and such like—are always an amalgam of fact and value.
- One of those elements (facts) is necessarily intersubjectively shared, the other (values) not.
- For the sorts of reasons sketched above, Bayesian arguments give people compelling reasons to revise their factual beliefs in the light of other people's credible reports regarding things (such as facts) that they necessarily share in common.
- Bayesian arguments, however, give people no reasons to revise their evaluative assessments in the light of other people's value judgements, which there is no reason to think that they necessarily do or should share.

In short, what is wrong with Bayesian models that ask us to update our beliefs in the light of others' votes-cum-reports is that those votes mix two things—facts and values—only one of which (others' assessments of the facts of the matter) we have any reason to take into account in updating our own beliefs.

Thus, for example, suppose we are considering a proposal to take $10,000 dollars away from everyone in our country with surnames beginning with the letters *A* to *F* and to divide the proceeds among everyone with surnames beginning with the letters *G* to Z. (Suppose also you are prohibited from changing your surname!) The former group opposes the plan, to a person; and the latter approves of the plan, to a person. So the plan wins, by a ratio of something like 20 to 6. Still, the size of that majority in no way provides the losers with any reason to revise their beliefs. The dispute never was over beliefs— matters of fact regarding what the impact of the policy would actually be. Everyone agreed about *that*, all along. The disagreement was purely over values: whether it was good or bad to do what the alphabetical redistribution scheme was clearly going to do, which was to take

---

[51] In a struggle among diverging interests, after all, their gain is necessarily to some extent our loss.

money from earlier-alphabet people and transfer it to later-alphabet people.

Logically, Bayes operates on beliefs and those alone. When building our mathematical models of politics, we seize upon votes as the closest convenient analogues to beliefs. But convenience of modelling badly misleads us, here. Votes are a bottom-line affair. In them are mixed beliefs of the sort that genuinely belong in Bayesian models, alongside evaluational judgements that do not.[52] For a proper application of Bayesian reasoning to politics, we need to pull back from that bottom line and apply those Bayesian arguments to the factual components of political judgements alone.

Disaggregating facts and values, even just in our own minds, is not always easy. But what that seems to suggest is that that is what we should be trying to do in democratic conversations with one another. Revising our bottom-line judgements, just because there are lots of other bottom-line judgements lined up against us, is crazy. But revising our assessments of the facts upon which our bottom-line judgements partially rest, in the light of other people's assessments of those same facts, is required by rationality itself.

Thus, it is in the factual underpinnings of the reasons that people give for their votes, rather than in their votes themselves, that Bayesian updating ought rationally to get a grip on people, politically. That is something that has to happen in the conversation that surrounds voting, rather than something that happens in immediate consequence of the vote itself. This provides yet another argument for extended discussion, rather than a 'rush to political judgement', pressing things to premature closure by calling for an early vote to settle matters once and for all.

This sort of argument also, importantly, provides a way of rationalizing (in strictly Bayesian terms) both majority rule and persisting opposition to the verdict of the majority. The epistemic power of majorities, when dealing with intersubjectively shared facts, is what underwrites the rationality of majority rule. Their lack of any epistemic authority, when it comes to matters of evaluations, is what underwrites the rationality of persisting opposition.[53]

---

[52] Or anyway not necessarily: moral realists who think there is an objectively correct fact of the matter where values are concerned, too, would of course be perfectly comfortable treating facts and values identically in Bayesian calculations.

[53] Note that this proposition sets on its head received wisdom that democracy ought to deal with matters of 'principle', leaving matters of factual detail (of 'administration') to experts to judge (cf. Lindsay 1929: 54).

Conclusion

On certain plausible accounts of what is going on in politics, even relatively modest majorities ought to prove rationally compelling, even
for people who had been firmly of some different opinion. Bayes's
Rule shows how rational consistency requires people to abandon
opposition, in such circumstances.

That conclusion of Chapter 6 poses a serious challenge for democratic theory. The challenge is to rationalize democratic rule, understood as giving people some rational reason to comply with the
majority's will, without derationalizing persisting opposition—which
seems part and parcel of democratic rule, too.

This chapter has shown that no amount of tweaking of the basic
Bayesian model seems likely to produce that desired result. Persisting
opposition remains irrational in Bayesian terms, pretty much whatever
we do. Many of the more overtly political rationales for persisting
opposition cannot deliver the desired goods, either. Some of them
give us reason for regarding opposition as 'legitimate', without giving
us any reason for regarding it as rational (in a narrowly Bayesian
sense, at least). Others rationalize opposition, but in ways that make
that opposition seem undemocratic (impervious to any further argument or reason). Still others rationalize opposition, but in ways that
derationalize majority rule (making political outcomes purely the consequence of power plays among factions driven purely by narrow
sectoral interests).

Only a few of the arguments that I canvass seem to hold any real
promise for underwriting the rationality of persisting opposition.[54]
The most general one holds that Bayes–Condorcet style reasoning
ought be confined to the factual bases people give for their votes, and
to that component of their votes alone. That in turn implies that we
must attend to the *reasons* people give for their votes, rather than just
adding up the votes themselves.

Where political disputes centrally involve values as well as facts,
some other way of accessing and assessing those value dimensions of
the dispute is required. Merely aggregating votes can be a powerful
way of resolving purely factual disputes. But for resolving disputes
with a value dimension, other techniques are required. It is to those
that I now turn.

---

[54] 'Persisting' as distinct from recurring sporadic opposition, of the sort rationalized
above. The other strong argument, which is applicable only in relative special circumstances
(which may, or may not, also be relatively common), rationalizes persisting opposition in
terms of segmented information pools.

Value Democracy

Political action, like all intentional action, is an amalgam of belief and desire, fact and value. Democratic disputes might sometimes have a purely factual side to them, and where they do the information-pooling at the heart of the democratic process can go far towards rationally resolving them. For purely fact-finding purposes, merely aggregating votes and noting the size of the majority is all the democracy that we need.

Where values are also at stake, however, all that changes dramatically. The proofs that vouchsafe the truth-tracking power of democratic politics are formally inapplicable; and some other form of democratic politics, beyond sheer aggregation of votes, is required. Rather than looking merely to the 'bottom line'—how people vote, individually and collectively—we need to be sensitive to inputs and the reasons people give for how they vote, if we are to address value-laden components of democratic disputes. We need to understand one another, imagining ourselves in their place. And we need to extend that courtesy not only to our proximate social circle but—if we are to be truly democratic—to all those who might be affected by our actions and choices. That is true whether they lie outside the boundaries of our polity, of our era, or even of our species. In what follows, my model of 'democratic deliberation within' is offered as being ideally suited to that demanding task.

CHAPTER 8

Input Democracy

Power and the Politics of the Bottom Line

Democrats rightly worry about 'the politics of the bottom line': who gets what, when, how.[1] They press for reforms to political procedures and practice with those questions of 'power over the bottom line' clearly in view.

This focus is found across the whole gamut of democratic theory and practice. For democratic activists, the whole point of expanding the franchise was to give the lower classes some real power over the outcome, not merely to satisfy the niceties of some empty formalism. Likewise, the point of 'one person one vote' electoral reform (eliminating 'rotten boroughs' and their contemporary equivalents) was deeply pragmatic as well as importantly symbolic. So too were requirements of regular, free and fair elections, of campaign spending limits, of free speech and association, and so on. All those are obvious requirements of procedural rectitude.[2] But they were all also supposed to carry some very practical political consequences. All were supposed to serve, in their various ways, to equalize the power of citizens over ultimate political outcomes. Among academic political scientists, a similarly hard-headed focus on the bottom line is built into the notion of power itself (power is the 'production of intended *effects*',[3] after all); and that focus was epitomized in the sorts of 'power studies' that once virtually defined the discipline.[4] Pragmatically, the aim of electoral reform

---

[1] Lasswell 1950.   [2] They all figure in e.g. Beitz's (1989) 'theory of political fairness'.
[3] Russell 1938; emphasis added. Or, again: 'power represents resources and ability to influence *results*' (Power and Democracy Project 2000: 14; emphasis added).
[4] In empirical power studies, from Charles Beard's (1913) analysis of the American founding to Floyd Hunter's (1953) study of Atlanta and Robert Dahl's (1961) of New Haven, a central focus was always on the bottom line—on the extent to which formally democratic procedures are circumvented in their actual functioning by concentrations of

lobbies around the world is to institute voting rule on the grounds that it more nearly equalizes the 'power' of each voter.[5]

Now, equalizing power over the bottom line is an important political project. Nothing I say here is intended to denigrate it. But another model of democracy also deserves a respectful airing. This alternative model focuses on inputs rather than outputs. It aims to give everyone (or, alternatively, every distinct affected interest) a 'voice'—that, rather than necessarily an equal (understood as 'equally effective') 'say' over the ultimate outcome. I shall call this 'input democracy', in contrast with 'output democracy'.[6] Those terms mark a distinction between a concern with different stages—early and late—of the political process.[7]

Of course input and output democracy *are* causally connected, as democratic activists have long appreciated. Democratic activists campaigning for extensions of the franchise or 'one person one vote' are, in the first instance, urging that everyone should have equal inputs into the process. But as I have said, they do so in the clear (and far from groundless) hope that people will thereby acquire more nearly equal power over political outcomes as well.

While the two models I shall be distinguishing are thus empirically intertwined, they are analytically distinct. And the analytics can sometimes be of practical consequence as well. After sketching the central concerns of the two models generically, I shall present Schumpeter's model as the paradigmatically output-oriented account. I then go on to sketch what might be regarded as a paradigmatically input-oriented

power and influence. Almost invariably they are, and the democratic reformer's task is then to come up with some prescription for equalizing real power over the final results—through giving different people power over different domains (Dahl 1961; Walzer 1983) or through consciousness-raising (Lukes 1974; Gaventa 1980) or whatever.

[5] As measured through the Banzhaf index or the Shapley–Shubik index or some other. See e.g. Dummett 1985, 1997; Morriss 1987: pt 4; Barry 1989: esp. ch. 9; Taagepera and Shugart 1989.

[6] There are precursors in the existing literature (Riker 1983; Scharpf 1999: ch. 1), but all draw the distinctions slightly differently than I do here. Dworkin's (2000: 186) notion of 'equal distribution of political power', for example, straddles what I want to regard as input and output considerations, touching as it does upon issues of both who gets a vote and how votes get aggregated. Although oriented towards very different problems, my own earlier discussion of 'input' and 'output filters' is broadly consistent with my present usage: output filters (such as entrenched rights) operate at the tail end of the political process, barring certain sorts of enactments from emerging as laws; input filters (such as prohibitions against hate speech, on the floor of the legislature or elsewhere) block certain inputs from the political process from the start (Goodin 1986: 77–81).

[7] There are also of course various 'middle' stages of the political process, where inputs are transformed into outputs; and much democratic theory of a procedural or deliberative sort focuses on that part of the process. In those middle stages of the process, however, input and output values are inevitably intertwined, and the contrast here in view is therefore better evoked by focusing on the limiting cases.

contrast with it. The latter, although an analytic construct, is loosely modelled on and represented by the sort of 'consultative democracy' characteristic of the Nordic countries and, indeed, of 'corporatist' and 'consociational' democracies worldwide.

Against a Preoccupation with Outputs

The Larger Problem with Majority Tyranny

One of the classic complaints against majority voting, recall, is the risk of 'majority tyranny'. To prevent majorities from oppressing 'persistent minorities', we have to find a way of somehow circumscribing the authority of majorities, whether by a bill of rights specifying what not even majorities can do, or through institutional devices (bicameralism, federalism, single transferable votes, or separate electoral registers) which, in effect, give minorities a veto. Democrats are more or less apologetic about the need for such devices.[8] But however brave a face democratic theorists may put on the situation, these devices none the less represent democratic constraints on the operation of democracy. Their necessity inevitably constitutes a clear limit to the application of principles of majoritarian democracy.

All that is exceedingly familiar. What I now want to suggest is that this embarrassing risk of majority tyranny is not just an incidental artefact of one particularly unfortunate (namely, majoritarian) specification of the democratic decision rule. Instead, I argue, it derives from an output-oriented approach to democratic theory more broadly.

What all output-oriented approaches share is an emphasis upon finding some social decision rule—some way of aggregating votes—which is privileged from a democratic point of view. If democratic theorists succeed in that task, then there is no arguing with the deliverances of that rule. It points to the right thing to do: end of story.[9]

---

[8] Unnecessarily so, perhaps. We might unapologetically say that 'respect for persons' requires us *both* to count everyone's vote equally *and also* not to act disrespectfully or tyrannically towards people, no matter how the vote has gone.

[9] Of course, no matter is ever 'closed, once and for all', in a democracy. No sovereign can bind its future self; any past decision, whether of the Parliament or of the electorate, can always be reopened. Hence there will always, in practice, be future opportunities for inputs. Still, special procedures are typically required for re-opening matters once they have been settled, even in this provisionary way. In a parliamentary setting, for example, under *Robert's Rules* and similar rules of procedure a motion to reconsider will only be entertained from someone who voted on the winning side in the last vote and who has now changed her mind.

That represents what can be called 'the arrogance of aggregation'. And that claim to ultimate decisiveness constitutes, I submit, the real culprit. 'Majority tyranny' is just one specific instance, one particular way of filling out the formula. But the tyrannical nature of decision rules arises from their claim to 'ultimate decisiveness', whether the decision rule in question is majoritarian or super-majoritarian or multi-tiered. The problem is that once the aggregation has been done, on whatever basis, that is the end of the matter.[10] Further considerations can no longer be brought into play: all has been said and done. That assertion of 'ultimate decisiveness' is the true 'arrogance of aggregation', and the problems it causes are quite independent of whatever way in which the aggregation is accomplished.

Against the Arrogance of Democratic Aggregation

A central claim of input democrats is that there must be more to a legitimate political process than can be captured in any mechanical aggregation process. What we should be doing in the political process is evaluating the competing claims of various parties on their merits. That must be a genuinely reflective process: internally contemplative in the first instance, interpersonally discursive in the second.[11]

No purely mechanical process can be reflective in the ways that are required to track (and in that way responsively and responsibly adjudicate) the claims and counter-claims that lie at the core of the political process. A person's vote summarizes his or her opinion only crudely and with much loss of nuance. Aggregations of many people's votes lose more information, yet again.

Note, though, how easily mechanical analogies trip off the tongue in discussions of decision rules and voting procedures. We talk of 'weighing' interests and arguments; of 'balancing' them; of 'aggregating' them, in ways that conjure up images of cranking the handle of an old-fashioned adding machine.

Far from being just loose language, this is actually the standard way of thinking about the democratic process across a wide range

[10] Inputs, however numerous and one-sided, cannot in and of themselves be tyrannical, in this sense of closing off further inputs and further deliberations.

[11] The American political system was supposed to be 'one of deliberation rather than aggregation', Sunstein (1993*b*: 242–3) says. 'The Framers insisted that existing views might be a product of partial perspectives, of limited experience, or of incomplete information. People engaged in democratic discussion should "meet others from the different parts of the Union, and consult". People should be "open to the force of argument".' This is especially clear in debates in the first Congress refusing to give citizens as part of the Bill of Rights a 'right to instruct' their congressional representatives. See similarly Cohen 1989, 1998.

of democratic theory. In his justly famous paper on 'A Paradox in the Theory of Democracy', for example, Richard Wollheim explicitly invites us to:

envisage Democracy in terms of a certain machine... Into it are fed, at fixed intervals, the choices of the individual citizens. The machine then aggregates them according to the pre-established rule or method, and so comes up with what may be called a 'choice' of its own. Democratic rule is said to be achieved if... the most recent choice of the machine is acted upon.[12]

And Jeremy Waldron repeatedly invokes the image of the 'Wollheim machine' in his discussion of how to make law in the face of disagreement.[13] Self-styled 'public choice' theorists talk in equally mechanistic terms: voting, for them, produces a 'summation of preferences';[14] more technically, 'a collective choice rule' is represented as a 'function' which serves to transform individual preference orderings into a unique social preference relation.[15]

What is crucial about all these mechanistic democratic aggregation procedures, from the present perspective, is that they are authoritative and decisive. They settle things. Taking preferences (or votes or whatever) as inputs, they crank out 'the right answer'. As long as the procedures for aggregating accord equal weight (or power or whatever) to each person's inputs, output-oriented democrats will typically suppose that the determinations of these procedures rightly represent the end of the matter.

How Much Legitimacy Does Aggregating Votes Confer?

At the end of the day, democratic procedures are expected to yield a determinate outcome.[16] When a decision is required before agreement has been reached, the way in which democrats of all stripes move towards a decision is by aggregating opinions through voting of some sort or another. Even self-styled 'deliberative democrats' who adamantly oppose aggregative models of democracy in general thus occasionally find themselves resorting to a mere show of hands.[17]

The issue between output- and input-based models of democracy lies not in whether or not votes are eventually taken and aggregations

---

[12] Wollheim 1962: 76; quoted approvingly in Waldron 1995: 337.

[13] Waldron 1999*b*: ch. 6.   [14] Riker 1961.   [15] Sen 1970: 35–6.

[16] Ordinarily, anyway. There are some things that we can afford simply to leave unsettled (Sunstein 1996). But those presumably are the exception rather than the rule; and in any event, note that even in Sunstein's examples there is always a determinate outcome as regards the case at hand (just not as regards the *ratio* underlying it).

[17] As in Principle I.4 in Cohen 1989: 23.

performed. Rather, the issue lies in how commonly and casually that is done; in how conclusive the aggregation is to taken to be; and in the relative weight of legitimacy accorded outcomes by the aggregation itself, as compared to other elements of the decision process.

Output-democrats are perfectly comfortable in aggregating early, and in regarding the results of those aggregations of votes as utterly determinative of legitimate policy. Their models, after all, suppose that the primary claim that any decision has to being democratically legitimate lies in certain attributes of the aggregation procedures—specifically, in how equal is the power accorded to each voter over the final decision. From this output-oriented perspective, aggregating votes is not an unfortunate necessity or a last resort. On the contrary, it is the primary locus of democratic legitimacy. In the purple prose of Adam Przeworski, 'It is the result of voting, not of discussion, that authorizes governments to govern, to compel'.[18]

Like deliberative democrats, input-democrats more generally accept that from time to time they might have to resort to settling things by aggregating votes. But they settle things in that way only as a last resort. And they do so without any illusion that attributes of the aggregation procedure can in and of themselves completely underwrite the democratic credentials of the decision process. For input-democrats, it is the openness of the process to everyone's inputs (as much as, or more than, how those inputs are rendered into outputs) that makes the process truly democratic.

Of course, to confer a final blessing on the results of any input-democratic process, a final vote (if only a call for 'unanimous consent') is characteristically taken. But when the input-democratic process has worked well that final vote serves merely as final ratification of decisions which have been reached—and legitimated—primarily through those other means.

Hence the difference between input- and output-oriented models of democracy. Both may (and maybe even characteristically do) end up voting on things. But whereas output-democrats suppose that the final vote is the be all and end all to the legitimation of the decision, input-democrats see the primary locus of legitimacy as lying elsewhere. Like output-democrats, input-democrats might *in extremis* end up genuinely 'settling things' by aggregating votes. But they resort to those blunt instruments only when strictly necessary, and without any illusion that mere aggregations of votes will necessarily be ultimately determinative or fully legitimating.

---

[18] Przeworski 1998: 142; 1999: 40; cf. Cohen 1989; Dryzek 2000: 38 ff.

Input-democrats attach much more importance to what precedes the vote. They see it as a moral mistake to 'rush to a vote', gratuitously foreclosing further inputs and deliberation in circumstances in which we could well afford to take more time for further discussion. Output-democrats, in contrast, assess everything in terms of the 'bottom line': the vote, and the equal power that is manifest in it. Rushing for that bottom line as if nothing else mattered, and regarding the question as firmly closed and the outcome as fully legitimate as soon as a bottom-line vote count has once been taken, truly constitutes the 'arrogance of aggregation'.

Institutional Embodiments: Contrasting the Limiting Cases

Institutionally, of course, there are a great many different ways of operationalizing democratic aggregation rules. From the perspective of output-oriented theories of democracy, however, what matters across all those variants is simply equalizing (in so far as possible) power (or influence or whatever) over the ultimate resolution, across the entire citizenry. As shorthand, let us dub this output-oriented desideratum one of 'equal power over the bottom line'.

This fixation on the 'bottom line' leaves output-oriented theories of democracy open to a range of institutional forms that would be anathema to other theories of democracy. Input-oriented theories are relatively more interested in the whole process of decision, and they would be relatively more unaccepting of institutional forms that gave the people power (even if it were perfectly equal power) over just the very last stage of the process. That would be absolutely fine by output-oriented theories, in contrast, just so long as power at that point really were equal.

Schumpeterian Democracy: An Output-oriented Paradigm

To make the contrast concrete, note that output-oriented theories of democracy are capable of endorsing Schumpeterian democracy in a way input-oriented theories are not. Suppose that the 'competitive struggle for people's votes' really does give each voter equal power over elected officials and, through that, over the policies that they enact.[19]

---

[19] Schumpeter 1950: ch. 12. Dahl's (1956: ch. 3) formal characterization of 'polyarchy' is essentially the same. The Schumpeterian model is now taken to constitute the principal alternative to populist democracy (Quinton 1967: ch. 9; Plamenatz 1973: ch. 4), and

(That is a tall claim: but let us grant it for the sake of argument, here.[20]) Were that the case, then the demands of output democracy might be satisfied: everyone might have 'equal power over the bottom-line outcome'. And that might be true, even though there is nothing remotely democratic about inputs into the processes of policy development.

The hallmark of Schumpeterian democracy, recall, is that all the work of policy development is all done within teams of elites constituted as political parties. Those teams prepare policy packages which they then offer to voters at the election. The role of voters is confined simply to choosing among the policy packages put to them by those competing teams. Within this starkly Schumpeterian vision, voters themselves have absolutely no input: they merely exercise control over outputs, through their control over which team is installed in government.[21]

To coin a slogan, output-democrats say, 'What matters is what happens at the end of the day, not what happens along the way'. Of course, output-democrats are not stupidly insensitive to agenda-setting and the ways in which some outputs can be ruled out right from the start. All of that clearly does matter—to the outputs, among many other things. What output-democrats would say is this: as long as everyone has equal power over what eventually comes out of the political process, it does not matter how the process produces that result.

Thus, Schumpeterian parties which anticipate what *would* be people's reactions could serve the purposes of output-democrats equally well as real people inputting their real preferences—just so long as the anticipations of parties (at least one of them) prove accurate. Similarly as regards agenda-setting: Schumpeterian parties setting agendas for themselves, in anticipation of people's reactions but without any actual input at that point from people themselves, would be just fine with output-democrats—again, just so long as those anticipations prove accurate in the end.

Within Schumpeter's model, the 'competitive struggle for people's votes' is supposed to provide the mechanism which ensures these results. That is what provides parties with the motivation to try to anticipate people's preferences correctly; that is what presumably ensures

economic theorists of democracy profess substantially unqualified allegiance to it (Riker 1983; Przeworski 1999).

[20] Cf. Macpherson 1977: ch. 4.

[21] Or in an even more watered-down variant, policy might be developed wholly within a government bureaucracy under ministerial direction, with voters being asked merely to indicate retrospectively their approval (or otherwise) of what has transpired during the incumbents' period in office (Fiorina 1981).

that parties whose anticipations are more accurate in those regards are selected for office, and those whose anticipations are systematically less accurate are weeded out.

Whether or not the mechanism actually works that way is of course an empirical question. There are reasons aplenty for doubt, ranging from imperfect information among voters to barriers to entry leading to imperfect competition among parties. My point here is an analytic rather than an empirical one, however. Supposing the competitive struggle for people's votes really did have the effects envisaged by Schumpeter, then that thin form of democracy would be all that output democrats would strictly require.

Consultative Democracy: An Input-Oriented Paradigm

Whereas Schumpeterian democracy might be the most dramatic embodiment of output democracy, Scandinavian-style consultative democracy might be regarded as the most dramatic embodiment of the input-democratic ideal.

My model of consultative democracy will be a pastiche, compiled from various secondary sources and papering over interesting differences among the Nordic countries. Furthermore, although constructed out of Scandinavian materials in the first instance, the model is not confined to Scandinavia. Lowi's 'interest group pluralism' in the US, Beer's Britain 'in the collectivist age', Lijphart's 'consociational democracy' and even Schmitter's 'corporatist intermediation' all seem substantially similar in respects which are highly relevant to the distinction I here want to draw.[22] Furthermore, many of those other versions of the model have their natural home in polities characterized by deep divisions, thus confirming that the applicability of the model is nowise confined to societies as homogeneous as Scandinavian ones are typically presumed to be.

Scandinavian politics (and 'consensus models' more generally[23]) display various attributes, most of which are beside my present point. Thus, for example, there is a drive for compromise (if not literal consensus), in place of overt conflict.[24] There is bargaining, but its tone is accomodative rather than adversarial.[25] The political style is

---

[22] Lowi 1969; Beer 1965; cf. Goodin 1982*a*; Lijphart 1975, 1999; Schmitter 1977.

[23] Lijphart 1999: chs. 2–3.

[24] Rustow 1955: ch. 8; Eckstein 1966: 194; Torgersen 1970; Elder *et al.* 1982; Anton 1969: 94; 1980: ch. 8.

[25] Mansbridge 1980. Thus, for example, remarking upon 'the predominant decision-making style' in Norway, Eckstein (1966: 158–9) speaks of 'the high valuation of very

'inclusionary' rather than exclusionary. Representation is proportional rather than majoritarian. And so on.[26]

True and important though all that is, it is another feature of Nordic democracy upon which I here want to focus. That is its broadly consultative nature.[27] In his classic essay describing the interplay of 'numerical democracy and corporate pluralism' in Norway, Stein Rokkan describes how

> the Cabinet has increasingly had to take on the role of *mediator* between the conflicting interests in the national community ... [I]t can rarely if ever force through decisions solely on the basis of its electoral power but has to temper its policies in complex consultations and bargains with the major interest organizations. ... [T]he government has over the years built up a large network of consultative boards and councils for the representation of all the relevant interests.[28]

Cynically, that may be thought to be only a matter of trying to coopt into the decision process groups which could block subsequent implementation of any of its decisions.[29] And from the point of view of genuinely participatory democracy, certainly it is embarrassingly true that Scandinavian-style consultative democracy is based on groups rather than citizens.[30] Again, let us leave all that to one side and concentrate instead upon consultation as a generic practice.

Consultation involves what Johan P. Olsen calls a process of 'sounding out'—that, as distinct from a process of 'voting'.[31] Rather than pressing matters to a prompt resolution, decision-makers take their time. They feel each other out; they tentatively float ideas; they adjust

broad agreements, a kind of collegiality in a much wider sense. This involves ... a stress upon the reconciliation of men of different interests and persuasions, a tendency to treat even opponents as colleagues. The depth of that value is reflected in the language: the Norwegian word for a body of rules is *vedtekt*, and that word derives from *vedta*, "to agree to"; a decision resulting in a rule thus is not something that a decision maker takes but something that affected parties manage to agree on'.

[26] Strøm 1990: ch. 6; Kvavik 1976; Shaffer 1998.

[27] This may be related to those other features, either as cause or consequence: that is a matter I here want to leave simply as an open question.

[28] Rokkan 1966: 107–8; emphasis added. The pattern is not confined to Norway: see e.g. Damgaard and Eliassen 1980; Gustafsson and Richardson 1980.

[29] Selznick 1949; Anton 1980: 163–5. Rokkan 1966: 108; as he says elsewhere, 'Votes count, resources decide' (Rokkan 1975). This is just the old principle, which Przeworski (1999: 48–9) says he borrows from Condorcet, that we ought to 'place authority where lies the force'.   [30] Ruin 1974; Buksti and Eliassen 1979.

[31] Olsen 1972, 1983: 112–15, building on a sketchy model developed for very different purposes by Thompson and McEwan 1958: 30. Lindblom's (1965) bargaining-style model of partisan mutual adjustment might be substantially similar in this respect.

their own positions in light of what they anticipate the reactions of others will be. Through successive mutual adjustments of that sort people converge: not so much on common preferences, perhaps, as on common perceptions of the feasible set. When the feasible set has become sufficiently small, the choice largely tends to make itself.[32] Votes, when they come, turn out to be substantially anti-climatic.

The most concrete manifestation is the 'remiss' procedure. (While the description that follows is specific to Sweden, similar procedures are found, to a lesser albeit still significant extent, throughout Scandinavia.[33]) In Sweden, proposals for any major policy changes are submitted 'to all parties or organizations likely to be affected by the proposals, or likely to have an interest in responding to them. . . . [O]n major proposals the "affected organizations" can quite literally number in the hundreds'. In 1974, for example, 'more than 5000 remiss comments were generated for the 188 government bills submitted'.[34]

The Commissions channelling these consultations—perhaps seventy-five new ones each year, each of them sitting for perhaps two-and-a-half years—typically contain representatives of political parties and interest organizations who 'keep their respective leaderships informed about developments'.[35] Although the process is highly open to group inputs, in other respects it operates very much 'in a completely closed circle'.[36] The operative rule is, 'Fight in private'.[37] The upshot is that 'by the time the public debate gets started—in connection with the publication of the Commission report—consensus has often been reached on essential points'.[38]

One may well raise an eyebrow—or more—at the way in which 'vitally important discussions between the political parties, interest organizations and government in a democratic society are carried on

---

[32] Cf. Elster 1986a: 22.

[33] Lægreid and Roness 1996; Kvavik 1976: ch. 4; Elder *et al.* 1982: 182–3; Damgaard and Eliassen 1980.

[34] Anton 1980: 163–4. This leads to a distinctive sort of policy-making style: 'policymaking is extraordinarily *deliberative*, involving long periods of time during which more or less constant attention is given to some problem by well trained specialists. It is *rationalistic*, in that great efforts are made to develop the fullest possible information about any given issue, including a thorough review of historical experiences as well as the range of alternative suggested by scholars in and out of Sweden. It is *open*, in the sense that all interested parties are consulted before a decision is finally made. And it is *consensual*, in that decisions are seldom made without the agreement of virtually all parties . . .' (Anton 1969: 94).

[35] Meijer 1969: 109, 114.   [36] Meijer 1969: 114.

[37] Anton 1980: 173. The process of producing a 'consensus' report from the Commission often involves suppressing some arguments which some, but not all, members of the Commission regarded as compelling reasons for their supporting the Commission's recommendations.   [38] Meijer 1969: 115.

behind closed doors and out of the view of the public'.[39] Democratically speaking, perhaps such consultations ought not be confined to group representatives but ought instead to be opened to individual members of the public at large at a much earlier stage of the proceedings. It is no part of my brief here to defend those particulars of Nordic democracy—or even to assert that my reading of the secondary sources is as accurate as a characterization of the way things there actually work (or ever worked).

My aim instead is to extract from these materials a stylized account of how an idealized form of consultative politics might work. For those purposes, I propose to leave it as an open question who is to be consulted: whether just directly affected parties or all interested parties; whether just representatives of groups or all members of the groups; and so on. I propose also to leave open the question of how the results of the consultation actually affect the policy process: whether the opinions offered are regarded merely as advice or something stronger (warnings or threats or promises); whether the consultation is to be regarded as a straw poll or as being more binding; and so on.[40] I propose, finally, to leave open the aim of the consultation: whether it is supposed to produce a consensus or merely to canvass opinion. Let us set aside all those issues, in order to try to envisage what consultation *as such* might accomplish for us, democratically speaking.

Bracketing out all that, what we are left with is simply this. First, consultation functions to generate inputs into the policy process. Secondly, the broader the consultation the broader—the more varied, but also the more representative—the inputs. 'Equality of inputs' (or, more weakly still, perhaps just 'equality of opportunity for inputs') is the distinctively democratic feature of input democracy.

What impact those inputs might actually have on the eventual outcome depends upon various further features of the policy process and how it translates inputs into outputs. Hence it remains an open question whether increasing opportunities for input in this way actually gives people greater (much less equal) 'power over the bottom line'.

For output-oriented theorists whose primary notion of democracy is 'equal power over the bottom line', increasing opportunities for input in these ways does not necessarily (though it may well contingently) produce any increase in democracy. From another perspective, though, it makes perfectly good sense to describe such consultative procedures as 'democratizing' the policy process. The broader the consultation, the more people and groups whose opinions are represented in the

---

[39] Meijer 1969: 115.   [40] Anton 1980: 118–19.

policy process; the broader the consultation, the more representative the representations, both in their 'central tendency' and in their variation around that central tendency. And those consequences of the consultative process surely do speak to deep democratic concerns.

Just as Schumpeterian democracy constitutes an extreme case of what output-democrats might be prepared to endorse, so to do 'toothless consultations' constitute an extreme case of what input-democrats might be prepared to endorse. Democratizing the process, even if it that has no systematic linkage to democratizing the outputs, might at a pinch be sufficient to satisfy input-democratic ends.[41] Concretely, input-democrats might be happy with Scandinavian-style consultative politics, even if being consulted provides no assurance that people's opinions will have any impact on the eventual decision.

Why Inputs Matter, Democratically

Such a flaccid form of input democracy might seem deeply inconsequential. Making submissions which others are obliged to receive, and maybe even to read—but which they are perfectly at liberty then to ignore—might seem to amount to little more than idle talk.

Any such supposition would be wrong, I think. Inputs can alter outcomes, even when there is no realpolitik reason to think that they can, through their workings on our internal reflective processes. Before proceeding to that argument, however, let me first offer what I regard as a compelling analogy—an analogy to the democratic right of free speech—to suggest that input democracy might be absolutely central to the democratic process, even if it were to make no material difference to outcomes.

Democratic Free Speech: An Analogy

That analogy is just this. Notice that the toothless consultation just described has exactly the same structure as the 'right to free speech'— which is something we ordinarily (and rightly) regard as absolutely central to democratic politics.

There are various ways to ground the right to free speech. One is in the speaker's right to speak; another is in the listener's right to hear.[42] Whichever way we run the story, however, the crucial thing to notice

---

[41] In asking *Why People Obey the Law*, Tyler (1990) similarly finds that that has much more to do with people's perceptions of process values having been respected than with their substantive agreement with the statute.   [42] Sunstein 1993: esp. ch. 5.

is that listeners are never *obliged* to listen.[43] Your right is to a soapbox, not to an audience.

Nevertheless, we think the right to speak freely is absolutely central to democratic government. Why? Because democracy entails both a right for citizens of a democracy to try to influence one another and a right for citizens to try to find out what one another thinks.[44]

We may think it unfortunate if people do not exercise those latter rights. We may think our fellow citizens are remiss—or even that our democracy is in peril—if people do not seek out and listen to one another's opinions in that way. We may think it is a good idea to engineer things in such a way as to encourage them to do so.[45]

Still, democratically desirable though it may be for ordinary citizens to listen to one another, we would never think of imposing a legal duty upon them to do so, or of sanctioning them for failing to do so. In no country in the world is political inattentiveness a hanging (or even a fining) offence. In no country in the world is it even so much as a misdemeanour to fail to read the daily newspaper.[46]

Thus we think the right to speak freely is democratically crucial, even if no one is necessarily listening—and hence even if what we say does not necessarily make any material difference to the decisions that eventuate. All of which is just to say that the theory of democratic free speech is predicated on precisely the assumption that the right to make input matters, even if your input makes no material difference to the outcome.

A Condition Necessary but Not Sufficient?

The conventional way of making sense of that curious fact would be to say that free speech is a necessary but not sufficient condition of democracy. There are good reasons for thinking that the political system cannot be democratic unless people are allowed to communicate with one another freely; but while democracy surely requires that much, it requires more than that as well. It requires that political outputs

---

[43] In Hohfeldian terms, your 'right of free speech' entails a correlative duty on others 'not to interfere with your speaking freely': not a duty 'to listen to what you have to say'.

[44] Not to mention the right to tell one's representatives what one thinks, which is how the Australian High Court magicked up a right of free political speech from the Australian Constitution's guarantee of 'representative government' (Mason *et al.* 1992).

[45] Through doctrines that streets and parks—and, in the extension Sunstein (2001) proposes, cyberspace—are public places, open to all.

[46] Even (indeed, especially) where it is an offence to fail to vote, there is no obligation to do so in an informed manner. Nowhere in the world is compulsory voting conjoined with a literacy test.

be 'systematically responsive' to the preferences that citizens thus express.[47] And the same would presumably be true of input democracy, by extension: that too may be a necessary condition for democracy; but equally surely and for the same reason, it cannot be a sufficient condition. Or so the conventional wisdom would suppose.

Of course as I said at the outset, input democracy is contingently closely connected with output democracy. Democratizing inputs contributes mightily to democratizing outputs. Expanding the franchise is quintessentially a matter of giving everyone an input; but doing so helps to give everyone equal power over the bottom line as well. Ensuring that elections are not bought ensures that the process is open to inputs of everyone, not just prospective purchasers; but that also obviously helps to promote output democracy, understood as equal power over the bottom line as well. Efforts to deny media magnates undue influence in elections protects the inputs of ordinary people, but it also helps to equalize their power over the bottom line. In all these ways, measures designed to democratize inputs also democratize outputs, and conversely.

Or, again, consider the problem of agenda-setting. Nothing can emerge as the output of a democratic process unless someone has first put it onto the agenda;[48] there, most dramatically, outputs are tightly constrained by inputs. Indeed, throughout the decision process more generally, which options are selected depends upon inputs— what arguments are offered, what pressures applied, and so on. Given all these ways in which inputs shape outputs, the best way to achieve output-democratic goals might well be to equalize inputs. At the very least, input-oriented strategies would seem to form a very important part of any larger strategy for equalizing power over outputs.

Output democrats would insist that they do not constitute the whole of the story, though. Democracy cannot be 'inputs all the way down', simply because at the end of the day inputs must be transformed into outputs; and how democratic the regime will be depends crucially (even if perhaps not wholly) upon the character of the rules governing that process. In that crucial respect, output democracy is not coterminous with input democracy. Rather, it adds something that input democracy cannot conceivably provide.

In so far as input democracy differs from output democracy, output-democrats would say, input democracy would seem to be necessarily

---

[47] May 1978.
[48] As Schattschneider (1960: 66) says, 'the definition of the alternatives is the supreme instrument of power'.

inferior, democratically speaking. To assert the contrary—that we should accord higher priority to input democracy than to output democracy, when the two diverge—would seem perverse in the extreme. It would seem to amount to saying that it is more important for people to have a voice than for the people to have any ultimate, determinative say in what happens to them. That seems plainly contrary to the fundamental democratic impulse. Whatever reason democrats have for wanting people to have input into processes, the same reasons must surely lead them to want the outputs actually to be responsive to those inputs—and indeed to be systematically rather than just incidentally so.

How Inputs Might Matter

One way of overcoming that sense of perversity is to point out how input democracy might actually contribute towards ensuring that sort of 'systematic responsiveness' which is required by output democracy.[49]

My suggestion, which will be elaborated much more fully in Chapter 9, builds on the proposition that inputs systematically shape outputs through the dynamics of political discourse. The very process of discussion inevitably serves to reframe the issues for interlocutors, systematically causing each to take into account the preferences and perspectives of each other.

The point is not merely that discourse leads to convergence, though. The deeper point is that this process of convergence is systematically responsive to the preferences and perspectives of everyone involved, in precisely the way democratic aggregation procedures are crucially supposed to be from the output-democrat's perspective. The fact that the process operates internally (within each interlocutor's head) rather than externally (through some vote-counting machine) is surely of no consequence, democratically speaking. Democratically, what matters is systematic responsiveness: and that, I argue, can be accomplished at either site.[50]

---

[49] There might of course be various other advantages to consultative procedures, quite apart from these effects. Among them would be ensuring citizens continuing influence over rulers between (and not just at) elections, inculcating civic virtue and binding citizens and groups participating in the consultations to the results of those consultations.

[50] The character of the community is certainly different, and arguably more desirable, where people are responding directly to one another's plight in their own internal reckonings, rather than merely trusting to some external mechanisms to ensure that the polity as a whole will be responsive to their needs and desires. Measured purely in terms of

Hard-headed realists might scoff. An anecdote along those lines is recounted in Andrew Shonfeld's *Modern Capitalism*:

I recall a British trade union leader after an organized visit to Sweden—there were several such visits undertaken by the British trade union movement in the early 1960s in an attempt to discover the secret of Swedish labour's success— expressing his frustration over the whole business. The secret was either too banal or too opaque to yield to intelligent investigation. 'All they can tell you when you ask them how they do it', he said, describing some particularly difficult decision which involved the concerted action of competing interest groups, 'is: "We has a meeting". *We has a meeting!* I'd like to see how they'd make out with our blokes over here'.[51]

But let scoffers reflect for a moment upon what actually goes on when one 'has a meeting', where one is obliged to sit through an 'exchange of views'. Of course it is possible just to argue your own brief and ignore theirs altogether, 'turning a deaf ear' to the other. More typically, though, the requirements of the context require you at least to pretend you are listening, engaging and answering one another in good faith. And even if you are doing so only half-heartedly or strategically, you inevitably end up at least partially internalizing the other's point of view.

Some discourse theorists and deliberative democrats might want to dress this up as a higher-order tenet of communicative ethics. Serious communications are arguably governed by strict norms, among them listening and responding in good faith to what one another is saying.[52] But there is no need for anything nearly so grand or nearly so high- minded. This 'internal-reflective' aspect of deliberation—this 'putting oneself in the place of the other'—is a much more mundane feature of conversation in all forms. It is what allows us to make sense of one another's utterances at all.

As I shall argue more fully in Chapter 9, it is also something that can happen in non-discursive settings. Having to engage with another, face-to-face, might force us to try to 'put ourselves into the place of the other'. But we might be led to do so merely by being obliged to read submissions from another: that too might lead us to try to internalize the other's perspective, if only (in the first instance) in order just to make sense of the written words.

responsiveness, though, outcomes might be about the same whichever of these ways they are achieved.

[51] Shonfield 1965: 199.   [52] Habermas 1995: 117; Midgaard *et al.* 1973.

Mutual Co-optation

What democratic theorists often fear about consultative practices is that they will result in 'co-optation'.[53] Oppositional groups will be incorporated into the process; having participated in the process of making the decision, they are held 'hostage' to it and cannot decently repudiate it. That is a deft political trick for stilling dissident voices, which is why democratic theorists are so wary of it.

That trick can easily backfire, though. Just as gerontologists tell us aged couples can fall into patterns of 'co-dependency', so too can the co-optor and the co-optee in administrative politics. When engaged in protracted consultations, each comes to internalize the perspective of the other.[54] Neither party is inclined to force the other into a corner, not because the other has the power successfully to resist, but rather because the first party is no longer quite so convinced that that is the right thing to do. It is not that the other party has a 'veto': it is just that the other party is seen, suddenly, as genuinely 'having a point'.[55]

This model might provide an alternative account of what goes on in Scandinavian consultative democracy. From the outside, anyway, it is hardly credible that political authority is so fragile that all the multi-farious groups that are consulted have power to block implementation of policies, and therefore strictly *need* to be squared in advance for any power-political reason. Even if they did, it is hardly credible that it would systematically take two or more years to cut a deal with them all, through the ordinary processes of political bargaining.

Much more plausibly, what are going on there would seem to be genuine conversations, where everyone genuinely comes to see (if not completely internalize) each other's point of view, and genu-inely comes to feel some internalized need to try to accommodate it in the ultimate resolution. That is to say, the 'mutual co-option' inev-itably involved in genuine political discourse is what is driving the phenomenon.[56]

Notice, now, the consequence of all that from an output-oriented perspective. The initial consultation may have been a relatively tooth-less proceedings. The groups being consulted might have had no real

[53] Selznick 1949; Goodin 1980: 52–6; Saward 1992.

[54] Consider e.g. the evidence from psychology labs that people are substantially more inclined to cooperate with one another in Prisoner's Dilemma games if they have had a chance for just a little incidental small talk before the game begins (Orbell *et al.* 1988).

[55] There are of course some people whose viewpoint we do not regard as legitimate and we do not want to internalize, in this way. Appreciation of the inevitably cooptive effects of conversation presumably is what underpins the 'no platform for racists (etc.)' position of many otherwise liberal opponents of free speech.   [56] Cf. Goodin 1980: 105–8.

power outside the process to make trouble for policy-makers; they may have been given no real power within the process to block or delay decisions there, either. The procedure might have been wholly 'toothless' in that respect. Still, once it got under way, the process of 'mutual co-optation' might afford otherwise powerless people some real power over the policy process and the outputs that eventually emerge from it.

That power might *de facto* rather than *de jure*, and the dynamics might be more mental than material. Still, power is power, and more subtle forms are often all the stronger for that very reason.

Conclusion

Most of democratic theory is devoted to equalizing power of a particular sort: power over political outcomes. The forms of power inequality that concern us are many and varied, as are democratic devices designed to rectify them. We want to insulate political outcomes from inequalities of status; and towards that end we institute rules of 'one person one vote' and secret ballots. We want to insulate political outcomes from inequalities of wealth; and towards that end we institute prohibitions against buying offices or votes. Various other devices described from time to time as democratic—ranging from public education to public broadcasting to second chambers—might all be seen in similar fashion as being designed, essentially, to prevent political outcomes from being influenced by factors we regard as illegitimate.

Without in the least wanting to denigrate all those important efforts, I have here drawn attention to another way in which we might go about democratizing the political process. That approach focuses on democratizing the inputs to the process, rather than focusing on the outputs.

We cannot do away with democratic aggregation rules, and output-democrats rightly insist that those should accord everyone equal power as nearly as possible. Input-democrats agree but add that aggregation is not the be all (even if perhaps it is, by definition, at least an interim end all) of democratic politics. We can and should try to avoid pre-emptive resort to the mechanical aggregation of opinions, for as long as possible. We should try to encourage genuine conversation and to let a genuine consensus emerge where we can; we should abstain from forcing matters prematurely to a conclusion, in so far as we possibly can.

By insisting that we should 'discuss while we can, vote when we must', input-democratic thinking marks a sharp contrast to our ordinary output-democratic inclination to look only to the bottom line. If the analysis I have been offering is correct, however, democratizing inputs might go some considerable distance to democratizing outputs—and systematically so, given the logic of conversational dynamics in consultative situations. As I shall show in the next chapter, this constitutes the best account of what 'deliberative democracy' is really all about. And, as I shall go on to show there, that same model might be extended from democratic consultations to democratic imaginings, empathy importantly supplementing actual conversation in 'democratic deliberations within'.

CHAPTER 9

Democratic Deliberation Within

Two Types of Deliberation

The focus of deliberative democrats is ordinarily on deliberation in its 'external-collective' aspect.[1] That is perfectly understandable. After all, democracy is quintessentially a manner of *collective* decision-making, in which everyone participates on an equal footing. Deliberation cannot dispense with 'the other' without compromising its democratic credentials.

Nevertheless, deliberation also has a familiar 'internal-reflective' aspect to it.[2] Deliberation consists in the weighing of reasons for and against a course of action. In that sense, it can and ultimately must take place within the head of each individual. True, the sort of give-and-take involved in that process is fundamentally argumentative, and hence discursive;[3] so perhaps deliberation, even in this internal-reflective mode, is invariably modelled upon, and thus parasitic upon, our interpersonal experiences of discussion and debate. Still, it remains significant how very much of the work of deliberation, even in external-collective settings, must inevitably be done within each individual's head—or so I shall here be arguing.

In their practical political proposals, deliberative democrats naturally concentrate upon ways of democratizing external-collective deliberation. Deliberative democrats seek outcomes which will be regarded as democratically binding and which will thereafter form the basis of (at least partially) 'collective intentions'.[4] They suppose that outcomes will be democratically legitimate only so far as they emerge

---

[1] Represented by Aristotle's 'deliberative speaking' in the *Rhetoric* (1984*a*: 1, 3–4).
[2] Found in e.g. Aristotle's *Nicomachean Ethics* (1984*b*: 4) and Hobbes's *Leviathan* (1651: ch. 6).　　　　　　　　　　　　　　　　　　　　　[3] Hampshire 2000.
[4] Gutmann and Thompson 1996: 4–5; Richardson 1997.

through external-collective processes of deliberation involving a free and equal exchange among everyone who will be affected by them.[5]

That ideal seems eminently feasible in small-scale societies where face-to-face interactions are the norm.[6] In large-scale mass societies, they are not and cannot be. Recall Dahl's back-of-the-envelope calculation, which I alluded to in Chapter 1: 'if an association were to make one decision a day, allow ten hours a day for discussion, and permit each member just ten minutes—rather extreme assumptions . . . —then the association could not have more than sixty members'.[7] Added to the constraints of time and numbers are the 'problems of distance' and the complications arising from the distinctive perspectives associated with distant others who must be represented in any genuinely democratic deliberation across an extended polity.[8] The challenge facing deliberative democrats is thus to find some way of adapting their deliberative ideals to any remotely large-scale society, where it is simply infeasible to arrange face-to-face discussions across the entire community.[9]

Solutions to that problem are not easily found. After briefly surveying various flawed attempts to rescue external-collective forms of deliberative democracy from the problems of time, numbers, and distance, I offer a counterproposal. My suggestion is that we ease the burdens of deliberative democracy in mass society by altering our focus from the 'external-collective' to the 'internal-reflective' mode, shifting

[5] Manin 1987; Cohen 1989: 21–3; 1996: 99–100; Benhabib 1994; Dryzek 1990, 2000.

[6] Laslett 1956. As Lindsay (1929: 23) says: 'It is a commonplace of political theory that direct democracy became impossible when the size of the community outgrew the limits of a single public meeting. But long before that limit is reached most members of the community have ceased to take any part in the discussion or to contribute anything to the meeting. No one can really do business at a big meeting. Men can say Yes or No to cut and dried proposals, or compelling and spellbinding speeches may turn votes, but the real discussion and largely the real government is in the hands of the committee who prepare the business.'   [7] Dahl 1970: 67–8.

[8] Contenting ourselves with getting all the positions on the table, as distinct from all persons to the podium, is one way of mitigating these problems. My proposals below can be seen as one way of doing that.

[9] James Madison thought that 'a democracy . . . must be confined to a small spot' whereas 'a republic may be extended over a large region', precisely because 'in a democracy the people meet and exercise government in person' whereas 'in a republic they administer it by their representatives and agents' (Hamilton et al. 1787–8: no. 14). See similarly Dahl and Tufte (1973) and Mansbridge (1980: chs. 19–20). Even face-to-face assemblies cease being deliberative when they become too large, with speech-making replacing conversation and rhetorical appeals replacing reasoned arguments. As Madison (or perhaps Hamilton) wrote in *The Federalist*, 'In all very numerous assemblies, of whatever characters composed, passions never fail to wrest the sceptre from reason. Had every Athenian assembly been a Socrates, every Athenian assembly would still have been a mob' (Hamilton et al. 1787–8: no. 55). Cf. Cicero, *De Officiis* (1991: 2. 48) and Madison, in *The Federalist*, nos 62 and 63 (Hamilton et al. 1787–8).

much of the work of democratic deliberation back inside the head of each individual. In defence of that proposal, I recall that such internal mental processes play a very major role even in ordinary conversational settings. It is a small step from there to suggesting that empathetic imagining can be an important supplement to, and at the margins can occasionally substitute for, interpersonal conversation in the sorts of deliberations which democrats desire across mass societies.

Deliberation, on this account, is less a matter of making people 'conversationally present' and more a matter of making them 'imaginatively present' in the minds of deliberators.[10] This revised understanding of deliberation has the effect of prioritizing what might otherwise seem peripheral to modern democratic theory. No doubt democrats always regard it as a presumptively good thing to democratize all corners of society, the arts along with everything else. But seeing empathetic imaginings as central to the deliberative processes of mass democracies sensitizes us to conditions surrounding the production and distribution of crucial aids to those imaginings, conspicuously among them the literary, visual, and performing arts. Ensuring the broad representativeness and generalized uptake of those representations is, on the model of democratic deliberation propounded here, of capital importance.

Internal-reflective modes of deliberation can never literally replace external-collective ones. For one thing, in practice the two modes are inextricably intertwined. Making others imaginatively present is essential to understanding what they are saying to us; so too can making them conversationally present constitute a powerful impetus for making them imaginatively present, as well. Politically, a deliberation conducted entirely within people's imaginations, however expansive it may be, would still lack the sort of ratification by others required for it to count as fully democratic. Conversely, a procedure in which people fail to internalize the perspective of one another qualifies as democratic only in the most mechanical of ways: without properly registering what one another is saying, it will be not an exchange of reasons but merely a count of votes.

Thus, internal-reflective deliberation is an important supplement and complement to external-collective deliberation in the political realm. To be properly democratic, its results must at some point or another be validated through procedures of the external-collective sort. Still, appreciating the proper role that internal-reflective deliberation

---

[10] After the fashion of Benedict Anderson's *Imagined Communities* (1983). See, more generally, Gilbert Ryle's discussion of 'imagination' (1949: 8).

may and indeed must play in deliberation can help to relieve many of the burdens plaguing external-collective deliberation in modern mass societies.

Unsuccessful Adaptations

Previous solutions to the problems that large-scale mass society poses for deliberative democracy rely upon one or another of four basic strategies. One pair works by limiting the *number of people* with whom you have to deliberate, a second pair by limiting the *level of inputs from others* with which you have to deal. Both seem likely to fail, for one reason or another.

Seriality: Disjointed Deliberation

If we are too numerous to deliberate together all at the same time, then one solution is Aristotle's suggestion that we 'deliberate, not all in one body, but by turns'.[11] Here is one way. Break us down into groups sufficiently small to allow genuine deliberation within each of them; and then let the upshots of those deliberations serve as inputs to subsequent deliberations among other groups, similarly constituted. Let us call this a model of 'serial' or 'disjointed deliberation'.

That is how the 'common law' has been supposedly discovered by English juries since the twelfth century.[12] A variation on that model appeals to certain sorts of postmodernists, whose preferred solution to the increasingly fractured social world is a 'directly deliberative polyarchy' involving 'a plurality of modes of association'.[13]

The trick with this general approach lies, of course, in somehow articulating all those separately deliberating bodies' judgements with one with another. Many ways of doing so are not particularly democratic. The deliberations of local English assizes were rendered into a unified common law across the realm by having the same small set of judges (twenty-five in all) travel up and down the country presiding over all proceedings. Sir Matthew Hale was pleased to report that

those men who are employed as justices ... have had a common education in the study of law ... [I]n term-time ... they daily converse and consult with one

[11] Aristotle, *Politics* (1984d: 1298^a 13).

[12] Berman 1983: 448–9. Even today, the jury is virtually the sole institution which 'regularly calls upon ordinary citizens to engage each other in a face-to-face process of debate' (Abramson 1994: 8).

[13] Cohen and Sabel 1997. See similarly Cohen and Rogers *et al.* 1995; Hirst 1994; Benhabib 1994: 35; Young 1997.

another; acquaint one another with their judgements, sit near one another in Westminster Hall, whereby their judgements are necessarily communicated to one another…[B]y this means their judgements and their administrations of common justice carry a constancy, congruity and uniformity one to another….[14]

Deliberative democrats are unlikely to share Hale's enthusiasm. From their perspective, whatever directly deliberative gains were secured by introducing juries in the first place would be largely nullified by entrusting to such a small and closed elite the task of blending all those lower level deliberations into a single nationwide common law.

The upper English judiciary constitutes only the most dramatic instance of a problem plaguing models of disjointed deliberation quite generally. Most of them seem to aggregate the inputs of highly democratic groups at the ground level through a hierarchy whose own directly democratic deliberative credentials are substantially less secure. Habermas, for example, proposes that the 'oppositional public sphere' serve as the source of deliberatively democratic inputs which are then fed into, and coordinated through, the ordinary political sphere—which Habermas himself, of course, regards as itself being very far indeed from directly deliberatively democratic.[15] Or for another example, consider Cohen and Sabel's proposal for the outputs of 'directly deliberatively democratic polyarchies' at the local level to be fed into a 'peak-level' meta-deliberation among all those groups: once again, however equal the groups might be within that meta-deliberation, the incorporation of that extra layer of deliberation itself makes that scheme less 'directly deliberative', and hence less democratic in that sense.[16] Much the same might be said about the various other mediating institutions—ranging from political parties to legislative subcommittees to high courts—which have from time to time been proposed as key agents in the deliberative process.[17]

I can see only one way in which the inputs of a plurality of groups could be blended together in a fashion that genuinely would be both directly and deliberatively democratic. Suppose each of us is a member of many different 'groups'. (Nothing hangs on the nature of those groups: they might, as with juries, be nothing more than random sortitions of the population.) Suppose furthermore that each of us overlaps any given other in only a small fraction of our group

---

[14] Hale 1716, quoted in Simpson (1973: 96). See also Berman 1983: 449.
[15] Habermas 1992: ch. 8; see similarly Dryzek 1996. Ackerman and Fishkin's (2002) 'Deliberation Day' shares this feature, as well.   [16] Cohen and Sabel 1997: 326.
[17] See, respectively, Cohen 1989: 31–2; Bessette 1994: esp. ch. 6; Uhr 1998: esp. ch. 4; Rawls 1993: 231–40.

memberships.[18] Then there might be a 'web of group affiliations' which links (indirectly: perhaps very indirectly) everyone with everyone else in a dialogue which effectively straddles the entire community.[19] Thus, for example, if each of us were a member of just five groups containing twenty others each, and none of us overlapped any other more than once, then our judgements would on these assumptions be merged directly or indirectly with those of 20^5 or 3,200,000 others.

That way of linking all the groups could, in principle, be both deliberatively and directly democratic. In practice, however, the crucial presuppositions underlying that model are unlikely to be met. Whereas the model of overlapping group affiliations presupposes that everyone is a member of some (indeed, several) groups, each of which approximates the deliberative ideal, in the real world altogether too many people are 'socially excluded', participating in no such groups at all.[20] Others are 'socially segregated', participating in only the same small sets of deliberative groups with the same other people, over and over again. In so far as either is the case, there will be no 'serial deliberation' indirectly linking all members of the community.

Substitution: Ersatz Deliberation

The first strategy of 'disjointed deliberation' substituted deliberation within partial, overlapping groups for deliberation across the entire community. A second strategy, which I dub 'ersatz deliberation', instead substitutes deliberation within a *subset* of the community for deliberation across the *whole* of the community.[21]

How the subset is identified and how the substitution is justified are interconnected issues. The subset is supposed to be representative—typical, 'a fair sample', 'a microcosm'[22]—of the larger set. Substituting its judgement for that of the larger is justified, in turn, on the grounds that the considered views reached through deliberation within that smaller group will be representative (an accurate reflection) of the views that would have been reached had similar processes been feasible within the larger group.[23]

---

[18] Something like this is suggested by Young 1995: 157.

[19] Simmel 1955: esp. pp. 125–95.   [20] As discussed in Ch. 10 below.

[21] To be sure, deliberators genuinely deliberate in these processes. The only question—which is what is meant to be signalled by calling the process 'ersatz'—is the extent to which the deliberations of the subset can adequately substitute for those of the whole.

[22] Mill 1861: ch. 5, p. 228. In Lord Boothby's delightful formulation, 'Ideally, the House of Commons should be a social microcosm of the nation. The nation includes a great many people who are rather stupid, and so should the House' (quoted in Birch 1977: 268).

[23] Thus e.g. in their deliberations behind the closed doors of the Philadelphia Convention the Founding Fathers self-consciously couched their arguments in terms of what 'ought to

The clearest example of this sort of 'ersatz deliberation'—the substitution of deliberation within a smaller group for that within an unwieldily large one—is of course representative democracy.[24] Legislatures are regularly styled as 'deliberative assemblies', in contrast to 'popular' ones (and even within the legislature, the less numerous house is standardly styled the 'deliberative' chamber[25]). But recent innovations like 'citizens' juries' and 'deliberative polling' are other instances of the same broad class of model.[26]

All these models of ersatz deliberation involve, at root, substituting a subset for the whole and letting the subset deliberate on behalf of the whole. The generic problem with all of those schemes lies in ensuring the *continuing* representativeness of the subset, once the deliberation gets under way. Naturally, people change their minds over the course of the deliberation (it would hardly be a genuine deliberation at all if they did not, at least sometimes[27]). The question is whether people who started out being representative of the wider community, in all the ways we can measure, are also representative of that wider community in the ways in which they *change* over the course of the deliberation.

On the face of it, that seems unlikely. From everyday life we know that different conversations with different participants (or with the same participants interjecting at different points) proceed in radically different directions.[28] Given the path dependency of conversational dynamics, and the sheer creativity of conversing agents, it beggars belief that any one group would come to exactly the same conclusions by exactly the same route as any other.[29] (Lawyers say it is a 'well known secret' that 'no two juries and no two judges are

occur to a people deliberating on a Government for themselves, ... in a temperate moment, and with the experience of other nations before them' (Madison 1840: entry for 26 June 1787, pp. 193–4).

[24] Pitkin 1967; Manin 1997: esp. ch. 6.

[25] Madison, *Federalist*, nos. 62 and 63 (Hamilton *et al.* 1787–8).

[26] Fishkin 1991, 1995; Coote and Lenaghan 1997; Smith and Wales 1999.

[27] Elster 1998*b*: 8–9.   [28] Tully 1999.

[29] Cf. Fishkin's (1995: 220) report of deliberative polls done for three different local public utilities in Texas. There he is pleased to report that in all three cases the shift in opinion, pre- to post-deliberation, was in the same *direction*. But the *absolute numbers* none the less diverged wildly. In one case, fully half of the respondents thought post-deliberation that 'investing in conservation' was the 'option to pursue first', whereas in another case under a third thought so. In one case, over a third still thought post-deliberation that 'renewable energy' should be the top option, whereas in another case less than a sixth thought so. Clearly, these deliberating groups ought not be regarded as interchangeable. Nor, in consequence, does this evidence inspire confidence in the general strategy of 'ersatz deliberation', treating smaller deliberative groups as microcosms capable of literally 'substituting' for deliberation across the whole community.

alike'.[30]) Yet that is what strong advocates of ersatz deliberation must be claiming to be at least approximately true, in insisting that deliberations within a representative subset will genuinely mirror, and can therefore substitute for, deliberations across the whole community.[31]

Restricting Inputs: Emaciated Deliberation

Whereas the first pair of strategies cope with the problem of mass society by reducing the *number of people* deliberating together, the second pair of strategies cope with the problem by reducing *how much they communicate* to one another. The first variation on this model is one of 'emaciated deliberation', which facilitates mass deliberation by reducing the density of the signals and hence the deliberative load each participant has to bear.

Legislative assemblies, for one familiar example, streamline their proceedings by imposing limits on the length or number of speeches.[32] One effect (among others) is to limit how much speakers can say, and hence to restrict how much input deliberators have to take into account. Rules of 'germaneness', of course, serve even more directly to filter the quantity (as well, obviously, as the quality) of inputs into legislative deliberations.[33]

Another version of this same basic strategy is 'mediated deliberation', where some intermediary filters what messages get passed along to others within the larger community. In international negotiations, intermediaries facilitate agreement by restricting the messages passed among parties to the negotiation (omitting gratuitous insults, groundless threats, and so on).[34] In modern mass society, much the same sort of 'mediated deliberation' occurs through the agency of the mass media, which strictly limits how much information anyone can impart to (or impose upon) everyone else.[35]

Facilitating mass deliberations by 'restricting inputs' into them poses some obvious problems, however. Unless we have some reason for supposing that we are screening out only inputs which are irrelevant

---

[30] Kalven and Zeisel 1966: 474. Even where mock juries come to the same verdicts, as Cass Sunstein tells me they often do, they do so through very different lines of collective reasoning.

[31] At most, they might be taken as 'recommendations' to be fed back into those broader community-wide deliberations (Fishkin 1995: 162).

[32] Limiting the length of interventions is the more modern way, limiting the number of them the older. British parliamentary practice traditionally was that 'none may speak more than once to the matter' (Jefferson 1766: 89).

[33] Jefferson 1766: 89–90.   [34] Young 1967.

[35] Page 1996. 'Seconds' played a similar role in the old *code dueletto*; Wyatt-Brown 1982.

or superfluous[36], restricting inputs leaves us deliberating in ignorance to some greater or lesser degree. Our cognitive capacities, which rely upon informational inputs, are more or less undernourished. (Hence the term 'emaciated deliberation'.) In the limiting case of a 'democracy of soundbites', we are deliberating on the basis of so little as to make it hardly a case of deliberation—of seriously reflective 'weighing and judging reasons'—at all.

Selective Uptake: Blinkered Deliberation

Participants in Habermas's 'public sphere' are ideally supposed to 'engage' with one another.[37] Maybe they actually did in the coffee-houses of seventeenth-century London.[38] Most of the institutions of the contemporary public sphere, however, are more like Habermas's other great paragon of the early public sphere, the broadsheet news-paper. 'When Addison and Steele published the first issue of the *Tattler* in 1709', Habermas tells us, 'the coffee-houses were already so numerous and the circles of their frequenters already so wide that contact among these thousandfold circles could only be maintained through a journal'.[39] At that point, participants in the public sphere were no longer engaging directly with one another at all.

The problem is not merely that their interactions were mediated through the broadsheet, with the consequent problems as already sketched. There is a further problem. Contributors to broadsheets— and, come to that, people holding forth in coffee-houses as well—are not so much 'talking to one another' as they are 'posting notices for all to read'. Others might (or might not) take note of them, and reply. In

---

[36] As arguably we do with germaneness rules in the legislative case, for example.

[37] Habermas 1962: esp. pp. 31–43; 1964; 1992: esp. chs. 7–8. See also Taylor 1993.

[38] Even there they engaged directly but not particularly deeply, judging from Hazlitt's later account, 'On Coffee-House Politicians' (1869). There he writes that coffee-house politicians 'are like an oyster at the ebb of the tide, gaping for fresh *tidings*' (p. 263). Among them, 'The Evening Paper is impatiently expected and called for at a certain critical minute: the news of the morning becomes stale and vapid by the dinner-hour. ... It is strange that people should take so much interest at one time what they so soon forget:—the truth is, they feel no interest in it at any time, but it does for something to talk about. Their ideas are served up to them, like their bill of fare, for the day' (p. 262). In coffee-houses, 'People do not seem to talk for the sake of expressing their opinions, but to maintain an opinion for the sake of talking. ... It is not conversation, but rehearsing a part' (pp. 268–9). 'Men of education and men of the world ... know what they have to say on a subject, and come to the point at once. Your coffee-house politician balances between what he heard last and what he shall say next; and not seeing his way clearly, puts you off with circumstantial phrases, and tries to gain time for fear of making a false step' (p. 269).

[39] Habermas 1962: 42.

so far as they reply in like fashion, they too are essentially just posting other notices for all to note (or not), in turn.

What we find in the public sphere, in short, is not so much 'public deliberation' as 'deliberation *in public*'. Beijing's 'Wall of Democracy' provided democracy of a sort. And democracy of that sort—the free broadcasting of opinions—might be one important precondition of any genuinely deliberative democracy. But merely posting notices on billboards or the internet, or shouting out opinions from a soapbox in Hyde Park, does not in and of itself constitute communication, much less full-blown *deliberative* democracy. British parliamentary practice prohibits reading out of written speeches for precisely that reason:

When orators confine themselves to reading out what they have written in the silence of their study, they no longer discuss, they amplify. They do not listen, since what they hear must not in any way alter what they are going to say. They wait until the speaker whose place they must take has concluded. They do not examine the opinion he defends, they count the time he is taking and which they regard as a delay. In this way there is no discussion ... Everyone sets aside whatever he has not anticipated, all that might disrupt a case already completed in advance. Speakers follow one another without meeting; if they refute one another it is simply by chance. They are like two armies, marching in opposite directions, one next to the other, barely catching a glimpse of one another, avoiding even looking at one another for fear of deviating from a route which has already been irrevocably traced out.[40]

For democracy to be truly deliberative, there must be uptake and engagement—other people must hear or read, internalize and respond—for that public-sphere activity to count as remotely deliberative.[41] Furthermore, for that public-sphere to count as richly democratic, it must be the case that most people are actively engaged in this sort of give-and-take with most other people.

Theorists of the public sphere, in short, solve the problem of how to deliberate democratically in mass societies by compromising the conditions that make the processes deliberative. In guaranteeing the free and equal expression of opinions in the public sphere, they guarantee everyone a voice but no one a hearing.

Another Approach: Deliberation Within

All of those previous proposals for making deliberative democracy work in the context of mass society focus on the 'external-collective'

---

[40] Constant 1815: ch. 7, p. 222.   [41] On uptake see Pocock 1973.

side of deliberation. They all suppose that the key to making democracy deliberative is making everyone 'communicatively present', in some sense or another. But in any large society, it is impossible to do that literally, and none of the substitutes suggested so far seems very satisfactory. My proposal is to try to make the 'internal-reflective' aspect of deliberation do more of the work for us.

Understanding One Another

Begin by recalling how very much of what goes on in a genuine face-to-face conversation is actually contained inside the head of each of the participants, anyway. Language itself must be public rather than private, to be sure. But the point remains that most of the work in interpreting the utterances of others—decoding the literal meaning, and enriching that literal meaning pragmatically in light of contextual information—is actually done within the hearer's own head.

When trying to understand what others are saying, we start by assuming that they are trying to talk sense. We assume, at least as a first approximation, that they mean by their utterances roughly what we ourselves would have meant by them.[42] We are prepared to treat provisionally as true, for the purposes of any given conversation, that set of propositions which seem to constitute the most coherent way of construing the background assumptions underlying the assertions our interlocutor is making.[43]

In ordinary conversation, people do not tediously elaborate complete syllogisms. (Nobody listens, if they do.) Instead, people characteristically talk more or less 'loosely'.[44] They make more-or-less cryptic allusions to more full-blown arguments. 'Catching the other's drift' in ordinary conversation is substantially a matter of completing the other's syllogism in your own mind, working out the various 'implicatures' contained within the other's utterances.[45]

How exactly we make sense of 'other minds' is a large and philosophically contentious issue.[46] But whatever more particular story we tell, the general idea is invariably that we make sense of others, their utterances, and their actions, by mentally 'putting ourselves in the other's place' in some sense or another. 'Simulation theorists' envisage

---

[42] Austin 1979: 115; Davidson 1984.   [43] Lewis 1979.

[44] Sperber and Wilson 1986.

[45] That is how 'conversational implicature' works (Grice 1975, 1989: esp. 22–40, 138–44, 269–82).

[46] On related disputes in the philosophy of mind, see Currie 1999; Peacocke 1994; Davies 1994; Davies and Stone 1998.

us 'understanding other minds from the inside' in a lightly theorized way.[47] 'Theory theorists', as the name implies, envisage us doing so in a much more theoretically laden manner.[48] Either way, much of the work involved in making sense of what others are saying in ordinary discourse necessarily goes on in the hearer's own head.

Discourse and Imagination

Discourse theorists know perfectly well that this is how ordinary conversation proceeds. Indeed, they make much of the fact. Habermas, for the most famous example, describes discourse ethics as 'rest[ing] on ... a joint process of "ideal role taking"' in which 'everyone is required to take the perspective of everyone else, and thus project herself into the understandings of self and world of all others'.[49] That is how he hopes to secure the sort of 'intersubjectivity' that is so central to his larger project.

It is precisely that process of imagining yourself into the place of the other which discourse theorists hope interpersonal discourse will set in motion. But note well: the process which discourse theorists valorize is this 'internal-reflective' one. The 'external-collective' process of discourse and debate is, even for discourse theorists, merely a means of setting this other more 'internal-reflective' process in motion.[50]

Having to answer to another in person might well be one good way of getting that process going. But it is hardly the only. Sometimes 'answering to oneself' might suffice, instead. Suppose our imagination has been fired by some film or fiction; we have been led by those artifices to imagine vividly what it would be like to be *them*, or to be in *that* situation; we ask ourselves, 'What we would say, *then*?'

Stimulating the Imagination

The precise mechanisms by which that works is the subject of much debate in literary theory and art criticism.[51] The fact that some such

[47] Heal 1998. 'Lightly theorized', but still none the less theorized: we need some grounds for supposing they are like us in relevant respects, for example.

[48] Block 1980. 'Folk psychologists' assume we attribute to others the same sort of psychology of beliefs and desires which, upon introspection, we find that we ourselves have; and we assume that they will act on their peculiar beliefs and desires in standard sorts of ways, under standard sorts of provocations, just as we ourselves would do. See Jackson and Pettit 1990; Pettit 1996: esp. chs. 1–2, 4, and postscript; Braddon-Mitchell and Jackson 1996.

[49] Habermas 1995: 117.

[50] As Young (1997: 39) aptly remarks, *apropos* Habermas, it is not just a matter of intellectually registering the perspective of the others but rather of 'imaginatively' projecting oneself into their position.

[51] For philosophical treatments, see Wollheim 1984: esp. chs. 3–4; Currie 1995; Scarry 1995.

process does seem to be at work seems incontrovertible enough, though, judging simply from our own everyday experience as readers, viewers, and listeners.[52]

One particularly striking example is the way in which 'slave narratives'—autobiographical accounts by freed slaves, vividly evoking their experiences in bondage—served the abolitionist cause.[53] Perhaps there are only a very few fictions which could literally be said to have changed the course of history, *Uncle Tom's Cabin* being one and *Passage to India* perhaps another.[54] But some such 'expanding of people's sensibilities' occurs in all good writing.[55] Literary theorists regard it as something of a commonplace that 'historical and social events as mirrored in the plots of Stendhal, Dickens or Tolstoy had a realness, an authenticity deeper than that conveyed by the journalist or professional historian. ... The art of Balzac is a *summa mundi*, an inventory of contemporaneous life. A man can learn half a dozen professions by reading Zola.'[56] And so on.

It is not just that fiction (and art more generally) might, and often does, contain allusions to social, economic, political, and historical facts, and in that way might serve certain didactic purposes. The larger point is that those lessons come packed with more emotional punch and engage our imagination in more effective ways than do historical narratives or reflective essays of a less stylized sort. 'Artists', John Dewey says, 'have always been the real purveyors of news, for it is not the outward happening in itself which is new, but the kindling by it of emotion, perception and appreciation. ... Democracy will have its consummation when free social inquiry is indissolubly wedded to the art of full and moving communication.'[57]

That is not just to say that novelists are more evocative writers than historians or essayists (true though that may be, too). Rather, they fix their focus on the particular—one person or one action or one period—and they introduce generalities by way of anecdotes, episodes viewed from that particular perspective.[58] That vivid evocation of the particular, in turn, has important consequences for the uptake of works of art. Inevitably, we find it relatively easy to project ourselves imaginatively into the place of some specific (fictitious but grounded) other. It is necessarily harder to project ourselves imaginatively into

---

[52] It may well be that one's own 'sense of oneself' is similarly constructed out of some such internal narrative (Taylor 1989: esp. ch. 2; MacIntyre 1981).   [53] Smith 1998.

[54] Such is the claim of Scarry (1996: 105).

[55] This, and the political implications flowing from it, form recurring themes in the writings of Martha Nussbaum (1990, 1995, 1997).   [56] Steiner 1967: 420.

[57] Dewey 1927: ch. 5, p. 184.   [58] Aristotle, *Poetics* (1984c: 1459^{a}17–1459^{b}8).

the inevitably underdescribed sorts of amorphous and abstract others which are the stock in trade of historians and social scientists.

Conduct the experiment for yourself. Is it not ever so much easier to imagine yourself Jean Valjean, given what all Hugo has told us about him, than it is to imagine yourself a generic 'prisoner of the Bastille' on the basis of what historians have told us about that place and its denizens? Intellectually, generalizations may be easier both to convey and to grasp; but emotionally and imaginatively we respond better to more fully described particulars than to generalities which abstract from the details that make those particulars more evocative.

That fiction 'takes us out of ourselves' in this way is intrinsic rather than incidental to the enterprise:

The very form of the novel arises from and embraces conflicts of character, values, interests, circumstances and classes. And ... that only seems to work well, as Sartre pointed out in his *What Is Literature?*, when the author ... can empathize with and portray plausible social diversity. Where, he asked, is there a great totalitarian novel? That was not just a contradiction in terms but a psychological impossibility.[59]

The 'unique value of fiction' lies in its 'relatively cost-free offer of trial runs ... In a month of reading, I can try out more "lives" than I can test in a lifetime'.[60]

Poets from Wordsworth to Eliot have harboured some such ambitions, aspiring to produce work that 'enlarges our consciousness or refines our sensibility'.[61] Some such role has been played, from time to time, by social realist art, by photojournalism and by radio plays. Nowadays it is played most commonly by television, film, and video.[62]

Imaginary Deliberations and the Deliberative Imagination

My proposal is simply that we make use of those familiar phenomena to enhance democratic deliberations in large-scale societies. No doubt there is much more we can do to make everyone else 'communicatively present', even in such settings. Ultimately, however, there are strict limits to the extent to which everyone really can be communicatively present all at once in large-scale mass societies.

[59] Crick 1989: 17. See also Steiner 1963: 29.
[60] Booth 1988: 485; cf. Scarry 1996: 104.
[61] Eliot 1943: 18, 20. See similarly Wordsworth 1820.
[62] Called by Steiner (1967: 420) 'the imagination of the new media of direct knowledge and graphic reproduction'.

Rather than merely bemoaning that fact, let us instead try harder to make everyone else 'imaginatively present' in the minds of each of the deliberators. Private fictions, I submit, can serve important public functions. Through the exercise of a suitably informed imagination, each of us might be able to conduct a wide-ranging debate within our own heads among all the contending perspectives.

Such internal dialogues can never wholly substitute for public ones. However well-informed our imaginings, we will always need to cross-check the views we attribute to others against those views they actually profess themselves to hold. However astute our imaginings and extensive our internal dialogues, at some point or another we must let others speak, and vote, for themselves if our deliberations are to carry any genuinely democratic warrant.

Still, where society is not small enough to allow genuine conversational exchanges among all the relevant public, internal-reflective dialogues are a useful aid helping to inform external-collective ones. Certainly they seem at least as helpful as the other suggestions that are typically offered by deliberative democrats for overcoming the constraints of time, numbers, and distance in large-scale society.

Furthermore, precisely because they do not require people to speak for themselves, internal-reflective deliberations might hope to secure better representation of the communicatively inept or the communicatively inert than external-collective deliberations ever could. The limiting case is future generations, discussed more fully in Chapter 11 below.[63] But just note for now that our actions and choices today clearly affect them; and according to ordinary democratic canons everyone affected ought have a say in our deliberations. However, the unborn cannot speak for themselves. It is a great virtue of internal-reflective deliberations that they do not need to do so. Future people need not be physically present in order for them to be imaginatively present.[64]

Dangers of Internal Deliberation

Internal-reflective deliberations suffer many obvious drawbacks compared to external-collective ones. One is the obvious absence of an insistent 'other' who is pressing her perspective upon you.[65] Some

[63] Laslett and Fishkin 1992. Other communicatively inert interests which we arguably ought to take into account include other species, also discussed in Ch. 11 below.

[64] Furthermore, since the whole internal-reflective process proceeds by everyone imagining themselves into the place of others, no special warrant is required for each of us to imagine ourselves into the place of people in the future.   [65] Ryan 1998: 473.

people and their perspectives might be ignored altogether; others might end up being more-or-less parodied because the too-pat representations of them we have inside our heads pass unchallenged. People whose situations are prototypical and familiar may be represented tolerably well in our internal deliberations; those whose situations are peculiar in some way often will not.[66] And so on.

All of that is true enough. That is why external-collective deliberation is superior to purely internal-reflective deliberation, where society is sufficiently small to make external-collective deliberation genuinely possible. But where societies are of a size such that genuinely democratic collective deliberations are not possible, anyway, we are operating in a world of 'second-best'. The alternative strategies for making external-collective decision procedures more directly deliberatively democratic all suffer from various drawbacks as well. My hope is merely that, by supplementing external-collective deliberations with internal-reflective ones, some of the errors and omissions inevitable in each mode might compensate for and cancel out one another.

Attending to the Other

Consider the many ways in which internal-reflective deliberations seem necessarily inferior to ideal-case external-collective ones. We might, for example, be worried over 'who is included' in the deliberations. In external-collective settings, deliberative democrats are at pains to ensure that everyone who will be affected is a party to the deliberations. With internal-reflective deliberations, in contrast, each deliberator inevitably populates her own imaginary internal universe as she will.

Of course we might exhort her to be as inclusive as she can, to try very hard to engage imaginatively with as many different sorts of people as might genuinely be affected by the decision. We might even send her a pile of books or photos or videos, as an aid to that process. But there seems little that we can do from the outside to *make* the full range of others present to her mind's eye, in the way we might hope to make all appropriate others physically present in external-collective deliberations of the more ordinary sort.

Remember, however, the context of my present argument. I have suggested we turn to internal-reflective deliberation precisely because (or, rather, in so far as) the group of people affected is too large literally to make them all physically present and still have a meaningful

---

[66] Schober 1998; Benhabib 1992*a*.

deliberation. Thus, what we should be comparing is, on the one hand, the representativeness of the population which we would conjure up in our mind's eye with, on the other hand, the (effective) representativeness of the second-best methods of external-collective deliberation surveyed above.

No doubt our imagination will always be imperfect, and some people will be left out of deliberations based on internal-reflective processes alone. By the same token, however, those other second-best methods of external-collective deliberation are imperfect too; and some people or positions will always be unrepresented or inadequately represented in them as well. All these second-best mechanisms run analogous risks in that respect. We can only hope that the voices omitted by the one can be captured by the other, when we use internal-deliberative processes to supplement external-collective ones in these settings.

Even where others are physically present in external-collective deliberations, of course, that does not necessarily mean that we will be genuinely responsive to them and their concerns. We can always turn, shrug our shoulders or walk away.[67] We can always turn a blind eye or deaf ear.[68] Input is no assurance of uptake. Indeed, recalling how heavily ordinary conversation depends on internal representations, one might even say that 'internal presence' is just as much a precondition of effective representation in external-collective deliberations as it is in internal-reflective ones.

Understanding the Other

In real conversations between real people, there is a constant cross-checking and renegotiation of meanings.[69] That facilitates interlocutors' understanding of one another. People who are merely overhearing a conversation sometimes find it hard to understand what is going on, precisely because they cannot interject into the conversation to cross-check their own understandings of what others mean to be saying.[70]

In real conversations, a code of dyadically shared meanings emerges. That simply cannot happen in imaginary conversations with imagined

[67] Ryan 1998: 473.

[68] As Averill Harriman famously did, in ostentatiously switching off his hearing aid when Soviet negotiators launched into one of their standard harangues. I owe this anecdote to my old friend and teacher, Robert Ferrell.

[69] As in Tilly's (1998: 495) representation of conversation as necessarily involving 'continuously negotiated communication'.

[70] Schober and Clark 1989, confirming a speculation by Sartre 1950: 50.

people of the sort that occur in the 'internal-reflective' deliberative mode. There, we are essentially having a conversation with ourselves. If we are sufficiently imaginative, we might envisage our 'imaginary other' correcting us in ways akin to those in which actual others might. But inevitably that is a pale shadow of the vigorous sort of cross-checking and cross-fertilization which occurs in any actual conversation. No single individual's imagination, however rich, will be able to mimic what occurs in the perfectly ordinary course of events in conversations among real people with genuinely different perspectives.

Much the same is true of mass deliberations as well, though. In dyadic conversations, each speaker can sensitize the other to her own particular perspective, one-on-one. In mass deliberations, what typically happens is that some speak and many listen. Hopefully those who speak are broadly typical of many others who do not.[71] But in any moderately large group there can be no realistic hope of each person individually negotiating meanings with each particular other, anyway.

Thus, while 'internal-reflective' deliberations may look seriously deficient in the sorts of shared understandings they nurture when compared with conversational dynamics in dyads or small groups, once again that is not the relevant comparison. The proposal here is to let internal-reflective deliberations inform and supplement external-collective ones in large groups. In settings of that sort, discursive dynamics are very different from conversational dyads anyway. There, the sorts of intensely negotiated meanings which we find emerging in conversational dyads will be largely missing. There, external representations risk being just as stylized, just as oriented towards the prototypical, as are the representations which figure in people's internal imaginary reconstructions of social life.[72] Once again, we can only hope that by allowing internal-reflective mechanisms to supplement external-collective ones, their respective errors and omissions might compensate and correct for one another's.

Representing the Other

As if in direct reply to my proposal to let internal deliberation do much of the work of external, reading doing much of the work of talking,

---

[71] If only in their atypicality: in a representative sample, the fact of diversity ought to be represented even if not all the diverse components can be individually represented.

[72] They inevitably reflect the 'generalized' more than the 'concrete' other, in all the other's concrete forms, in the terms of Benhabib 1992a.

Montaigne protests:

Studying books has a languid feeble motion, whereas conversation provides teaching and exercise all at once. If I am sparring with a strong and solid opponent he will attack me on the flanks, stick his lance in me right and left; his ideas send mine soaring. Rivalry, competitiveness and glory will drive me and raise me above my own level.[73]

Certainly we can sympathize with that sentiment. Playing chess against yourself is far less satisfactory than playing against someone else (or even a good computer). Everything is too pat, too devoid of surprise. That seems as true of cooperative games like conversation as of competitive games like chess. No one can imagine someone else's interests, position, and perspective as richly as that person herself experiences them. There is therefore a compelling case, pragmatically as well as symbolically, for the 'politics of presence': for all different sorts of people being physically present during deliberations that affect their interests, rather than just having their interests 'represented' by others.[74]

Once again, however, that ideal seems to be compromised by the realities of large-scale societies. The circumstances here in view—the circumstances under which I envisage external-collective deliberation being importantly supplemented by internal-reflective—are circumstances in which there are too many different people involved for all of them to be effectively present in deliberations.

At best, we might (through what I have called 'ersatz deliberation') substitute one or a few members of the group for all other members of that group.[75] Such a substitution might be satisfactory if the groups were so homogeneous that a few members really were representative of the group as a whole. (In the limiting case if each were a literally identical token of the type, utterly interchangeable with every other, then a single representative from each group would suffice.) Most theorists of group difference would baulk at the sort of 'essentialism' implied by that, however.[76] They shun the 'generalized' in favour of the 'concrete other'.[77] And one implication of that is that no small set of representatives can truly stand in for groups as a whole, as the politics of presence would require.

How much this will impinge on external-collective deliberative processes depends in part on how many different groups there are to be

---

[73] Montaigne 1580: bk 3, essay 8, p. 1045.   [74] Phillips 1995.
[75] That is precisely what Phillips (1995: esp. ch. 6) calls for: 'group representation'.
[76] Young 1995.   [77] Benhabib 1992*a*.

represented and in part on how many individuals it takes to represent tolerably well each of those groups in its full complexity. But in any large-scale society, we can probably assume moderately high levels both of inter-group pluralism and of intra-group heterogeneity. And that multiplicity would be compounded yet again, if geographical situatedness itself proves to be an important dimension of identity and difference, as theorists of the 'politics of place' contend.[78]

The upshot would seem to be, once again, that in any large-scale society external-collective deliberations are necessarily very far from ideal. That deliberation cannot effectively give every distinct voice a hearing: second-best short-cuts of one sort of another will inevitably be required; and something will inevitably be lost in the process. Something would also inevitably be lost in trying to replicate some such conversation within one's own mind, in internal-reflective mode. But once again, hopefully the omissions and errors of the one might cancel and correct those of the other, when we supplement external-collective deliberations with internal-reflective ones.[79]

Finding Time for the Other

Finally it might be argued that, in any large-scale mass society, internal-reflective deliberative processes would fall prey to the same pressures on time and attention as do external-collective deliberative processes. In the latter case, the problem is that we lack the time to *have* the requisite conversations with all others. In the former case, it might be said, there is a perfectly parallel problem: we lack the time to *imagine* those conversations, either.

Certainly it is true that 'attention' is a strictly limited resource, imposing severe constraints on our deliberative capacities, but those constraints have greater impact on external-collective methods of deliberation. The mechanism by which we attend to others in that way is through oral or written communications, and we can listen to only one speaker or read only one thing at a time. That makes the external-collective deliberative process a more radically serial process than is internal-reflective deliberation.

Suppose we manage successfully to 'internalize' the perspectives of various others, through having imaginatively projected ourselves into their position on some previous occasion. Then perhaps we might even

---

[78] Malpas 1999.

[79] True, in situations of great heterogeneity we might find it hard to imagine ourselves in a very different other person's position: but that compromises our capacity for understanding what the other is asserting in external-collective deliberations as well.

be able to 'see' the situation from those many different perspectives at once without any conscious effort. If those other perspectives have been internalized in some strong way, applying them is 'second nature' to us. No deliberate act of will is required to evoke them; no deliberate focusing of our attention on them is involved. 'Seeing' things from all those various other perspectives is something we might hope to do simultaneously.

Again, there is no guarantee that people will 'internalize' any (much less all) other relevant perspectives in this strong way.[80] The point is merely that they might. If they do, that would significantly ease the cognitive constraints involved in attending to many others, once again making internal-reflective deliberation an invaluable supplement to external-collective modes.

Informing the Democratic Imagination

Important practical consequences follow from recognizing all these ways in which internal, imaginary discourses can serve as important aids to democratic deliberation. Concerns which might otherwise seem peripheral to our democratic theory—concerns to do with the production and consumption of the representations and images upon which our imaginings work—suddenly become central.

On the one side are familiar questions about access to means of modern mass communication. On the other side are equally familiar questions about 'for whom does one write?'[81] Who is the audience, the reference group? Who are the subjects, and how are they represented?[82]

Those are not just arcane disputes within cultural studies. Instead, they are absolutely crucial issues for democracy as it is inevitably practised in modern large-scale societies, where (as I have been arguing) representations inside the head can count for almost as much as representation within the legislative chamber. The art forms out of which we construct those representations are potentially as potent, politically, as are the elections out of which we construct legislative majorities.

---

[80] And if they internalize some but not all other perspectives, there is of course then a risk that their internal-reflective deliberations will be biased accordingly.

[81] Sartre 1950: ch. 3.

[82] In terms of democratizing culture (or, rather, of enlisting cultural artefacts in the service of democracy), it is not so much a matter of 'high culture' against 'low' as it is of 'broad' against 'narrow'.

Some of the public policy implications of that insight are rather banal. Of course democracy naturally requires well-stocked public libraries and public funding of the arts.[83] Art and literature are at least partly public goods which would be undersupplied by ordinary market forces; we ought therefore to subsidize creativity, in so far as we can.[84] We ought to 'take art to the people' rather than locking it away, making public museums 'forums, not temples'.[85] All of that is obviously important in generating and disseminating the sorts of representations which will serve as crucial aids to the sorts of internal-reflective deliberations that I am here proposing.

Equally importantly, though, we must ensure the representativeness of those representations. When supplementing external-collective deliberations with internal-reflective ones, we are in effect enfranchising images. If we want that process to serve democratic ends, we obviously need to ensure that the images thus enfranchised are as extensive as required really to represent the diversity of experiences extant across the communities to be affected by those deliberations.[86]

Not all of those experiences are pretty. Not all are intellectually edifying or morally uplifting. Some will be sad or depressing or downright obnoxious. Still, all deserve a voice in the democratic cultural space, in so far as that feeds into internal-reflective deliberation—or anyway all do, to just the same extent that they deserve a literal voice in the political space of external-collective democratic deliberations. (In so far as we have good democratic grounds for censoring 'hate speech', we ought to be prepared to ban its other cultural manifestations as well.[87]) From the present perspective, we have no more grounds for confining our public concern, and public subsidies, purely to more 'elevated' forms of cultural expression than we do for confining our political attention purely to the expression of 'elevated' opinion.

Merely producing diverse representations is not enough, though. We must also ensure that those diverse representations are widely diffused throughout the deliberative community. 'Despite ... the emphasis on artistic multiculturalism in the United States, it sometimes appears that Asian-American literature is being read by Asian Americans, Afro-American literature by Afro-Americans, and Euro-American literature by Euro-Americans.'[88] Narrow-band imaginings thereby fostered will hardly aid the cause of genuinely democratic deliberation.

---

[83] Gutmann 1987: ch. 8; Netzer 1978; Banfield 1984; Carnegie Commission on the Future of Public Broadcasting 1979.   [84] Dworkin 1985.

[85] Edelman 1995; Adams 1999.   [86] Brighouse 1995; Dworkin 1985.

[87] Lowenstein 1938.   [88] Scarry 1996: 104.

That is to specify a set of desiderata for cultural policy in a deliberative democracy. How exactly those desiderata might best be met undoubtedly varies from place to place and from one period to the next. In interwar Britain, cheap Penguins and the BBC performed broadly this function with some considerable success; and it has long been hoped that some combination of public broadcasting and public subsidies for the performing arts might have a similarly 'broadening' function elsewhere around the world.

Similarly, social mixing within primary and secondary schools—through 'comprehensive' schools in postwar Britain and racially integrated schools in post-*Brown* America—were championed in no small part for the 'lessons in diversity' that they would impart. Much has been written on the evils of racially or ethnically segregated communities, and the mutual ignorance and misunderstanding that they breed. Those segregations are largely the products of public policy, and they can typically be overcome only with the aid of public interventions.[89] Various specific policy interventions can contribute greatly to ensuring people are exposed to a broader social mix of people, in schools and workplaces, entertainments, and incidental encounters of everyday life.

It is obviously far easier to imagine what the world looks like from the perspective of a black person or an immigrant or a person from some religious minority if you actually know people like that personally. Merely riding the bus together might not be quite enough to fire the imagination; merely going to the same school, or living next door to one another, might not be quite enough.[90] But social mixing of those minimal sorts constitutes a necessary first step towards firing the imagination in the ways 'democratic deliberation within' would require.

How these models might be adapted to the peculiar circumstances of contemporary broadcasting and publishing, work and schooling—and how they might be extended beyond those realms—constitute major policy challenges. The first step in addressing those challenges, however, lies in recognizing the many and varied purposes which were supposed to be served by those older social forms (cheap Penguins, the BBC, and socially mixed neighbourhoods), and what exactly it is therefore that we are wanting to recreate in some new guise. Mechanisms for informing and extending our social imaginings are, I suggest,

[89] Myrdal 1944: esp. ch. 29; Downs 1973; Massey and Denton 1993; King 1995; Rae 2001.

[90] Indeed, 'casual' contacts often have the tendency of reinforcing stereotypes (Myrdal 1944: 651); so in the very first instance, those more casual forms of social mixing might actually make things worse.

one of the things that deliberative democrats ought to be seeking in whatever new social arrangements are proposed.

From Democratic Deliberation to Democratic Legitimacy

Deliberation is supposed to have an *end*, it is supposed to *resolve* something.[91] Occasionally deliberation yields a decision directly, as when a genuine consensus has emerged. But deliberative assemblies even of the most ideal sort more typically have to force a decision, announcing an end to the deliberations and calling for a vote.

That final show of hands is what is crucial in conferring democratic legitimacy on the decision. However free and equal the preceding discussion may have been, the democratic credentials of the ultimate decision would be deeply suspect had it merely been left to the chairperson of the meeting to summarize the 'sense of the meeting', with no ratification from others.[92] But however crucial that distinctly non-deliberative final show of hands may be in providing *democratic legitimacy* for the decision, it is the preceding discussion which renders that decision a *democratically deliberative* one.

Thus, even in the most pristine directly democratic deliberative assemblies, democratic legitimacy typically derives from one source and democratic deliberativeness from another. Internal-reflective and external-collective deliberative processes, I submit, stand in a similar relation to one another.

Internal-reflective deliberations are not a substitute for, but rather an input into, external-collective decision procedures. That is so, in the first instance, because internal deliberations cannot in and of themselves yield any collective determinations. Beyond that necessary analytic truth stands another deeper democratic one. Purely private acts of internal deliberation, however expansive or empathetic they may be, can never have a fully democratic warrant until they have secured public validation of one sort or another. Democratizing our internal reflections—rendering them more expansive and more empathetic—contributes to the democratic quality of the process as well, making it more democratically deliberative. But some external-collective act is eventually required to confer democratic legitimacy on any conclusions we reach.

Just as in a small assembly the requirements of deliberative democracy may be met by a free-ranging discussion of the issues culminating

[91] Hobbes 1651: ch. 6.

[92] As, lore has it, was the traditional practice of the Cabinet Secretary in Britain.

in a distinctly non-deliberative show of hands, so too in large-scale mass societies the requirements of deliberative democracy may be met by expansive internal-reflective deliberations culminating in a distinctly non-deliberative visit to the poll booth. And the more democratically deliberative our internal reflections manage to be, the less it will matter that external-collective decision procedures can never be as directly deliberatively democratic as we might like in large-scale mass societies.

CHAPTER 10

Representing Excluded Interests

Once upon a time, 'democratic inclusion' was regarded as mainly a matter of expanding the franchise. Suppose you saw democracy as a merely mechanical process of taking a vote, aggregating votes, and declaring a winner. All you had to do was to bring everyone in, give them a vote, and let them look after themselves in the ensuing electoral fray.[1]

As our concerns with 'social exclusion' have broadened, however, our faith in that simplistic model of democratic inclusion has waned. Mere inclusion, as per the mechanistic model of aggregative democracy, is not enough to meet all our new concerns. Some affected interests will always be left out through those sorts of processes. 'Democratic deliberation within', I shall argue, offers the best way—and with the necessarily mute interests discussed in the next chapter, the only way—to address those new democratic concerns.

The Importance of Inclusion

As a matter of pure logic, issues of inclusion and exclusion are absolutely central to democracy. The constitution of the *demos* ('who is in and who is out?') is necessarily 'the first question that any political community must answer about itself'.[2] As a matter of political practice,

[1] This seems to be the view of e.g. Key and Crouch 1939: 442: 'In a broad sense legislation is the culmination of the political process. Theoretically the conflict in the interests of large groups of citizens is adjudicated and settled, by the balancing of strength and claims, within the lawmaking machinery of government under conditions conducive to a degree of deliberation and compromise. The effective functioning of the machinery of legislation implies an equitable representation in the lawmaking body of all interests concerned and a fair chance for measuring the relative strength of their claims and demands by the entire assembly. Only in this way can lost causes be quieted, popular demands be met and generally acceptable and workable lines of policy be evolved.'

[2] Walzer 1993: 55. See similarly Dahl 1979, 1989: ch. 9; Shklar 1991.

distributions and redistributions inevitably take place primarily among those who are within the bounds of the community thus constituted; hence issues of inclusion and exclusion are central to distributive justice, as well.[3] As a matter of contemporary politics, feminists, multiculturalists, and other 'theorists of difference' increasingly phrase their demands in similar terms of the inclusion of groups which have historically been marginalized or excluded.[4] So too have various social policies (to do with housing, education, employment, and, most particularly, poverty itself) recently been re-oriented—or perhaps just redescribed—as steps toward 'social inclusion', integrating and 'mainstreaming' previously marginalized individuals, families, and communities.[5]

'Social exclusion' thus serves as a potent rallying cry, both politically and programatically. Politically it reflects and reinforces the mobilization of the socially downtrodden, and philosophically it seems to catch much of what is morally obnoxious about their oppression. Programmatically, the notion promises to link together a great variety of social concerns, tracing them to common (or anyway cognate) causes and prescribing identical (or anyway analogous) cures.

Attractive though the notion of social exclusion is in all those ways, in the end I think that that phrase misdiagnoses the problem and misprescribes the cure for most of the social ills to which it refers. The problem is not that too many people, or the wrong people, have been 'left out'; the proper remedy not merely to make democratic communities more 'inclusive', at least not in the standard way. Instead, the problem of exclusion is that there *is* an inclusive community, be its catchment broad or narrow, that makes certain sorts of rather grand claims for itself. If *that* is the problem, then the solution is not to make democratic communities more inclusive but rather to change their nature, making them at one and the same time both less exclusive and less inclusive.

There are various institutional arrangements along those lines to which we might ultimately aspire. 'Democratic deliberation within',

[3] Walzer 1983: ch. 2.

[4] For feminist treatments, see particularly Minnow 1990; Young 1990; Fraser 1994. On difference and multiculturalism, see Young 1990: esp. 53–5; Kymlicka 1995. On recognition, see Taylor 1992; Habermas 1993; Tully 1995.

[5] Jordan 1996; Balibar 1992. On European Union applications, see Room 1995: 105–6. In France and much of the European Union social policies for *les exclus* are discussed, not in terms of 'inclusion', but rather in terms of 'insertion'; to Anglophone ears, that seems to imply that the 'excluded' are being regarded philosophically as objects rather than subjects (or juridically as subjects rather than citizens) for purposes of social policy (Evans et al. 1995).

practised on a suitably expansive scale, will be a necessary concomitant of such institutions in the long run and—as I will argue—it would be the best substitute for them in the short run.

Underlying Intuitions

In motivating people, it is crucial to be able to appeal to deeply rooted and widely shared moral intuitions. It is, for example, a great if seldom-spoken strength of John Rawls's theory of 'justice as fairness' that it builds on powerful intuitions about the indubitable fairness of familiar practices of fair division (such as the rule, 'You cut, I choose', when children are cutting up a cake).[6]

At its most banal, talk of 'social exclusion' similarly evokes deeply rooted intuitions traceable to slights in the schoolyard. We keenly recall the pain that comes from being cold-shouldered and cut out of the games of our schoolmates. Intuitively, we all know it to be plainly wrong to be unnecessarily hurtful in such ways to other people around us.

Furthermore, such slights might be more consequential than at first they seem. Many of the grander 'sources of human misery'—plague, pestilence, poverty, famine, war, torture, and so on—may actually be traceable to social exclusion of one sort or another. Amartya Sen shows how being excluded from lucrative war work, rather than any objective shortage of rice, was the cause of so many Bengalis starving in the great famine of 1943.[7] Being excluded from privileged social groups might, in one way or another, be likewise to blame for much of the poverty, pestilence, and social violence that certain social groups experience today.

Americans of Kennedy's generation talked of *The Other America*, those who missed out on the benefits of the long boom of the 1950s and 1960s.[8] Today's talk focuses on the 'homeless' as the most conspicuously 'left out' among the domestically disadvantaged.[9] At the same time there are all those foreigners who are being 'kept out', most conspicuously among them those who want to immigrate but are not allowed to enter and those who, having gained entry, are frustrated in their desire to be allowed to participate fully in our society, on the same terms as everyone else. The plight of both those groups is also effectively evoked by the same phrase, 'social exclusion'.

[6] Rawls 1958, 1971.   [7] Sen 1981.   [8] Harrington 1962.
[9] Waldron 1991; Jencks 1994.

That usage points to yet another source for intuitive repugnance toward social exclusion. It is simply *rude* to slam a door shut in the face of someone poised to pass through it. It is simply rude—a violation of norms of hospitaliy familiar from Homeric Greece forward[10]—not to take proper care of your guests. Stretching as it does across cases of would-be immigrants and guestworkers, talk of 'social exclusion' can avail itself of these further intuitive resources as well.

The Hidden Costs of Inclusion Talk

Marginality: An Unintended Focus

What we seek, when demanding a more 'inclusive' conception of the community, is the mainstreaming of those who are presently marginalized. If that is our aim, though, couching those demands in terms of 'exclusion' and 'inclusion' may well be strategically counterproductive. Built into the very logic of those concepts, I shall argue, is a focus on precisely that marginality which those who politically invoke values of 'inclusion' hope to transcend.

Consider, first, the way these terms function in ordinary discourse wholly outside any political context. We make a hotel booking 'for the nights of 2 May to 5 May, inclusive'—the word 'inclusive' there serving to mark the endpoints, the boundaries, the margins of our stay. Or we tell our children to 'include Sammy in your game'. The function of the word 'include', once again, is to instruct the kids to stretch their playgroup at the margins. Or the British Navy declares an 'exclusionary zone' around the Falkland Islands, thus delimiting boundaries beyond which normal shipping would not be permitted to pass. Or white Americans form exclusive clubs or neighbourhoods through restrictive membership rules and 'exclusionary zoning' strictly delimiting who will be allowed to enter and what they will be allowed to do when they do.[11] Or trade negotiators institute 'exclusive economic zones', denying anyone outside that club access to their markets.

Much the same fixation on policing boundaries seems to characterize political appeals couched in inclusionary terms. Far from moving us beyond marginality—far from helping to take 'the excluded' to the very centre of social life—political appeals couched in terms of 'inclusion of the excluded' only succeed in pushing them 'just over the line'. No doubt it matters greatly what side of the line people are on: whether,

---

[10] Finlay 1978.   [11] Downs 1973: ch. 6; Massey and Denton 1993.

as migrants, they are allowed in or kept out of the country; whether, as workers, they are allowed in or kept out of the labour market; whether, as residents, they are allowed in or kept out of the social safety net. Important though it is to be on the 'right side of the line' in all those respects, the point remains that couching the argument in terms of 'inclusion of the excluded' constitutes an argument for pushing them 'just over' the line. They remain borderline.[12] As long as they are on the 'right side' of the line, though, there is nothing in this language or in the logic standing behind it that would help us address our larger concerns about social marginality.

Inclusion Entails Exclusion: An Unintended Concession

A second danger is best expressed in the familiar post-Wittgensteinian deconstructivist thought, traceable to Derrida himself, that there can be no outside without an inside.[13] 'Exclusion' implies 'inclusion': and, by the same token, 'inclusion' implies 'exclusion'. For every 'inside', there is something which is 'outside'. Expand its catchment as we may, inclusion as a practice only makes sense (politically, most particularly) against the background of something or another simultaneously being 'excluded'.[14]

Talking about 'the excluded', in terms that suggests that the problem is simply that those who have been excluded should be included, suggests that the boundaries of inclusiveness have been wrongly drawn. But on that way of looking at things, it is only the *location* of the boundaries that is in question. The legitimacy of the *existence* of boundaries—that some should be outside, in order for others to be inside—is analytically, if only implicitly, conceded by this way of putting things. Keen though we may be to alleviate the disadvantages of those who are presently excluded, we ought not consent casually to that larger implication of this way of structuring our political debates.

The Political Functions of Inclusion Talk

Many familiar political projects have been recently subsumed within the larger crusade against 'social exclusion', with demands for

---

[12] Worrying about including the excluded, we are inevitably preoccupied with 'the boundaries of citizenship' (Spinner-Halev 1994).   [13] Derrida 1978.

[14] The term 'all inclusive' is not so much meaningless as pointless: membership of a set, or a group, ceases to be of much interest when membershp is coterminous with the entire population.

'inclusion' taking the place of many older demands for participation, for citizenship, and for free movement and open borders. In each of these cases, something important seems inevitably to be lost in the translation. All those other political projects, I shall now argue, would be better understood, and better pursued, in their own original terms.

Inclusion as Code for Participation

Inclusion sometimes seems to be just another way of restating all the same points as democratic theorists had couched, in previous periods, in terms of the value of 'participation'. The classic appeal was for participation in the political realm.[15] And one way of stating what participatory democrats were demanding was the inclusion of a much broader section of the community among those wielding effective power and influence in the political sphere.[16] Arguments for participatory democracy were often allied with—sometimes implying, other times being implied by—arguments for 'shopfloor democracy' and 'workers' control.[17] And that too could be understood as a demand for the inclusion of the workers themselves among those wielding effective power and influence over what happened within their workplaces.

Allied to those older participatory themes that people *should* participate more fully and effectively in various aspects of social life are a raft of newer arguments to the effect that people *do* participate more fully, effectively, and productively in various aspects of social life than is currently recognized, either in societal self-conceptions or more especially in social reward structures. Advocates of paying an unconditional 'basic income' to (virtually) all adults often describe it as a 'participation income'.[18] The point is that there are lots of people—those undergoing education and training, rearing children or caring for those incapable of caring for themselves or participating in various other unpaid forms of 'social work'—who, although unpaid, are hardly idle. They participate actively and productively. They ought to be included among those who are valued, and rewarded, by society as a whole.

Arguments for inclusion thus dovetail with arguments for participation in political life, in the workplace, in economic and social life more generally. The temptation, and current trend, is to let the more

[15] Classic works in this tradition include: Dahl 1970; Pateman 1970; Barber 1984.

[16] This aspect of the argument finds its fullest and most explicit discussion in Phillips's *The Politics of Presence* (1995).

[17] The connections are evident in Pateman (1970: chs. 3–5). See also: Schweikhart 1980; Dahl 1985; Greenberg 1986.

[18] Commission on Social Justice, UK Labour Party 1994; Atkinson 1995*b*, 1996.

expansive term 'inclusion' subsume all those older arguments and concerns. But that gets the relationship between those two propositions exactly the wrong way around. In truth, it is arguments for participation which should properly be seen to be subsuming arguments for inclusion.

Certainly one of the things participatory theorists demand—and must demand, given the deeper logic of their arguments—is the inclusion of the previously excluded among those *eligible* to participate in various fora of concern to them. But for participatory theorists, *mere* inclusion would never be enough. What they want is not for everyone to be eligible to participate but rather for everyone to be actively participating. Mere inclusion, mere eligibility, is just too passive a notion to capture all that participatory democrats want to promote.

Inclusion as Code for Citizenship

Sometimes 'inclusion' seems to be just another way of restating all the points previously couched in terms of expanding notions of democratic 'citizenship'.[19] The citizenship story, in the form made famous by T. H. Marshall, is one of how more and more people have over time come to enjoy more and more rights and liberties, privileges and prerogatives, as the ordinary complement of citizenship, understood as 'basic membership' in the political community. First came civil rights, then political rights, and then most recently economic rights. First such citizenship rights were extended to only a small set of male subjects of noble birth, then to most men of independent means, and then most recently to everyone regardless of race, gender, or social standing.[20]

Familiar though such stories may be, tales of expanding notions of citizenship were never terribly compelling, *analytically*. They may or may not trace an identifiable historical pattern, of broader or narrower applicability.[21] Yet there was never any compelling analytical account of why change must always proceed in those directions.[22] Why should

---

[19] Arguments for participation and citizenship often merge, with notions of 'republican citizenship', for example, having at their core the vision of a 'citizen as someone who plays an active role in shaping his or her society through public discussion'. See Miller 1995; Shklar 1991.

[20] Marshall 1949: 70–134. Among those picking up on those themes in recent debates, see Mann 1985; King and Waldron 1988; Balibar 1992: 99–168; Pixley 1993; Klausen 1995. For critical surveys, see Kymlicka and Norman 1994; Somers 1994: 67–83.

[21] Some say Marshall just wrote English history into his theory of citizenship, just as Rawls was later to write the American constitution into his theory of justice and the Virginia Statute of Religious Liberty into his theory of political liberalism.

[22] Except perhaps in so far as Marshall had implicitly underlying his overall thesis the implicit class dynamic teased out in Somers 1994—though even then there is far more

it always, necessarily, be a matter of *expanding* citizenship? Expanding citizenship in some directions or dimensions is perfectly consistent, logically, with its being contracted in others. Why should the 'expansion of citizenship' entail expanding numbers of *new citizens*? Rather than incorporating more and more people as citizens, we might merely have expanded the prerogatives of already existing citizens. Why, *substantively*, should the expansion of citizenship rights have necessarily proceeded from legal to political to economic citizenship? Finally, why were those *particular* rights and liberties, privileges, and prerogatives associated with each style of citizenship? Economic citizenship, for example, might more naturally have been associated with rights to a fair share of social capital rather than merely with rights to welfare benefits.

Arguments for inclusion are superior to that citizenship story in that there is no implication of any necessary evolutionary sequence. There is no necessary order in which steps towards inclusion have come, nor inevitably that any (much less all) of them necessarily have to happen at all. Arguments about inclusion are claims, not predictions. What rights should be taken to be constitutive of membership is, in the language of inclusion, a matter for political disputation, not something to be adduced from the cunning of history. In these ways, the shift from citizenship talk to inclusion talk seems to mark clear progress in the discourse of politics.

However, there is also a clear price to be paid for shifting to terms of the 'inclusion of the excluded'. Citizenship had the great virtue of referring, logically, to a 'single-status moral community'. One is either a citizen or one is not. If one is a citizen, one is a full citizen, vested with all the rights and prerogatives of any other citizen.[23] 'Second-class citizenship' is an oxymoron, intended to be seen as such by minority-rights campaigners couching their political complaints in those terms.

Whereas talking in terms of citizenship fixes attention on what is common and central, on what all citizens share, talk of 'inclusion' and 'exclusion' fixes attention on boundaries and margins, on what differentiates one class of persons from another. The focus, in the first instance, is on what differentiates citizens from non-citizens. But citizens themselves will inevitably differ to a greater or lesser extent along

---

variability in the specific ways in which class politics play themselves out than this deterministic account would allow, as is evident from Karl Marx's account of 'The Civil War in France' (1871: 526–7).

[23] Formally, at least, everyone is equally entitled to consular protection when abroad, to sue in a court of law, to vote, and to petition government. In practice, of course, some people are for various reasons better able to avail themselves of those formal resources.

the same dimensions. Suppose, for example, the rule of citizenship is *jus sanguinis*, those born of citizen parents are themselves citizens. Then the same focus on blood which differentiates citizens from non-citizens will similarly serve, incidentally, to differentiate 'old blood' from 'new', those who can trace their roots back many generations from relative new-comers and social upstarts. Important social distinctions can thus be implicitly sanctioned by practices which present themselves as purely juridical ones.

Such informal seepage from the legal to the social is not the only problem, however. There is another way in which a single-status community is hard to sustain, even in formal legal terms, once we begin talking of 'inclusion and exclusion'. Talk of citizenship focuses on the core, and in so doing sustains a view of citizenship as a concept with insistently off/on characteristics. When thinking about inclusion and exclusion, in contrast, we are inevitably preoccupied with the margins and boundaries—and there, treating marginal peoples marginally becomes a wholly apt response. Citizenship claims are therefore necessarily strong claims (one is a *full* citizen, if one is a citizen at all), in ways that inclusion claims are not, or anyway certainly not necessarily.

Thus, in so far as inclusion claims are in fact just a code for citizenship claims, they are an emaciated form of the claim in question. Compared to those stronger claims of citizenship, mere claims for 'inclusion' risk being too easily satisfied and too naturally subverted.

Inclusion as Code for Free Movement

Finally, 'inclusion' sometimes seems to be just another way of making many points which, until recently, would have been couched in terms of free trade and open borders.[24] The argument there is essentially that we should resist any temptations to exclude foreign influences—whether in the form of people or goods, investments or ideas. Instead we should take an open, welcoming, 'inclusive' attitude towards foreign peoples and things.

Moralists of a universal cosmopolitan sort simply presume the desirability of such policies.[25] Exclusion and discrimination against 'outsiders' stands roundly condemned as sheer favouritism toward kith and kin, wholly arbitrary, and therefore wholly odious from a moral point of view.[26] Universalists regard that intuition as a fundamental

[24] Bader 1995; Brubaker 1992; Castles 1992, 1994: 3–28; Bauböck 1994*a*,*b*.
[25] Carens 1987; Goodin 1992*b*.
[26] That root idea underlying Rawls's 'Justice as Fairness' (1958) and *Theory of Justice* (1971) is elaborated most fully in Barry's *Justice as Impartiality* (1995).

moral primitive, as indubitable a proposition as they can find upon which to ground any moral theories at all. And the practical relevance of that presumption is revealed all too clearly in the way anti-immigrant sentiment often seems motivated by racism, pure and simple.[27] The moral obnoxiousness of the morally arbitrary is clearly revealed when we discriminate against people for no more reason than the colour of their skin.[28]

Inclusiveness seems to be the bottom line, the policy prescription that follows from such moral universalism. Here again, however, the fit is less than perfect. What moral universalism demands is *full* inclusion. The aim, there, is to bring the disadvantaged ('the excluded') into the mainstream—into the very centre of the social life of the community. As my earlier analysis of the notion of inclusion suggested, however, inclusion is merely a matter of 'bare' inclusion. Inclusion, as such, is a just matter of 'getting people over the line'. There is nothing in that notion which implies (or is even compatible with) insisting on getting them all the way to the centre.

Consider immigration debates, for example. Even among the most liberal-minded friends and champions of the migrant's cause, one sort of reason is characteristically given for allowing foreigners to enter the country and a very different battery of reasons for according them ordinary economic and social rights once they are there. Using the term 'inclusion' to cover both cases gives the appearance of thematic unity. In practice, however, inclusion-cum-entry ends up being justified very differently from inclusion-cum-social-citizenship.

In much the same way, emancipation brought American slaves 'one kind of freedom'. But couched as abolitionist arguments were purely in terms of the wrongness of *owning* other human beings, they did not readily roll on into arguments for giving newly freed slaves the sort of capital endowment they would need to be truly independent social actors. Having won the one argument but lost the other, black sharecroppers in the American South remained condemned to a status substantially akin to slavery for the rest of the nineteenth century.[29]

Much the same sometimes seems to be happening to certain sorts of migrants today. Having won the right to enter, but having yet to win the argument for full rights of social citizenship, they are condemned to a life perhaps only marginally better than that they escaped back home. And perhaps needlessly so: had both the arguments been joined from the outset, there is an undeniable risk that both might have been

---

[27] Balibar and Wallerstein 1988; Balibar 1992: 19–98; Bovenkerk *et al.* 1991.
[28] Wasserstrom 1964, 1977.   [29] Ransom and Sutch 1977.

lost; but by the same token, there is also a chance that both might have been won and the sad spectacle of 'guestworkers' avoided altogether.

Toward a Non-Exclusive Concept of Political Authority

For all those reasons, I think it is generally a mistake to (re)cast political arguments in terms of a demand for greater inclusion in a standardly exclusive sort of state. My larger counterproposal is that we start thinking, instead, more in terms of a less exclusive concept of the state.

Exclusivity undeniably has its uses. Children, we are told, need to feel that they have someone (typically but not necessarily parents) who cares more for them than anybody else in the world. Exclusive sexual relations seem similarly to speak to some deep human need. Be all that as it may, however, few of us, I submit, have ever felt the need to have anything like exclusive sexual relations with anything like a state.

Indeed, it is a curiously recent thought that people's primary identity should attach to their membership in a nation-state at all. In both France and Germany, that thought would have struck many as odd, virtually on the eve of the First World War.[30] The process now seems to be going in reverse, at least in Europe, with new notions of European citizenship growing up alongside those other notions (also still new, in any broader historical sweep) of national citizenship.[31]

That, I submit, is a model towards which we should be aspiring. We should be striving towards a world with multiple, overlapping memberships, with correspondingly multiple sources of identity, multiple sources of claims, and multiple places to lodge them.[32] My preference is a world of communities which are *internally less inclusive* and *externally less exclusive*.

Contrast that with the contemporary state system, which tries to partition the world (territories, and peoples tied to them) into a set of mutually exclusive and jointly exhaustive parcels. Everyone, ideally, is tied to some particular state—and, ideally, to only one state.[33] In this sort of world, each citizen has ultimately exactly one source of social

[30] Weber 1976; Brubaker 1992. Elsewhere nation-building occurred a little earlier, perhaps, but not much (Lipset 1963).

[31] Meehan 1993; Weiler 1995; Kostakopoulau 1996, 2001.

[32] Annette Baier's (1992) analysis of the 'virtues of resident alienage' is perhaps a step towards a moral theory of that sort of society.

[33] Stateless peoples and dual citizens pose problems of an oddly similar sort for this model: no state is charged with looking after the interests of the stateless; dual citizens might suffer similar neglect, in so far as each state leaves it to the other to look after citizens they share.

succour. Everything we need we must get from the state, or from those legally operating under licence from it.

That is the sense in which the state, as presently conceived, is *too inclusive*. It is not necessarily itself the only source of social succour available to any given citizen. But even if people get the help they need from family or friends or the open market, those other institutions operate only by leave of the state, the state claims a monopoly on the power to legitimate any other sources of social succour operating within its boundaries. The state is the all-purpose authorizer and legitimator, and it is the only one there is for any given community.

Furthermore, the state is obliged to acknowledge appeals from only those whom it recognizes as members of its community. That is the sense in which the state, as presently conceived, is *too exclusive*. It claims to do (or to subcontract others to do) all things for its people— but only for its own people. The state succours only its own. Those who are some other state's citizens are that other state's business, and no concern of ours.

The present state system can thus be seen as a system of clubs, with everyone being a member of exactly one club, from which they must get everything they need.[34] The alternative which I have in view (and which may be emerging in the backwash of notions like Euro-citizenship) can be conceived as a system of clubs, too. But in this alternative system, any given person can be a member of several clubs at once. There is no thought that we should (much less should have to) rely upon one club, alone, for all that we might need. There is no thought that we should give our full allegiance to one club alone. Instead, on this alternative model, we could be members of many different clubs, drawing on them and contributing to them in turn for many different purposes and many different kinds of support and assistance.[35]

That is, as I say, rather what the emerging European Union looks like: a system of multiple, overlapping 'sovereignties', with lots of different levels and places one might lodge an application or an appeal.[36] Some see that as movement towards European unification of a statist sort, toward the consolidation of a full-blooded European state (albeit,

---

[34] This is the myth that much contemporary international law attempts to sustain, in ways remarked upon by Bauböck 1994*a*.

[35] The advantages of having several credit cards in one's wallet are well recognized: this is just the political analogue.

[36] As does the international system more generally, with the fragmentation of sovereignty in the post-cold war era; see Camilleri and Falk 1992; Ruggie 1993. Bauböck (1994*a*: 206 ff.) offers a structurally similar model, albeit one cast in terms of multiple memberships for any given individual rather than multiple sovereigns exercising jurisdiction over the same subjects; see similarly Shachar 2001: chs. 5–6.

in the first instance anyway, one federal in structure); others see it as regression to more medieval, pre-state patterns.[37] Both suppose that the present patterns represent transitional arrangements, not likely to last.

Let us not pin too much, then, on present and perhaps passing features of the contemporary European scene. Another equally good illustration of what I have in mind can be found in the sort of 'welfare pluralism' practised within most advanced industrial states. The basic point, as the name implies, is simply that there are multiple sources of social assistance for those in need. The state's social services constitute one such source, but only one among many; operating alongside and in conjunction with public assistance are various forms of assistance from family and friends, charities, public and private insurance and pension schemes, and so on.[38]

In these systems of welfare pluralism, there is no thought that state-operated schemes should necessarily constitute the first, much less the only, source of assistance to any particular individual. They have no imperial ambitions, in that regard. They do not attempt to be all-inclusive, operating to the exclusion of other systems or subsuming those other more informal systems of welfare provision within their basic framework.[39]

What state welfare services *do* do, in regimes of welfare pluralism, is to provide a safety net. The basic function of the state system is to operate as a provider of last resort, guaranteeing that anyone not adequately catered for by other arrangements at least has basic needs met. In the case of social welfare provision, we immediately recognize that as absolutely crucial. Advantageous though a 'mixed economy of welfare' might be in various other respects, we would not dream of recommending loosening up systems of welfare provision *without* assigning the state (or some comparable agency) residual responsibility to care for those who find no one else to care for them.

A more flexible system of multiple, overlapping communities caring for their own is well and good—except for those whom no community is prepared to acknowledge as its own. That seems terribly trite and

---

[37] Somers 1994: 83 ff.

[38] Beresford and Croft 1984; Johnson 1987; De Swaan 1988. The World Bank (1994) and OECD (1997) rhetoric of alternative 'pillars' of welfare provision, and New Public Management (Kettl 2000) rhetoric of 'reinventing government' worldwide, is replete with such examples.

[39] Even in the privatized Chilean pension, which is the World Bank's (1994) model for the world, the state guarantee remains: you will never get out less than you paid in (even though, in the worst-case scenario, you might not get any interest on your investment).

obvious in the case of welfare pluralism. Why is it so much harder to
see, or anyway to sell, in international applications? There, too, we see
just the same danger of someone falling through the cracks constituted
by the system of multiple, overlapping clubs and communities that is
emerging out of the fragmentation of traditional sovereignty. There,
too, we will need some agency—be it national or international, transna-
tional or non-national—to take residual responsibility for those who
find no one else to take care of them.[40]

What such an agency needs to be charged with is residual responsibility, not overarching authority. It stands beneath, not above, the
other elements of this larger network. In introducing such a residuary
body, we would not be reintroducing political authority of any ordinary sort, nationally or internationally either. But loosening up overly
inclusive, overly exclusive notions of social organization, we do create
(or perhaps just recreate, or re-emphasize) the need for an agency with
a broad remit to pick up the pieces that inevitably get left behind.

What is called for, here, is hardly a world government. It is more
a lower authority than a higher one. In Michael Walzer's terms, it
answers much more the call of 'moral minimalism' than of moral
maximalism.[41] Moral minima might not count as a grand vision, perhaps—except, perhaps, to those miserable wretches who do not already
enjoy them.

'Democratic Deliberation Within' as a Concomitant, and a Substitute

What Chapter 9 described as 'deliberative democracy within' would
seem to have two distinct roles to play in this sort of process. One is as
a concomitant to such international institutions, once they are in place;
the other is as a substitute for them, until they are in place.

Democratic inclusion is a paradigmatic 'institutional fix'. If there are
some agents whose interests we should be taking into account in our
collective decision-making, but at present are not, then the inclusionary
solution is simply to give them a vote. Then we can go about our
democratic business in the ordinary way, simply aggregating votes.

Wherever we draw the line, however, some people are left on the
wrong side of it, and many others brought 'just over the line' are
minimally better off for that. The alternative political vision offered

---

[40] As we do, in a world of traditional sovereign states, to take care of stateless persons
(Goodin 1988).   [41] Walzer 1994: ch. 1.

suggests a more fragmented sort of social and political institution. Each person had more potential sources of social succour but, inevitably, less compelling claims against any particular one. Given that, some residual institutions are then required (both nationally and internationally) to serve as back-ups and safety nets, catching the cases that would otherwise fall through the cracks between those other institutional catchments.

There are likely to be aspects of such cases that particularly call for empathetic understanding, both on the part of administrators working within those programmes and on the part of democratic publics standing behind them. The cases that fall through the cracks of other institutions often will have done so because they are somehow peculiar: non-standard, atypical, out-of-the-ordinary. They often will be peculiar in the sense of being odd, eccentric, and sometimes flatly perverse and unappealing.

Cases which are easy to understand and to sympathize with will ordinarily be dealt with perfectly adequately by other institutions. Residuary institutional back-ups are there precisely to attend to cases that are less easy to understand or sympathize with. That makes it all the more important for people working within them and for publics standing behind them to exercise the skills of 'democratic deliberation within', trying assiduously to put themselves in the place of those peculiar others and see the world from their perspectives.

Important although 'democratic deliberation within' will be, even once such residuary institutions are in place, it is all the more important in the absence of any such institutions. 'Difficult cases' will still fall between the institutional cracks, both domestically and internationally. In the absence of anyone with institutional responsibility for attending to their interests, it is all the more important for democratic publics to be attuned to the interests of 'peculiar' others. It is all the more important for people to try to project themselves imaginatively into the positions of those whose life experiences are so unlike their own. Indeed, in the absence of such institutions, such 'democratic deliberation within' is literally the only way the needs of those people might be registered, politically, with anything like the force that they democratically deserve to be.

CHAPTER 11

―――

Representing Mute Interests

By imagining ourselves in the place of others, 'democratic deliberation within' enables us to bring their interests to bear on democratic
decision-making. Democratically desirable though that always is, it is
absolutely essential when the others are in no position to speak for
themselves in the ordinary course of democratic deliberations.

One group about whom that is true is the 'socially excluded', as
discussed in Chapter 10. Both as a cause and a consequence of their
social exclusion, such people lack any effective political voice. There are
other interests that stand even more dramatically outside the ordinary
political processes, though.

Future generations are one. They are ontologically precluded from
participating directly in current political decisions. People who are
not yet here cannot take part, here and now, in decisions that will
affect them once they get here. The same is as true, in different ways,
of non-human interests. They too are almost as necessarily incapable
of taking any direct role in democratic deliberations among humans.
Neither nature nor future generations can be incorporated into democratic deliberations in the ordinary way, simply by being given a vote
and left to speak for themselves.

'Democratic deliberation within' once again provides a mechanism
for including those most dramatically hard-to-include interests within
our democratic deliberations. Even if those interests cannot speak for
themselves, present people can imaginatively project themselves into
the position of others, be they in future times or different species.[1]

That they should do so follows from the familiar liberal democratic
principle of 'equal protection of interests', modified in two ways. On

―――

[1] Those two particular concerns lie at the core of green political theory (Goodin 1992*a*).
But the general issue, and certainly the first concern, should surely engage a wide range of
people who do not share a green worldview more generally.

one side, that familiar liberal democratic value premise can and should be buttressed by an expanded view of what sorts of interests should count. Specifically, natural objects and future generations are shown to have interests which are as deserving of protection as are those of current humans. On the other side, familiar liberal propositions about 'equal protection of interests' can and should be stretched to admit of novel mechanisms for politically securing that goal. Specifically, notions of 'encapsulated interests', discredited in other connections, can be rehabilitated for purposes of protecting future-oriented and non-human values. Those goals can be served, best and ultimately only, by the mechanisms of 'democratic deliberation within'.

An Expanded Sense of Interests

Future generations clearly have interests, or anyway they will have. So too do naturally occurring objects have value, and those values are in certain important respects akin to 'interests' of the sort standard democratic theory says should be politically represented along with all others. Or such will be my argument here.

That future generations (will) have interests of the relevant sort, which deserve equal protection from a democratic regime, seems straightforward. Making the same case for nature requires a little more elaboration.

The sorts of objective values which even moderately deep ecologists see as inhering in natural objects differ radically from the sorts of things we ordinarily think of as 'interests'. But here our habits of thought simply mislead us. Analytically, if not always in our ordinary habits of thought, there is a sharp distinction between 'interest' in the sense of 'what one *takes* an interest in' and in the sense of 'what one *has* an interest in'. Eliding the two is a clear conceptual error. It empties the space between the notion of a 'want' and an 'interest', thereby depriving the latter concept of any distinctive role or any independent analytic leverage. To do so is not only untrue to ordinary linguistic usage but is also, and more importantly, counterproductive of any interest-based political theory that tries to be more nuanced than the crassest form of hedonic (or, at best, preference) utilitarianism.

Kicking away those mentalist props—the illegitimate equating of having an interest with taking an interest—we are left with a notion of interests as much more akin to objective values. They may, on certain accounts, retain a certain *subsequent* subjective component. That is to say, those things we now deem to be objectively in someone's interests may be precisely those things in which we think s/he will, or may, later come to see as being subjectively of interest. (That clearly is the case with future generations, for example.) But those subjective warrants for the present ascription of interests will come only later, if they come at all. The only warrants we can have in the present for asserting that something is in someone's interests are considerations having to do with the objective attributes and values of those things, and with the ways in which those values and attributes relate to other values and attributes of other things in the world.[2]

Thus it seems fairly straightforward that all interests point to object-ive values. But perhaps not all objective values point to interests, or anyway not to interests that ought to be politically represented. That proposition points to two quite distinct claims which need be discussed in turn.

The latter claim—that there are certain interests which ought not to be represented politically—can be summarily dismissed. The whole thrust of modern democratic theory is to reject arbitrary delimitation of the subjects whose interests are to be politically considerable. The democratic slogan of the modern era firmly enjoins *equal consideration* of interests.[3] It is simply no longer acceptable to disregard certain interests, simply on account of whose interests they are (blacks' or women's or whomsoever's).[4]

I shall not reargue that hard-won case here. I merely register the victory and piggyback on it to say that the same goes for environ-mental interests and the interests of future generations. The case of future generations is trivially easy to make: they *will* have interests, in so far as they exist at all, even if they do not *yet* have interests (because they do not yet exist). In so far as natural objects have objective values that can properly be construed as interests, those ought to be politically represented just as any others. To deny them representation merely on account of whose they are would be as unac-ceptable as it would be to deny other interests representation because of whose they are. It would, in the contemporary phrase, amount to sheer 'human chauvinism'.[5] That form of chauvinism is as offensive

---

[2] Among them, perhaps, human cognitive structures, in ways which will be explicated below. Most defensible theories of interests build on this connection, as does my version of green value theory; but that is another story, told elsewhere. See Goodin 1992*a*: 41–54 and, on interests more generally, Goodin 1995*b*: ch. 1; Goodin and Gibson 1997.

[3] Dahl 1979; Beitz 1989.

[4] The partial, but discreditable, exception is foreigners; but even that disregard is typically (if often disingenuously) justified, through the thought that those interests are represented elsewhere, and it would be wrong to double-count by including them here as well as there.

[5] Routley and Routley 1979.

as any other, and for broadly the same reasons—reasons to do with showing arbitrary preference for some things over others with interests of their own.[6]

If we want to resist that conclusion, we must therefore resort to the other challenge—that not all objective values give rise to interests at all. But why should that be so? Clearly, it cannot have anything to do with the peculiar powers of agency ordinarily possessed by humans but not by animals or trees or rocks. The notion of an interest was concocted legally precisely for use in fiduciary settings where beneficiaries of a trust (underage minors and mental incompetents, as well as—obviously—babies yet to be born) lack ordinary powers of agency. If the notion of interests could not apply in such settings, then guardians and trustees would have nothing left legally to guide them in the exercise of their trust. Fiduciary duties and the law of trusts would simply disappear.

In the end, I suspect the reason we think of interests paradigmatically in connection with human beings (and perhaps cognate corners of the animal kingdom) is closely akin to the 'mentalist' move dismissed so summarily above. We intuitively suppose that objective goods do not themselves have interests. Rather, other sorts of beings partake of those objective values which they embody, and it is this potential for a particular sort of interaction between objectively valuable object and subjectively equipped appreciator to which the notion of interest refers.[7] This would explain why nonsentient beings, or sentient beings lacking certain cognitive equipment, might be said to lack interests of their own, even if it is none the less agreed that they possess objective value.

But while those things lack interests in their own right, their objective valuableness (when brought into conjunction with other beings with the right cognitive equipment) is what causes those things to be *in* the interests of those other beings. Thus there is still a tight connection between objective value and interests even on this analysis which tries, with some success, to drive a wedge between them. Objective values are the sources—indeed, the only sources—of interests. Any objective value may potentially come to be in some agent's interests, and only objective values may do so.

---

[6] The disanalogy, of course, is that all those other forms of chauvinism—racial or sexual or whatever—denigrate other *people* in some way or another. Perhaps what the principle in view requires is not equal consideration of interests *tout court* but merely equal consideration of each *person*'s interests. I return to this issue at the end of this section.

[7] This is to adapt to the context of interests arguments from Regan 1986; Goodin 1992*a*: 41–54.

It is not as if the interaction with the cognitive equipment of the value appreciator adds nothing in the process. In the parallel case in epistemology, it might credibly be claimed that truths are true independently of their being recognized as true.[8] The case of objective values-cum-interests is not like that. The interaction with cognitively equipped appreciators does add something, over and above the sheer existence of objective value; and whatever it adds transforms objective values into interests. The question is just what is the character of that which is added. There may be many ways of answering that question. However we do so, my point is just this: in the case of objective values, what is added through interaction with the cognitively equipped appreciator—whatever it is—is nothing of *value*. All the values were already there.

The question then arises, why should we respect interests, except because they are of value? And if all the value they contain is imparted by objective values, why respect interests rather than the values upon which they rest, in so far as those two differ? Interaction with cognitively equipped appreciators may be required to transform objective values into interests. But if no value, strictly speaking, is added in the process—and if the reason we respect interests is that they are of value—then that move has backfired. It has succeeded in driving a wedge between interests and objective values, but it has done so in such a way as to leave us with no reason to respect interests in preference to values. Quite the contrary.

At root, the issue comes down to this: why take political notice of what happens to be of value to people, presently, rather than just what is *of value*, and *timelessly* so? While people (and others cognitively similarly equipped) *have* interests, objective values *are* interests. Equal protection of interests, democratically understood, ought to extend to the interests as such rather than merely to the people who are their mere carriers. That is why our democratic theory is interest-regarding, rather than merely want-regarding. That is we institute all those forms of indirect democracy and democratic paternalism discussed in Chapter 3.

There may be a strong principled defence for respecting interests via respecting the people whose interests they are. Autonomy and dignity *are* values, as objective and as compelling as any others. But dignity and autonomy cannot credibly be said to be the *only* things with objective value in the universe. The more heavily we weight those values against others, the more we would want to rely on traditional mechanisms

[8] Others would deny that claim, of course: compare the various chapters of Dancy and Sosa 1992.

of respecting interests via respecting people whose interests they are, and the more we would be willing to tolerate imperfections in that as a system for securing full protection for all other potential values and interests. But it would be implausible to accord those values absolute priority over all others. And unless we do, we should be sensitive to imperfections in way of protecting other values and interests (of future generations and nature, for example), and we should be prepared to switch to some other better mechanism for securing full protection of all potential interests if those imperfections are sufficiently great and the alternatives sufficiently promising.

The Problem of Representing Mute Interests

That long excursus into the analytics of interests and objective values serves to establish the first key step of my argument, which is that the interests of non-humans as well as of future humans are as deserving of protection as are the interests of anyone or anything else.[9] The objective values which green theorists, and others, see in the future and naturally occurring objects can be seen as akin to interests of the sort which ordinary democratic theory demands be accorded equal consideration.[10]

At the level of political principle, the implications are clear enough. If (1) we are committed to a notion of democracy which centrally involves the equal consideration of interests, and (2) we accept that future generations and naturally occurring objects have objective value of some sort or another, akin to future human interests, then (3) ordinary democratic theory commits us to equal consideration of their interests, too.

At the level of political practice, however, implications are less clear-cut. Even accepting that our principles require us to try to ensure equal consideration for the interests of future generations and of nature, it is not at all obvious what might be the most appropriate political mechanisms for doing so.

At first brush, the ordinarily democratic impulse might seem to be of little help here. Over the centuries we have heard any number of arguments for extending the equal consideration of interests to an

[9] The interests of 'corporations' (as distinct from those of their employees or owners) are other examples of non-human interests, made justiciable in American constitutional law by the doctrine that 'corporations are persons' in the eyes of the law.

[10] 'Akin' here serves to straddle 'identity' and 'analogy'. Of course, it has been argued above that, in so far as nature's objective value differ from interests, they actually command more rather than less respect—so little harm will be done conflating the two cases in this way.

ever-widening range of subjects. The action implication standardly associated with those arguments has invariably been simply to extend the suffrage. If there are excluded subjects whose interests deserve equal consideration in political deliberations, then the obvious solution is literally to include them in those deliberations. The standard way to include excluded interests, politically, is simply to enfranchise them.[11]

Following that familiar formula would seem to suggest that we ought literally to 'enfranchise the future' and 'enfranchise nature' in order to secure equal political consideration for their interests. To many that will look almost like a *reductio ad absurdum*. 'Ballots for whales? Or babies not yet conceived? Absurd', they will scoff.

Whales do not talk: not to us, anyway. They do not mark ballot papers. They do not have interests—or anyway, they do not communicate them to us clearly enough for us ever to know whether someone entrusted with representing them is discharging that fiduciary responsibility well or badly. And as for people who have not yet even been conceived, they obviously can't vote or complain until they are among us.

Or so cynics might say.

From the point of view of a democratic theory committed to the equal consideration of interests, though, the central issue is precisely that of whether we can (and therefore should try to) surmise the interests of others, not whether others can enunciate their own interests for themselves. And on that key issue, things are not so straightforward as our cynic might suppose. Christopher Stone's telling comment is that it is a lot easier for my lawn to communicate to me that it would be in its interests to be watered than it is for 'the United States' to communicate to the Attorney General that it is in its interests for Al Capone to be prosecuted.[12] Like the Attorney General, those entrusted with protecting nature's interests can often enough surmise those interests tolerably well and act upon them politically with some confidence.

Representation of the interests of nature or future generations by others who are entrusted with their care will indeed be required. We cannot literally enfranchise future generations or nature and let them tend their interests for themselves, politically. A direct democracy of the birds and bees and boulders is simply not on the cards. But that is for much the same reason that a direct democracy involving all generations (Burke's living and dead and not yet born) is not on the cards, or that

---

[11] For examples, see Goodin 1992c: ch. 5; Bendix and Rokkan 1964.

[12] Stone 1973: 471. Or as Dryzek 1987: 207 puts it, 'If the topsoil on which my crops depend is shrinking, then clearly nature is "telling" me something.'

direct democratic representation of the interests of infants and mental incompetents is not on the cards.[13]

In all those cases the barriers to directly enfranchising those subjects are ones of practicality, not desirability. It is not as if those interests are less deserving of consideration. It is merely that their carriers cannot, for one reason or another, speak for themselves in pressing those interests politically. What is absurd is to suggest that they can—to suggest that we could read votes off the babbling of infants or of streams, either. But the absurdity of that suggestion does not translate into any absurdity in the idea that their interests *ought* to be represented, by others as necessary.

Thus, enfranchising nature and the future is indeed the ideal which we should hold firmly in view. We should do so in full knowledge that it is an ideal in the strongest sense of the term. It is infeasible, taken literally. But it is none the less desirable for its being infeasible in any literal sense. And that recognition, in turn, should lead us to start looking for mechanisms by which we might—less literally, less directly—approximate that ideal.

Incorporating Mute Interests in the Interests of Others

The vision of that infeasible ideal of literally enfranchising nature leads us to start thinking through forms of second-best democracy, tailored to realizing that unattainable ideal as best we practically can. My first proposal, here, is that we ought actually to re-evaluate a class of mechanisms we have historically learnt to loathe.

Those, generically, are mechanisms that involve incorporating or subsuming the interests of one agent within those of another. The basic idea is just this. Suppose that A's interests are wholly encapsulated within B's: everything in which A has an interest is also in B's interest, as well. Suppose, now, that B is enfranchised but A is not. Does that matter? Arguably not, because B—in using B's own vote to further B's own interests—will also, in effect, be looking after A's interests as well.

Historically, this model has found some distinctly disreputable uses. Slaves' and servants' interests were, in just such ways, encapsulated within those of the master. Pre-Edwardian wives, having no independent legal personality apart from that of their husbands, saw their interests similarly and quite literally incorporated within those of their

---

[13] They all have interests which we ought to protect, whether or not they might be said to have 'rights' strictly speaking. See Feinberg 1974.

husbands. And thanks to this model of incorporated interests just elaborated, politics—far from providing a remedy to those unfortunate facts of sociological subordination—served merely to reinforce them instead. The political inference drawn via that model from those sociological facts was that, so long as the subordinates' interests really were fully incorporated in those of an enfranchised master, then the master could be entrusted to exercise that franchise in such a way as to protect subordinates' interests as well as the master's own.

We rightly baulk at those examples, on various grounds. We baulk at the political inferences. Even if subordinates' interests are wholly encapsulated in their master's own, it is preposterous to suppose that the master will weigh those other interests fully on a par with the master's own in exercising the franchise. It may well have been in the interests of slave owners not to destroy their property by killing their slaves, but that did not stop them from beating and abusing them in a variety of less dramatic ways; and much the same would hold true for the sort of political protection extended to them through their interests being incorporated politically within their master's own.

Moreover, we baulk at the sociological facts being stipulated. There is something deeply wrong with social arrangements which allow one person—slave or servant or wife—to be so wholly subordinated to another as to make that model of 'subsumed interests' plausible. And we may well reject the political implications drawn by the model as a strategy for altering those sociological facts. We may well want to extend the franchise to presently subordinated groups in the hopes that giving them electoral independence will eventually lead to their greater sociological independence as well. Votes are, or can be, levers for forcing social change.

Such examples constitute only one side of the story, though. Slaves and servants and Victorian wives certainly do represent an unacceptable—illegitimate—side of incorporated interests. It is unacceptable (illegitimate) for them to be so wholly subordinated that their interests are wholly encapsulated within those of the master; and, furthermore, it is unacceptable (illegitimate), for their interests to be politically represented wholly through the votes of those whose interests incorporate their own.

There is, however, another side to the story. In a variety of other cases, it seems perfectly acceptable and legitimate for one person's interests to be sociologically encapsulated and politically incorporated within another's. In some such cases, we have no objections to one person's interests being politically represented by another, provided that person's interests truly and legitimately are somehow wholly incorporated within the other's.[14]

Consider in this connection the example, as classical as any of those others, of underage children. Minors (very young minors, anyway) are virtually nowhere enfranchised. That is not to say that they have no interests of their own; nor is it to say that those interests should not be considered in the political process. It is merely to say that—as discussed in Chapter 3—we assume that parents speak and act on behalf of their children. Parents have the vote, and we trust them to use it (at least in part) to protect their children's interests as well as their own. Parents are presumed (as husbands alone once were presumed) to cast their ballots on behalf of the whole household.[15]

Parental actions and choices, in politics as elsewhere, may serve well or badly those other interests which are subsumed within their own. Sometimes (perhaps often) we might suppose that the child's interests are better served by altering social arrangements so as to reconstitute the caring unit, substituting for the nuclear family extended families or foster care or collectivist child-rearing. In so far as we suppose that parents are inadequate representatives of their children's interests, in more political settings, we might concoct notions of 'children's rights' to be promoted by courts and others, acting as guardians of children's interests.

My point here is not that parents are perfect protectors of their children's interests, or that they are perfect political spokespersons for them either. My point is merely that someone has to take on that role. The incapacity of minors to be politically included in their own right, to speak for themselves in collective affairs, is not socially constituted to any important extent. There is nothing illegitimate in the social arrangements that lead to their interests being politically incorporated within and subsumed by someone else's. There is nothing illegitimate, in those circumstances, in letting such others speak on the child's behalf.

An even more dramatic example in much the same vein concerns future generations. The problem of trying to get a sensible statement of their interests from the merely immature pales when compared to the problem of getting any such statement from those not yet born. Transparently, they cannot speak for themselves. Their interests can

---

[14] Sometimes (as with almost-mature children or colonies) there is a 'developmental' case to be made for giving people the vote as a means of perfecting their skills, even if it makes no practical difference (in the short term) to political outcomes. Obviously, such Millean considerations are absent in the case of nature, however.

[15] Schoeman 1980; Van Parijs 1998.

only be made felt in current political deliberations by being incorporated into the interests of, and forming the basis of votes by, presently extant people.[16]

Both in the cases of young children and of future generations, the model of 'incorporated interests' seems legitimate largely because it seems inevitable. Assuming the interests of those people deserve to be taken politically into account at all (and it seems hard to argue that they do not), and given that those people (by reason of immaturity or nonexistence) are unable to speak for themselves, someone else simply has to be assigned to speak for them. Incorporating those (young or nonexistent) people's interests within someone else's may be decidedly second-best. But since the first-best solution of letting them speak for themselves is infeasible, our choice seems to be either to settle for some such second-best solution or else to resign ourselves to the even worse situation of their interests going unrepresented altogether.

The effect of those examples, as I see it, is to break down the view of democracy as necessarily entailing 'one person one vote', with each person representing his or her own interests and trusting to the aggregation process alone to yield the right result for us all. That is a familiar model, with many attractions but also many familiar problems.[17]

I do not want to belabour any of those familiar problems, which have grown increasingly fancy and complex. Nothing fancy or complex is required for my purposes here. The problems in that model to which I point do not derive from any peculiarities of the institutional processing of people's preferences. They derive instead from the antecedent conceptualization of persons and preferences.

At root, what I want to query is the image of democracy as necessarily entailing each person representing his or her *own* interests, and those exclusively. It might be empirically more realistic, as well as being morally and politically preferable, to think instead of democracy as a process in which we all come to internalize the interests of each other and indeed of the larger world around us.[18] Incorporating the interests of others within our own might not be such a bad thing, at least in so

---

[16] Likewise, perhaps the interests of foreigners can only or anyway best be made to be felt domestically only by being incorporated in the interests (though, for example, playing on the conscience) of those who are electors inside our own country. That was the upshot of Chapter 10 above.

[17] Among the latter are problems of agenda-setting, boundary drawing and gerrymandering—together with the raft of irrationalities which social choice theorists have exposed in virtually all aggregation rules.

[18] As suggested e.g. in Mansbridge 1990, as well as Ch. 9 above.

far as the alternative is that those interests would otherwise simply be ignored.

That would seem to constitute the best hope, practically, for the protection of both the natural environment and future generations of humans. Much though those interests may deserve to be enfranchised in their own right, that is simply impracticable. People, and people alone, can exercise the vote; the living, and the living alone, can exercise the vote.[19] The best hope for the interests of mute nature and the as-yet unborn is that their interests will come to be internalized by suffi-cient numbers of present people with sufficient leverage in the political system for those interests to secure the protection that they deserve.[20]

That is not to say that present people will necessarily internalize those interests completely or represent them perfectly. Still less is it to say that the legitimate interests of nature or the future (the interests which ideally should be politically represented on their behalf, in the present) are necessarily limited to the overlap that they have with the interests of even their greatest sympathizers. Slippage is inevitable. But politically it is also unavoidable. There is simply no other way in which the interests of mute nature or unborn persons can find political representation except through being politically incorporated within the interests of sympathetic people in the present who are capable of bringing political pressure to bear on their behalf.

From Participatory Democracy to 'Democratic Deliberation Within'

Our goal, here, is twofold. First, we must find some way of inducing people to internalize the interests of nature and the future; and second, we must find some way of inducing the political system to be maximally responsive to expressions of those interests.

Green political theorists have long expressed a fondness for particip-atory politics in decentralized settings, supposing that that would help to serve those ends. There has not been much theoretical or empirical warrant for those hopes, heretofore.[21] In what follows, I shall sketch some mechanisms that might help connect the participatory styles that greens prefer to the substantive outcomes that greens hope to achieve.

---

[19] Except in certain precincts of Chicago: and possibly the Maori lists in New Zealand (Mulgan 1999).

[20] Both electorally, and in other fora as well. *Amicus curae* briefs could be filed in the courts by 'friends of nature', for example (Stone 1973).

[21] As I have argued elsewhere (Goodin 1992*a*).

Having shown how direct participation in deliberative fora might help to promote these ends, I then go on to show that the mechanism by which that works does not necessarily depend on either participation or direct interpersonal deliberation; it can be achieved, as well and perhaps better, by 'democratic deliberation within'.

The System-level effects of Participatory Democracy

Participatory democracy does many things, when it works well. Perhaps most importantly, it serves to break down concentrations of power. The simple fact that political power is extended widely and exercised vigorously in such a system means that, in a participatory democracy, elites cannot insulate themselves from the consequences of their actions.[22] At the very least, it means that they cannot reliably get their own way without being called to question. People have to justify themselves to others in a participatory setting.

Two things follow from that, one at the systemic level, the other at the individual level. Both have potentially important consequences for the incorporation of mute interests, such as those of nature and the future, in the political process.

The way in which participatory democracy makes the political system more responsive to such interests is this. The more others there are who have to be given an explanation, the more likely it is that there will be someone among them who internalizes interests of those not among them (of nature or the future or anything else). The larger and more diverse the electorate, the more likely there is to be some nature-lover who is going to ask, 'What about the effects of all this on nature?' or there will be someone asking, 'What about the effects of all this on future generations?' If in a participatory democracy advocates must answer all comers, and if in a participatory democracy there is more likely to be someone coming at problems from the perspective of nature or future generations, then a participatory democracy would indeed be more likely to incorporate those interests.

That first system-level point mechanism works purely through the analytics of participatory democracy and the law of large numbers. The analytics of participatory democracy are such that, at least in the idealized limiting case, every proposal has to be justified to everyone: a unanimity (or virtual unanimity) rule prevails. The law of large numbers serves to guarantee that, at least among very large electorates, virtually every point of view is likely to be represented.

[22] Goodin 1992c: chs. 5 and 7.

Of course, such quasi-analytic truths may sometimes be empirically false. Real electorates are not so large and diverse as that: there
may, empirically, be no 'friends of nature' or 'friends of the future'
in any given constitutency (though reasons will be given below for
supposing that participatory democracy will also evoke those values,
among others). Furthermore, even the staunchest advocate of participatory democracy would allow us to close off discussion and come to a
decision well before absolutely everyone has been satisfied, well before
complete unanimity has been achieved. Where those limits of realism
begin to bite, and how hard, is an empirical question. But at least in
the limiting case it seems clear enough how participatory democracy
might make the political system more responsive to the interests of
nature and the future.

How Participatory Democracy Affects Individuals

This second, individual-level argument for thinking that participatory
democracy might serve environmental or future generational interests
goes like this. Among advocates of discursive democracy, it is a familiar proposition that having to defend our positions publicly makes
us suppress narrowly self-interested reasons for action and highlight
public-spirited reasons in their place.[23] We must do so, at least in our
public explanations, if we want to give reasons to which we expect
anyone besides ourselves to assent.[24]

But that depends, once again, upon the composition of the constitu-
ency in the forum in which actions are being advocated and defended.
It depends, specifically, upon the forum containing spokespersons for
the whole range of interests which we want to see represented in our

---

[23] These themes from Habermas are elaborated in e.g. Dryzek 1987: esp. ch. 15, 1990,
1992; Elster 1986b: 103–22. There are various concrete illustrations of such processes at
work. Consider the surprising findings from experimental psychology that players of
Prisoner's Dilemma games, allowed to discuss their situation among themselves before
choosing their moves, play the cooperative move significantly more often purely because
of that prior discussion period (Dawes *et al.* 1977, 1990; Orbell *et al.* 1988; Frey and Bohnet
1996). Or, for another example, consider the anthropological report of discussions among
villagers, whose positions were initially self-interested but came to be substantially more
public-spirited as the discussion progressed (Bilmes 1979).

[24] Logically, of course, it is perfectly possible to be utterly duplicitous in this matter,
choosing actions for reasons of self-interest but defending them publicly on grounds of
public interest. Psychologically, however, that seems hard to sustain over the long haul.
Ultimately, talking continuously in terms of the public interest leads us almost inevitably to
start thinking in terms of public rather than private interests as well (Goodin 1992c: ch. 7).
Even Kuran (1998), who is in other very respects very wary of these deliberative dynamics,
concedes that much.

deliberations. The mechanism ordinarily in view for driving discursive democracy from particular to generalized interests is some person shouting up from the back of the room, 'Why should I care about *that*?'[25] If this were all there was to the second argument, it would simply collapse back into the first.

The further fact to note—and what distinguishes this second individual-level mechanism from the first system-level one—is that there will always be a certain amount of *anticipatory internalization* in such settings. Knowing that they will have to be defended in the public forum, one will ask oneself, 'How would I justify this to X?', even before X even asks for an explanation.

To a certain extent, that sort of anticipatory internalization is nothing more than good political strategy. Certainly that is so where the 'X' in question is someone (or rather a representative of some interest) likely to be present in the forum in which the action will have to be defended. But such anticipatory internalization might occur even for interests that would not, and maybe even could not, actually *ask* for an explanation.

The idea is just this: once people get used to making their choices with a view of having to justify them publicly to all and sundry, they might just stop trying to calculate who is likely to ask what, when. Instead, they might simply internalize, peremptorily, all the possible interests that they can imagine coming into play in those discussions.

In those processes of 'anticipatory internalization', exactly whose perspectives get peremptorily internalized is an open question of an empirical sort. Clearly, it is a matter of great substantive consequence—particularly in the context of the concerns of the present chapter with 'necessarily mute interests'—whether that will extend only to the perspectives of people who can be anticipated to intervene in the discussions, or whether it will extend to all and sundry without much consideration of the likelihood of their actually intervening in the discussions. All the argument demonstrates is that there exists a plausible mechanism by which the need to defend one's position in public discourse might *make* one internalize interests that might not (and maybe cannot) actually be voiced.

---

[25] Note that the 'generalized' versus 'particular' interests which Dryzek, following Habermas, sees emerging from discursive interactions are purely human interests in nature rather than the interests of nature as such; Dryzek 1987: 207–8.

Envisaging the Absent Other: 'Deliberative Democracy Within'

To understand the mechanisms at work in this process, we do not need the full apparatus of 'discourse theory', as elaborated by Habermas and others. The argument appeals instead merely to the perfectly ordinary analytics of how conversation is possible at all, given the inscrutability of 'other minds'.

It is obviously impossible literally to look into another's mind, in order to surmise the exact intentions behind the other's utterance. Given that inscrutability of 'other minds', analytic philosophers of language say, we therefore rely on various interpretive aids in making sense of what one another is saying.[26] Among them are convergent conventions and principles of charity, common knowledge, and conversational implicature.

Accounts of exactly how all that works are many and varied. But common across all of them is the basic idea that we converse with one another by thinking the other's thoughts for ourselves, to the point of completing the other's thoughts in our own heads. Given the problem of literally getting inside another's head, we cannot do otherwise.

The important point, for present purposes, is just this. Suppose those mental gymnastics of putting oneself in the place of the other are as central as analytically they seem to be, even in ordinary conversation where the other is present. The same sort of processes can obviously be employed where the other is absent. Calling to mind some 'absent other', and imagining what that sort of person would say to us, is on this account broadly of a cloth with what is involved in trying to figure out what a present other is actually saying to us.

It is just as well that that is so. For it is precisely that mechanism that is and must be employed by 'friends of the earth' or 'friends of the future', in order to assess the interests of nature or future generations which they then take it upon themselves to represent in external-collective deliberative fora. And unless some people take it upon themselves to do precisely that, the interests of those unable themselves to participate in deliberative fora (like the natural environment and future generations) will go unrepresented there.

That is to say, first, that 'democratic deliberation within' is an essential element of any strategy for representing mute interests, through participatory deliberative politics or otherwise. That is how spokespersons for mute interests inform themselves of the content of

---

[26] As discussed above. For an example of how political scientists are coming increasingly to appreciate the importance of these analyses for their own work, see Sniderman (1993: 236–7).

those interests, which they then communicate to others in discursive, participatory fora.

That is to say, secondly, that there is no need for anyone to wait for a participatory deliberative forum in order to become informed of the legitimate claims of mute interests like those of the natural environment or future generations. All of us can, in principle, inform ourselves in just the same way that spokespersons for those interests in public fora inform themselves of what those interests consist in.

What exactly we should do to protect those interests is, at least in part, a technical question on which expertise of various sorts is clearly required. For exploring those issues, further external-collective investigations and deliberations might be required. But as regards the first essential step—informing ourselves as to the content of mute interests such as those of nature or the future—each of us is as able to perform that enquiry in an internal-reflective way as every other.

What matters, in short, is that mute interests be internalized, somehow, by people who are in a position to play a real role in political decision-making. Participation in some actual process of discourse might serve to prompt that; it might be an aid or an occasion for that. But it is not strictly necessary actually to engage with others, or even their representatives, to get some sense of what it would be like to be in their situation and how certain actions and choices might impact on them.

With the necessarily mute interests under discussion in this chapter, that is just as well. None of us (Dr Doolittle and seers apart) can actively engage in a discourse with them. The only way any of us have of taking their interests into account—the only way any of us have of feeding their interests into the democratic process—is through 'democratic deliberation within'.

CHAPTER 12

___

Conclusion

It is now time for short restatements on two fronts. First I comment briefly on how my model of 'democratic deliberation within' compares to, and improves upon, existing models. I then close by providing some brief indications of the scope of required changes to existing political practice.

What's the Point?

Among the more important stands in my model of 'democratic deliberation within' are these:

1. Aggregation is fine for facts, but deliberation is required when values come into play. So far as facts and beliefs about facts are concerned, simply adding up the votes will usually yield the right results; people ordinarily ought rationally to alter their own beliefs as to the facts of the matter accordingly, once the votes are in. But where values are also involved, the grounds for respecting mere aggregations of votes collapse.[1] More reflective and deliberative processes, taking account of reasons rather than merely counting people's own bottom-line votes, are then required.

2. Votes are good, reasons better. Voting is crucial for conferring democratic legitimacy, for settling disagreements that cannot be resolved in other ways. But reason-giving can help others *understand* your position, rather than merely 'noting' it and 'weighing it appropriately' in some aggregative machinery. Understanding your

___

[1] Ironically, the Waldron's *Law and Disagreement*—the greatest contemporary celebration of voting as the 'right of rights', and hence the proper way of settling disagreements—specifically pertains to 'principled diagreements' (1999*b*: 15–16). Those, on this analysis, are precisely the sorts of disagreements which merely counting votes cannot properly resolve.

position in this way enables others to appreciate and partly internalize it, in turn.

3. Conversation is useful, but imagination essential. In trying to understand the position of others, it is undeniably helpful to have active others pressing their points of view upon you and providing a cross-check on your own understandings of them. But direct, active interpersonal engagement of that sort is possible only in small groups, not in large polities. Even in small-group settings, much of the work of understanding others conversationally is done inside your own head, imaginatively projecting yourself into their place. Happily, that is something that can be done in the large as well as the small. 'Democratic deliberation within' thus provides a way of imaginatively projecting ourselves into the place of a great many (prototypical) 'others' with whom we can never speak, much less deliberate in person.[2]

4. 'Democratic deliberation within' asks us to assess what is 'the right thing to do, from all perspectives'. It asks each of us to internalize the perspective of each (prototypical) other.[3] It asks each of us to look at the situation from all those various perspectives, and to come to a judgement as to what is best from all those perspectives. But in saying 'what is best overall', or 'what is best for all', there is no sense of any 'community' or 'public interest' that is more than a function of the interacting interests of all those representative individuals, their preferences and perspectives.

5. 'Deliberative democracy within' is indeed a preference-respecting model of liberal democracy. Or, perhaps better, it is a 'preference-and-perspective-respecting' model. It is sensitive not just to people's desires but also to their beliefs. It offers a way of articulating both their assessments of facts and their judgements of values.

6. 'Democratic deliberation within' never in itself settles things, and cannot in itself provide full democratic legitimacy to any outcome. Acting in perfectly good faith, trying as hard as we might to internalize the perspective of all others, each of us invariably comes to slightly different conclusions as to 'what is best overall', from everyone's perspective. Inevitably we settle such disagreements in the ordinary democratic ways: by talking in the first instance, by voting in the second. 'Democratic deliberation within' should thus be seen as an

---

[2] This 'attending to the Other' lies at the heart of 'difference feminism' of various stripes, nicely surveyed by Lacey (1998: chs. 5–7).

[3] That is to say, each 'type' of other, rather than each and every other. In any large group, we will inevitably be confined mostly to envisaging representative others rather than individualized and idiosyncratic ones.

important concomitant to ordinary democratic processes, an essential supplement but nowise a substitute.

7. 'Deliberative democracy within' is a necessary component of ideal democratic institutions; it is an all-the-more-necessary component of second-best democratic institutions in the absence of those ideal arrangements.[4] Even in an ideally representative democracy—one that is as representative as it can possibly be—it is none the less desirable for 'democratic deliberation within' to be practised both by rulers (when interpreting what people say to them, in their submissions, petitions, letters, and votes) and by citizens (when holding their representatives to account, at periodic elections). Even in a democracy that is ideally inclusive and expansive—just as inclusive and expansive as it can be—it is none the less important for 'democratic deliberation within' to be practised by both rulers and citizens in order to internalize the perspectives of all the diverse interests represented within their community.

Important though 'democratic deliberation within' is even in those ideal cases of maximal democracy, it is all the more important in cases that fall short of the ideal. Wherever some people are denied direct representation in the political process—whether formally or informally, contingently or necessarily—it is all the more important for each of us to provide it indirectly, by internalizing the perspectives of those excluded others. It is all the more important that those of us with a vote should vote with their interests partly in mind, because they have no vote of their own to cast.

How Demanding Would it Be?

Retheorizing democracy is typically a visionary but ambitious activity. Its proposals for reform of our existing political structures and practices are often bold, but often wildly impractical.

Consider the precedents. Direct democrats urge us to put absolutely everything to a vote of absolutely all the people, perhaps through fanciful schemes of electronic voting and tele-democracy.[5] Participatory democrats urge us to put everything to a decision of all the people, assembled physically (not merely virtually) and engaged actively (not merely passively). Grass-root democrats urge us to devolve absolutely

---

[4] The 'general theory of second best', recall, does not say that second-best solutions are *necessarily* very different from first-best ones, merely that they might be (Goodin 1995*a*).

[5] McLean 1989; Budge 1996.

all decisions to participatory assemblies at the most local of levels. Lottery democrats urge us to choose our representatives utterly at random.[6] And so on.

Compared to those, the proposals of this book are modest indeed. They are perfectly capable of working within the received institutions of representative democracy. They are perfectly capable of working with periodic elections. They are perfectly capable of working with people whose perspectives and priorities are self-oriented, most of the time.

All that 'democratic deliberation within' strictly requires is that, when an election is called: (1) people take it upon themselves to try to think how the issues would look from other people's perspectives as well as their own, and (2) they vote on the basis of that 'overall' assessment.

Cynics might say that that in itself sounds pretty wishful. To such cynicism I offer two replies. First, that, or something very much like that, is how democratic theory has traditionally conceptualized the appropriate role of citizens. Traditionally, they are supposed to vote the good of the country rather than their own personal good.[7]

Secondly, I would add that there is empirical evidence that citizens do what they are normatively supposed to do in that regard. Careful analyses of political behaviour find that people do, indeed, vote the 'common good'—what is best for the national economy or the natural environment—over their own personal interests, in clear cases where the two action-premises pull in opposite directions.[8]

Unenforceable appeals to pure 'good will' are sure to induce high anxiety among realpolitik analysts. In *The Federalist*, Madison is among the first to acknowledge that such motives 'may...be insufficient to control the caprice and wickedness of man. But'—he goes on to ask, and I with him—'are they not all that government will admit, and that human prudence can devise?'[9]

While no great reform to basic political institutions or human character is required for 'democratic deliberation within' to work, that model does make some non-trivial demands one level down. At the level of processes, it recommends policy-making through actual deliberative engagements or other consultative procedures, wherever possible.

---

[6] Burnheim 1981*a*, *b*; 1985.

[7] e.g. Waldron (1999*b*: 14) begins by saying, 'I shall proceed throughout this book on the assumption that people sometimes or often do vote their considered and impartial opinions. It is by no means invariably true, but normative theory of law and politics needs an aspirational quality, and this is mine.'   [8] Kiewiet 1983; Rohrschneider 1988.

[9] Hamilton *et al.* 1787–8: no. 57, p. 387.

It recommends 'site visits', seeing for yourself what life is like in the places and among the people your actions will affect, rather than making policy from the centre oblivious to on-the-ground realities and impacts. Nothing fires the imagination, of policy-makers or anyone else, better than direct engagement with people whom they are trying to call up in their imagination.[10] However, it is essential for policy-makers and administrators also to remember that the whole point of speaking with these particular people is to help them conjure up, in their mind's eye, a whole raft of other people—similar in some respects but different in ever so many others—whom their policies will also affect.

At the level of public policy itself, the model of 'democratic deliberation within' emphasizes the importance of social mixing, and of various housing, education, and transport to facilitate that. It emphasizes the importance of cultural aids in informing the democratic imagination, and recommends a range of public services and subsidies towards that end. It emphasizes the importance of collective consumption—of doing things together, of public places and shared experiences—not to force us all to do or to be or to have the same things, but rather to sensitize to the many different ways we have of doing, being, and having.[11] In all these ways, and dozens more, 'democratic deliberation within' makes non-trivial demands on public policy and practice.

So too does 'democratic deliberation within' require people to make various changes in their behaviour, if not their basic character. It requires them to do lots of things in between elections to put themselves in a position, come the election, to internalize adequately the perspectives of all those around them (and indeed others at some distance, in various dimensions: spatial, temporal, species, and so on).

Those demands, too, seem relatively undemanding, though. For the most part, what is required for effective practice of 'democratic deliberation within' are things that are interesting and amusing in their own right. They typically count as entertainment. Even escapist television, films, and novels manage to stretch us, giving us practice at putting ourselves in place of others. Even just getting to know fictionalized others can help us to understand actual others on whose broad patterns of experience those fictions rest.

---

[10] In the office administering the American wage-price freeze in the early 1970s appeals which would have been rejected out of hand, had they come in writing, got a far more sympathetic hearing when presented in person (Kagan 1978: 152). Lobbyists have long known this, of course (Milbrath 1960). [11] Barry 1988; Sunstein 2001.

Cynics again abound. They say this makes democracy sound much too easy, that it trivializes something profoundly important. But if there are easy ways to evoke the sort of reflective, considered, empathetic responses upon which democracy depends, then surely so much the better.

REFERENCES

ABERCROMBIE, NICHOLAS, HILL, STEPHEN, and TURNER, BRYAN S. (1986), *Sovereign Individuals of Capitalism* (London: Allen & Unwin).

ABRAMSON, JEFFREY (1993), 'The Jury and Democratic Theory', *Journal of Political Philosophy*, 1: 45–68.

—— (1994), *We, the Jury* (New York: Basic).

ACKERMAN, BRUCE (1991), *We, the People* (Cambridge, Mass.: Harvard University Press).

—— and ALSTOTT, ANNE (1999), *The Stakeholder Society* (New Haven, Conn.: Yale University Press).

—— and FISHKIN, JAMES S. (2002), 'Deliberation Day', *Journal of Political Philosophy*, 10: 128–51.

ADAMS, ROBERT McC. (1999), 'Forums, Not Temples', *American Behavioral Scientist*, 42: 968–76.

ADORNO, THEODOR W., and HORKHEIMER, MAX, (1979), *Dialectic of Enlightenment*, tr. John Cumming (London: Verso/New Left Books).

ALESINA, ALBERTO, and ROSENTHAL, HOWARD (1996), *Partisan Politics, Divided Government and the Economy* (New York: Cambridge University Press).

AMIN, SAMIR (1976), *Unequal Development: An Essay on the Social Formations of Peripheral Capitalism*, tr. Brian Pearce (Hassocks, UK: Harvester Press).

ANDERSON, BENEDICT (1983), *Imagined Communities: Reflections on the Origin and Spread of Nationalism* (London: Verso).

ANDERSON, ELIZABETH S. (1991), 'John Stuart Mill and Experiments in Living', *Ethics*, 102: 4–26.

—— (1999), 'What is the Point of Equality?', *Ethics*, 109: 287–338.

ANDERSON, MIKAEL SKOU (1994), *Governance by Green Taxes* (Manchester: Manchester University Press).

ANTON, THOMAS J. (x1969), 'Policy-Making and Political Culture in Sweden', *Scandinavian Political Studies*, 4: 88–102.

—— (1980), *Administered Politics: Elite Political Culture in Sweden* (Boston: Martinus Nijhoff).

ARENDT, HANNAH (1958), *The Human Condition* (Chicago: University of Chicago Press).

ARISTOTLE (1984a), *The Complete Works of Aristotle*, ed. Jonathan Barnes (Princeton: Princeton University Press).

—— (1984b), *Nicomachean Ethics*, tr. W. D. Ross and J. O. Urmson, in Aristotle 1984a: ii. 1729–1867.

—— (1984c), *Poetics*, tr. J. Bywater, in Aristotle 1984a: ii. 2316–40.

ARISTOTLE (1984*d*), *The Politics*, tr. B. Jowett, in Aristotle 1984*a*: ii. 1986–2150.

—— (1984*e*), *Rhetoric*, tr. W. Rhys Roberts, in Aristotle 1984*a*: ii. 2152–2269.

ARNOULD, R. J., and GRABOWSKI, H. (1981), 'Auto Safety Regulation: An Analysis of Market Failure', *Bell Journal of Economics*, 12: 27–48.

ARROW, KENNETH J. (1963), *Social Choice and Individual Values*, 2nd edn. (New Haven, Conn.: Yale University Press).

—— and HAHN, FRANK (1971), *General Competitive Analysis* (San Francisco: Holden-Day).

ATKINSON, ANTHONY B. (1995*a*), 'Capabilities, Exclusion and the Supply of Goods', in K. Basu, P. Pattanaik, and K. Suzumara (eds.), *Choice, Welfare and Development* (Oxford: Clarendon Press), 17–31.

—— (1995*b*), *Public Economics in Action: The Basic Income/Flat Tax Proposal* (Oxford: Oxford University Press).

—— (1996), 'The Case for a Participation Income', *Political Quarterly*, 67: 67–70.

AUMANN, ROBERT J. (1976), 'Agreeing to Disagree', *Annals of Statistics*, 4: 1236–9.

AUSTEN-SMITH, DAVID, and BANKS, JEFFREY S. (1996), 'Information Aggregation, Rationality and the Condorcet Jury Theorem', *American Political Science Review*, 90/1 (Mar.): 34–45.

AUSTIN, J. L. (1962), *How to Do Things with Words* (Oxford: Clarendon Press).

—— (1979), 'Other Minds', in Austin, *Philosophical Papers*, J. O. Urmson and G. J. Warnock (eds.) 3rd edn. (Oxford: Oxford University Press), 76–116.

AVINERI, SHLOMO, and DE-SHALIT, AVNER (eds.) (1992), *Communitarianism and Individualism* (Oxford: Oxford University Press).

AXELROD, ROBERT (1970), *Conflict of Interests* (Chicago: Markham).

—— (1984), *The Evolution of Cooperation* (New York: Basic).

—— (1986), 'An Evolutionary Approach to Norms', *American Political Science Review*, 80: 1095–1112.

BACHRACH, PETER (1967), *The Theory of Democratic Elitism* (Boston: Little, Brown).

BADER, VEIT (1995), 'Citizenship and Exclusion', *Political Theory*, 23: 211–46.

BAIER, ANNETTE C. (1992), 'Some Virtues of Resident Alienage', in *Nomos XXXIV: Virtue*, ed. J. W. Chapman and W. A. Galston (New York: New York University Press), 291–308.

BAKER, WAYNE (1984), 'The Social Structure of a National Securities Market', *American Journal of Sociology*, 89: 775–811.

BALIBAR, ÉTIENNE (1991), 'Exclusion ou lutte des classes?', repr. in Balibar (1992: 191–205).

—— (1992), *Les Frontières de la Démocratie* (Paris: Éditions la Découverte).

—— and WALLERSTEIN, IMMANUEL (1988), *Race, Nation, Classe* (Paris: Éditions la Découverte).

BALLADUR, EDOUARD (1994), 'Mieux associer les citoyens', *Le Monde* (17 Nov.).

BANFIELD, EDWARD C. (1984), *The Democratic Muse: The Visual Arts and the Public Interest* (New York: Basic Books).

BARBER, BENJAMIN (1984), *Strong Democracy* (Berkeley: University of California Press).

BARRETT, MICHÈLE (1980), *Women's Oppression Today: Problems in Marxist Feminist Analysis* (London: Verso).

—— and MCINTOSH, MARY (1982), *The Anti-Social Family* (London: Verso).

—— and PHILLIPS, ANNE (ed.) (1992), *Destabilizing Theory: Contemporary Feminist Debates* (Oxford: Polity).

BARRY, BRIAN (1964), 'The Public Interest', *Proceedings of the Aristotelian Society (Supplement)*, 38: 1–18.

—— (1965), *Political Argument* (London: Routledge & Kegan Paul).

—— (1973), 'Wollheim's Paradox: Comment', *Political Theory*, 1/3 (Aug.): 317–22.

—— (1988), 'The Continuing Relevance of Socialism', in Robert Skidelsky (ed.), *Thatcherism* (London: Chatto & Windus), 143–58. Reprinted in Barry 1989: 526–42.

—— (1989), *Democracy, Power and Justice* (Oxford: Clarendon Press).

—— (1995), *Justice as Impartiality* (Oxford: Clarendon Press).

BARTHOLDI, J., TOVEY, C. A., and TRICK, M. A. (1989), 'Voting Schemes for Which it Can Be Difficult to Tell who Won the Election', *Social Choice and Welfare*, 6/2: 157–65.

BAUBÖCK, RAINER (1994*a*), 'Changing the Boundaries of Citizenship: The Inclusion of Immigrants in Democratic Politics', in Bauböck 1994*b*: 199–232.

—— (ed.) (1994*b*), *From Aliens to Citizens* (Aldershot: Avebury).

BEARD, CHARLES A. (1913), *An Economic Interpretation of the Constitution of the United States* (New York: Macmillan).

BEATTIE, JOHN (1964), *Other Cultures* (New York: Free Press).

BEER, SAMUEL H. (1965), *British Politics in the Collectivist Age* (New York: Knopf).

BEINER, RONALD (1983), *Political Judgment* (Chicago: University of Chicago).

BEITZ, CHARLES R. (1979), *Political Theory and International Relations* (Princeton: Princeton University Press).

—— (1983), 'Cosmopolitan Ideals and National Sentiment', *Journal of Philosophy*, 80: 591–600.

—— (1989), *Political Equality* (Princeton: Princeton University Press).

BELL, DAVID E., RAIFFA, HOWARD, and TVERSKY, AMOS (eds.) (1988), *Decision Making: Descriptive, Normative and Prescriptive Interactions* (Cambridge: Cambridge University Press).

BENDIX, R., and ROKKAN, S. (1964), 'The Extension of Citizenship to the Lower Classes', in R. Bendix, *Nation-Building and Citizenship* (New York: Wiley), 74–104.

BENHABIB, SEYLA (1992*a*), 'The Generalized and the Concrete Other: The Kohlberg–Gilligan Controversy and Moral Theory', in Benhabib 1992*a*: 148–77.

—— (1992*b*), *Situating the Self: Gender, Community and Postmodernism in Contemporary Ethics* (Oxford: Polity).

—— (1994), 'Deliberative Rationality and Models of Democratic Legitimacy', *Constellations*, 1: 26–52.

—— BUTLER, JUDITH, CORNELL, DRUCILLA, and FRASER, NANCY (1995), *Feminist Contentions* (New York: Routledge).

BENNETT, SUSAN D. (1995), ' "No Relief but upon the Terms of Coming into the House": Controlled Spaces, Invisible Disentitlements, and Homeless in an Urban Shelter System', *Yale Law Journal*, 104: 2157–2212.

BERESFORD, PETE, and CROFT, SUZY (1984), 'Welfare Pluralism: The New Face of Fabianism?', *Critical Social Policy*, 9: 19–39.

BERGER, PETER L., and LUCKMAN, THOMAS (1966), *The Social Construction of Reality* (Garden City, NY: Doubleday).

BERMAN, HAROLD J. (1983), *Law and Revolution: The Formation of the Western Legal Tradition* (Cambridge, Mass.: Harvard University Press).

BESSETTE, JOSEPH M. (1994), *The Mild Voice of Reason: Deliberative Democracy and American National Government* (Chicago: University of Chicago Press).

BICKFORD, SUSAN (1996), *The Dissonance of Democracy: Listening, Conflict, and Citizenship* (Ithaca, NY: Cornell University Press).

BILMES, J. M. (1979), 'The Evolution of Decisions in a Thai Village: A Quasi-Experimental Study', *Human Organization*, 38: 169–78.

BIRCH, A. H. (1977), 'The Nature and Functions of Representation', in Preston King (ed.), *The Study of Politics* (London: Frank Cass), 265–78.

BLACK, DUNCAN (1958), *The Theory of Committees and Elections* (Cambridge: Cambridge University Press).

BLOCK, NED (ed.) (1980), *Readings in the Philosophy of Psychology* (Cambridge, Mass.: Harvard University Press).

BLUSTEIN, JEFFREY (1982), *Parents and Children: The Ethics of the Family* (New York: Oxford University Press).

BOCK, GISELA, and JAMES, SUSAN (eds.) (1992), *Beyond Equality and Difference: Citizenship, Feminist Politics and Female Subjectivity* (London: Routledge).

BOHMAN, JAMES (1996), *Public Deliberation: Pluralism, Complexity and Democracy* (Cambridge, Mass.: MIT Press).

—— and REHG, WILLIAM (eds.) (1997), *Deliberative Democracy* (Cambridge, Mass.: MIT Press).

BOOTH, WAYNE C. (1988), *The Company We Keep: An Ethics of Fiction* (Berkeley: University of California Press).

BORDA, JEAN-CHARLES DE (1784), 'Mémoire sur les élections au scrutin par M. de Borda', *Mémoires de l'Académie Royale des Sciences année 1781* (Paris: l'Imprimerie Royale), 657–65. Tr. and reprinted in Sommerlad and McLean 1988: 122–8; McLean and Hewitt 1994: 114–19; McLean and Urken 1995: 83–9; Sommerlad and McLean 1988: 122–8.

BORLAND, PHILIP J. (1989), 'Majority Systems and the Condorcet Jury Theorem', *Statistician*, 38: 181–9.

BOVENKERK, FRANK, MILES, ROBERT, and VERBUNT, GILLES (1991), 'Comparative Studies of Migration and Exclusion on Grounds of "Race" and Ethnic Background in Western Europe: A Critical Appraisal', *International Migration Review*, 25: 375–91.

BOWLES, SAMUEL, and GINTIS, HERBERT (1986), *Democracy and Capitalism* (New York: Basic Books).

BRADDON-MITCHELL, DAVID, and JACKSON, FRANK (1996), *The Philosophy of Mind and Cognition* (Cambridge, Mass.: Blackwell).

BRENNAN, H. GEOFFREY (1995), 'Condorcet [review of McLean and Hewitt 1994]', *History of Economics Review*, 23 (Winter): 157–9.

—— (2001), 'Collective Coherence?', *International Review of Law and Economics* 21: 197–211.

—— and LOMASKY, LOREN (1993), *Democracy and Decision* (Cambridge: Cambridge University Press).

—— and PETTIT, PHILIP (1990), 'Unveiling the Vote', *British Journal of Political Science*, 20: 311–34.

BRENNAN, TERESA, and PATEMAN, CAROLE (1979), ' "Mere Auxiliaries to the Commonwealth": Women and the Origins of Liberalism', *Political Studies*, 27: 183–200.

BRIGHOUSE, HARRY (1995), 'Neutrality, Publicity and Public Funding of the Arts', *Philosophy and Public Affairs*, 24: 36–63.

BRUBAKER, ROGERS (1992), *Citizenship and Nationhood in France and Germany* (Cambridge, Mass.: Harvard University Press).

BUCHANAN, ALLEN E. (1978), 'Medical Paternalism', *Philosophy and Public Affairs*, 7: 371–90.

BUDGE, IAN (1996), *The New Challenge of Direct Democracy* (Oxford: Polity).

BUKSTI, JACOB A., and ELIASSEN, KJELL A. (eds.) (1979) 'Corporate Pluralism in Nordic Democracies', Special Issue of *Scandinavian Political Studies*, NS 2: 195–298.

BURKE, EDMUND (1774), 'Speech to the Electorate at Bristol', in *Writings and Speeches of Edmund Burke*, ed. Paul Langford (Oxford: Clarendon Press, 1980), ii. 95–7.

BURNHEIM, JOHN (1981a), 'Statistical Democracy', *Radical Philosophy*, 27: 5–12.

—— (1981b), 'Statistical Democracy', *Thesis Eleven*, 3: 60–71.

—— (1985), *Is Democracy Possible?* (Berkeley, Calif.: University of California Press).

BURNSTEIN, E., and SCHU, Y. (1983), 'Group Polarization', in H. H. Blumberg, A. P. Hare, V. Kent and M. F. Davies (eds.), *Small Groups and Social Interaction* (Chichester: Wiley), ii. 57–64.

BUTLER, JUDITH, and SCOTT, JOAN W. (eds.) (1992), *Feminists Theorize the Political* (New York: Routledge).

CAMILLERI, JOSEPH A., and FALK, JIM (1992), *The End of Sovereignty? The Politics of a Shrinking and Fragmenting World* (Aldershot: Elgar).

CARDOSO, FERNANDO HENRIQUE, and FALETTO, ENZO (1979), *Dependency and Development in Latin America*, tr. M. M. Urquidi (Berkeley, Calif.: University of California Press).

CARE, NORMAN S. (1984), 'Career Choice', *Ethics*, 94: 283–302.

CARENS, JOSEPH (1987), 'Aliens and Citizens: The Case for Open Borders', *Review of Politics*, 49: 251–73.

CARNEGIE COMMISSION ON THE FUTURE OF PUBLIC BROADCASTING (1979), *A Public Trust* (New York: Bantam).

CASTLES, STEPHEN (1992), 'The Australian Model of Immigration and Multiculturalism: Is it Applicable in Europe?', *International Migration Review*, 26: 549–67.

—— (1994), 'Democracy and Multicultural Citizenship: Australian Debates and their Relevance for Western Europe', in Bauböck 1994*b*: 3–28.

CAYTON, H. R., and DRAKE, ST. CLAIR (1946), *Black Metropolis* (London: Jonathan Cape).

CHAIKEN, SHELLY, WOOD, WENDY, and EAGLY, ALICE H. (1996), 'Principles of Persuasion', in E. Tory Higgins and Arie W. Kruglanski (eds.), *Social Psychology: Handbook of Basic Principles* (New York: Guilford Press), 702–43.

CICERO (1991), *De Officiis*, ed. M. T. Griffin and E. M. Atkins (Cambridge: Cambridge University Press).

CNUDDE, CHARLES F., and NEUBAUER, DEANE E. (eds.) (1969), *Empirical Democratic Theory* (Chicago: Markham).

COASE, R. H. (1974), 'The Market for Goods and the Market for Ideas', *American Economic Review (Papers & Proceedings)*, 64/2: 384–402.

COHEN, JOSHUA (1986), 'An Epistemic Conception of Democracy', *Ethics*, 97/1 (Oct): 26–38.

—— (1989), 'Deliberation and Democratic Legitimacy', in Alan Hamlin and Philip Pettit (eds.), *The Good Polity* (Oxford: Blackwell), 17–34.

—— (1996), 'Procedure and Substance in Deliberative Democracy', in Seyla Benhabib (ed.), *Democracy and Difference* (Princeton: Princeton University Press), 95–119.

—— (1998), 'Democracy and Liberty', in Elster 1998: 185–231.

—— and ROGERS, JOEL, *et al.* (1995), in E. O. Wright (ed.), *Associations and Democracy* (London: Verso).

—— and SABEL, CHARLES (1997), 'Directly-Deliberative Polyarchy', *European Law Journal*, 3: 313–42.

COLEMAN, JULES L. (1989), 'Rationality and the Justification of Democracy', in Geoffrey Brennan and Loren E. Lomasky (eds.), *Politics and Process: New Essays in Democratic Thought* (Cambridge: Cambridge University Press), 194–220.

COLEMAN, JULES L., and FEREJOHN, JOHN (1986), 'Democracy and Social Choice', *Ethics*, 97/1 (Oct.): 6–25.

COMMISSION ON SOCIAL JUSTICE, UK LABOUR PARTY (1993), *The Justice Gap* (London: Institute for Public Policy Research).

—— (1994), *Social Justice: Strategies for National Renewal* (London: Vintage/ Random House).

CONDORCET, MARIE JEAN ANTOINE NICOLAS DE CARITAT, MARQUIS DE (1784), 'Sur les élections par scrutin', *Histoire de l'Académie Royale des Sciences année 1781* (Paris: De l'imprimerie royale), 31–4. Tr. and reprinted in Sommerlad and McLean 1988: 119–22; McLean and Hewitt 1994: 111–13; McLean and Urken 1995: 81–3.

—— (1785), *Essai sur l'application de l'analyse à la probabilité des décisions rendues à la pluralité des voix* (Paris: De l'Imprimerie Royale [fascimile ed. New York: Chelsea, 1972]). Comprised of: Discours préliminaire, pp. i–cxci; *Essai*, pp. 1–304. Tr. and excerpted in: Sommerlad and McLean 1989: 69–80 (corresponding to Condorcet 1785: pp. lvi–lxx); Sommerlad and McLean 1989: 81–9 (corresponding to Condorcet 1785: pp. clxviii–clxxix); Sommerlad and McLean 1989: 90–108 (corresponding to Condorcet 1785: 119–36); Sommerlad and McLean 1989: 109–18 (corresponding to Condorcet 1785: 287–96); McLean and Hewitt 1994: 120–30 (corresponding to Condorcet 1785: pp. lvi–lxx); McLean and Hewitt 1994: 130–8 (corresponding to Condorcet 1785: pp. clxviii–clxxix); McLean and Urken 1995: 91–113 (corresponding to Condorcet 1785: 279–304).

—— (1788), 'On the Constitution and the Functions of Provincial Assemblies', tr. and excerpted in McLean and Hewitt 1994: 139–68; McLean and Urken 1995: 113–44; Sommerlad and McLean 1989: 129–66.

—— (1792), 'A Survey of the Principles Underlying the Draft Constitution', tr. and excerpted in McLean and Hewitt 1994: 190–227; McLean and Urken 1995: 145–50; Sommerlad and McLean 1989: 216–22.

CONNOLLY, WILLIAM E. (1991), *Identity\Difference: Democratic Negotiations of Political Paradox* (Ithaca, NY: Cornell University Press).

CONSTANT, BENJAMIN (1815), 'Principles of Politics Applicable to All Representative Governments', in *Political Writings*, tr. and ed. Biancamaria Fontana (Cambridge: Cambridge University Press, 1988), 171–305.

CONVERSE, PHILIP E. (1964), 'The Nature of Belief Systems in Mass Publics', in David Apter (ed.), *Ideology and Discontent* (New York: Free Press), 206–61.

COOTE, ANNA, and LENAGHAN, JO (1997), *Citizens' Juries: Theory into Practice* (London: Institute for Public Policy Research).

COPP, DAVID (1993), 'Could Political Truth be a Hazard for Democracy?', in David Copp, Jean Hampton and John E. Roemer (eds.), *The Idea of Democracy* (Cambridge: Cambridge University Press), 101–17.

CORDEN, W. M. (1977), *The Theory of Protection* (Oxford: Oxford University Press).

COSER, LEWIS A. (1974), *Greedy Institutions: Patterns of Undivided Commitment* (New York: Free Press).

COUGHLAN, PETER J. (2000), 'In Defense of Unanimous Jury Verdicts: Mistrials, Communication and Strategic Voting', *American Political Science Review*, 94/2 (June): 375–94.

CRICK, BERNARD (1989), *Essays on Politics and Literature* (Edinburgh: Edinburgh University Press).

CURRIE, GREGORY (1995), *Image and Mind: Film, Philosophy and Cognitive Science* (Cambridge: Cambridge University Press).

——(1999), *Meeting of Minds: Thought, Imagination and Perception* (Oxford: Oxford University Press).

DAHL, ROBERT A. (1956), *A Preface to Democratic Theory* (Chicago: University of Chicago Press).

——(1961), *Who Governs?* (New Haven, Conn.: Yale University Press).

——(ed.) (1966), *Political Oppositions in Western Democracies* (New Haven, Conn.: Yale University Press).

——(1970), *After the Revolution?* (New Haven, Conn.: Yale University Press).

——(1971), *Polyarchy* (New Haven, Conn.: Yale University Press).

——(ed.) (1973), *Regimes and Oppositions* (New Haven, Conn.: Yale University Press).

——(1979), 'Procedural Democracy', in *Philosophy, Politics and Society*, 5th ser., ed. P. Laslett and J. Fishkin (Oxford: Blackwell), 97–133.

——(1982), *Dilemmas of Pluralist Democracy* (New Haven, Conn.: Yale University Press).

——(1985), *A Preface to Economic Democracy* (Berkeley: University of California Press).

——(1989), *Democracy and its Critics* (New Haven, Conn.: Yale University Press).

——and LINDBLOM, CHARLES E. (1953), *Politics, Economics and Welfare* (New York: Harper & Row).

——and NEUBAUER, DEANE E. (eds.) (1968), *Readings in Modern Political Analysis* (Englewood Cliffs, NJ: Prentice-Hall).

——and TUFTE, EDWARD R. (1973), *Size and Democracy* (Stanford, Calif.: Stanford University Press).

DAHRENDORF, RALF (1958), 'Homo Sociologicus', in Dahrendorf, *Essays in Social Theory* (Stanford, Calif.: Stanford University Press, 1968), 19–87.

DAMGAARD, ERIK, and ELIASSEN, KJELL A. (1980), 'Reduction of Party Conflict through Corporate Participation in Danish Law-Making', *Scandinavian Political Studies*, NS 3: 105–21.

DANCY, JONTATHAN, and SOSA, E. (eds.) (1992), *A Companion to Epistemology* (Oxford: Blackwell).

DANIELS, NORMAN (1979), 'Wide Reflective Equilibrium and Theory Acceptance in Ethics', *Journal of Philosophy*, 76/5: 256–82.

DANIELSON, MICHAEL N. (1976), *The Politics of Exclusion* (New York: Comunbia University Press).

DAVIDSON, DONALD (1980), *Essays on Actions and Events* (Oxford: Clarendon Press).

——(1984), *Inquiries into Truth and Interpretation* (Oxford: Clarendon Press).

DAVIES, MARTIN (1994), 'The Mental Simulation Debate', in Peacocke 1994: 99–127.

——and STONE, TONY (1998), 'Folk Psychology and Mental Simulation', in Anthony O'Hear (ed.), *Current Issues in the Philosophy of Mind* (Cambridge: Cambridge University Press, for the Royal Institute of Philosophy, 1998), 53–82.

DAVIS, J. H., BRAY, R. M., and HOLT, R. W. (1977), 'The Empirical Study of Decision Processes in Juries: A Critical Review', in J. L. Tapp and F. J. Levine (eds.), *Law, Justice and the Individual in Society: Psychological and Legal Issues* (New York: Holt, Rinehart & Winston), 326–61.

DAWES, R., McTAVISH, J., and SHAKLEE, H. (1977), 'Behavior, Communications and Assumptions about Other People's Behaviour in a Commons Dilemma Situation', *Journal of Personality and Social Psychology*, 35: 1–35.

DAWES, R. M., VAN DE KRAGT, A. J. C., and ORBELL, J. M. (1990), 'Cooperation for the Benefit of Us—Not Me, or My Conscience', in Mansbridge 1990: 97–110.

DAY, PATRICIA, and KLEIN, RUDOLPH (1987), *Accountabilities: Five Public Services* (London: Tavistock).

DERRIDA, JACQUES (1978), *Writing and Difference*, tr. Alan Bass (London: Routledge & Kegan Paul).

DE SWAAN, ABRAM (1988), *In Care of the State* (Oxford: Polity).

DEWEY, JOHN (1927), *The Public and its Problems* (Chicago: Swallow Press, 1954).

DIAMOND, LARRY (1999), *Developing Democracy: Toward Consolidation* (Baltimore: Johns Hopkins University Press).

DOWNS, ANTHONY (1957), *An Economic Theory of Democracy* (New York: Harper).

——(1973), *Opening up the Suburbs* (New Haven, Conn.: Yale University Press).

DRYZEK, JOHN S. (1987), *Rational Ecology* (Oxford, Blackwell).

——(1990), *Discursive Democracy* (Cambridge: Cambridge University Press).

——(1992), 'Ecology and Discursive Democracy: Beyond Liberal Capitalism and the Administrative State', *Capitalism, Nature, Socialism*, 3: 18–42.

242   References

DRYZEK, JOHN S. (1995), *Democracy in Capitalist Times* (Oxford: Oxford University Press).

—— (1996), 'Political Inclusion and the Dynamics of Democratization', *American Political Science Review*, 90: 475–87.

—— (2000), *Deliberative Democracy and Beyond* (Oxford: Oxford University Press).

—— (2001), 'Legitimacy and Economy in Deliberative Democracy', *Political Theory*, 29: 651–69.

DUMMETT, MICHAEL (1985), *Voting Procedures* (Oxford: Clarendon Press).

—— (1997), *Principles of Electoral Reform* (Oxford: Clarendon Press).

DUNCAN, GREG J., GUSTAFSSON, BJÖRN, HAUSER, RICHARD, SCHMAUS, GÜNTHER, JENKINS, STEPHEN, MESSINGER, HANS, MUFFELS, RUUD, NOLAN, BRIAN, RAY, JEAN-CLAUDE, and VOGES, WOLFGANG (1995), 'Poverty and Social-Assistance Dynamics in the United States, Canada and Europe', in Katherine McFate, Roger Lawson and William Julius Wilson (eds.), *Poverty, Inequality and the Future of Social Policy* (New York: Russell Sage Foundation), 67–108.

DUNCAN, GREG J., with RICHARD D. COE, MARY E. CORCORAN, MARTHA S. HILL, SAUL D. HOFFMAN and JAMES N. MORGAN (1984), *Years of Poverty, Years of Plenty: The Changing Economic Fortunes of American Workers and Families* (Ann Arbor: Survey Research Center, Institute for Social Research, University of Michigan).

DWORKIN, RONALD (1985), 'Can a Liberal State Support Art?', in Dworkin, *A Matter of Principle* (Cambridge, Mass.: Harvard University Press), 221–33.

—— (2000), *The Sovereign Virtue* (Cambridge, Mass.: Harvard University Press).

EASTON, DAVID (1965), *A System Analysis of Political Life* (New York: Wiley).

ECKSTEIN, HARRY (1966), *Division and Cohesion in Democracy* (Princeton: Princeton University Press).

EDELMAN, MURRAY (1977), *Political Language* (New York: Academic Press).

—— (1995), *From Art to Politics: How Artistic Creations Shape Political Conceptions* (Chicago: University of Chicago Press).

EDGEWORTH, FRANCIS Y. (1925), 'The Pure Theory of Taxation', in Edgeworth, *Papers Relating to Political Economy* (London: Macmillan), ii. 100–16.

ELDER, NEIL, THOMAS, ALASTAIR H., and ARTER, DAVID (1982), *The Consensual Democracies: The Government and Politics of the Scandinavian States* (Oxford: Martin Robertson).

ELIOT, T. S. (1943), 'The Social Function of Poetry', in Eliot (ed.), *On Poetry and Poets* (London: Faber & Faber, 1958), 15–25.

ELSTER, JON (1976), 'A Note on Hysteresis in the Social Sciences', *Synthese*, 33: 371–91.

—— (1979), *Ulysses and the Sirens* (Cambridge: Cambridge University Press).

—— (1983), 'Belief, Bias and Ideology', in Elster, *Sour Grapes* (Cambridge: Cambridge University Press), 141–66.

—— (1986*a*), 'Introduction', in Elster (ed.), *Rational Choice* (Oxford: Blackwell), 1–33.

—— (1986*b*), 'The Market and the Forum: Three Varieties of Political Theory', in Elster and Hylland 1986: 103–32.

—— (1988), 'Consequences of Constitutional Choice: Reflections on Tocqueville', in Elster and Slagstad 1988: 81–101.

—— (1994), 'Argumenter et négocier dans deux Assemblées constituantes', *Revue Française de Science Politique*, 44/22: 187–256.

—— (ed.) (1998*a*), *Deliberative Democracy* (Cambridge: Cambridge University Press).

—— (1998*b*), 'Introduction', in Elster 1998*a*: 8–9.

—— and HYLLAND, AANUND (eds.) (1986), *Foundations of Social Choice Theory* (Cambridge: Cambridge University Press).

—— and SLAGSTAD, RUNE (eds.) (1988), *Constitutionalism and Democracy* (Cambridge: Cambridge University Press).

ELY, JOHN HART (1980), *Democracy and Distrust* (Cambridge, Mass.: Harvard University Press).

ERIKSON, ROBERT, and GOLDTHORPE, JOHN H. (1992), *The Constant Flux: A Study of Class Mobility in Industrial Societies* (Oxford: Clarendon Press).

ESTLUND, DAVID (1989*a*), 'Democratic Theory and the Public Interest: Condorcet and Rousseau Revisited', *American Political Science Review*, 83/4 (Dec.): 1317–22.

—— (1989*b*), 'The Persistent Puzzle of the Minority Democrat', *American Philosophical Quarterly*, 26: 143–51.

—— (1990), 'Democracy without Preference', *Philosophical Review*, 49: 397–424.

—— (1993), 'Making Truth Safe for Democracy', in David Copp, Jean Hampton and John E. Roemer (eds.), *The Idea of Democracy* (New York: Cambridge University Press), 71–100.

—— (1994), 'Opinion Leaders, Independence and Condorcet's Jury Theorem', *Theory and Decision*, 36/2: 131–62.

—— (1997), 'Beyond Fairness and Deliberation: The Epistemic Dimension of Democratic Authority', in James Bohman and Willian Rehg (eds.), *Deliberative Democracy* (Cambridge, Mass.: MIT Press), 173–204.

—— (1998), 'The Insularity of the Reasonable: Why Political Liberalism Must Admit the Truth', *Ethics*, 108 (Jan.): 252–75.

—— (2001), Deliberation Down and Dirty: Must Political Expression be Civil?', in Thomas R. Hensley (ed.), *The Boundaries of Freedom of Expression and Order in American Democracy* (Kent, Ohio: Kent State University Press), 49–79.

—— WALDRON, JEREMY, GROFMAN, BERNARD, and FELD, SCOTT (1989), 'Controversy: Democratic Theory and the Public Interest: Condorcet and Rousseau Revisited', *American Political Science Review*, 83/4 (Dec.): 1317–40.

ETZINOI, AMITAI (1993), *The Spirit of Community* (London: HarperCollins).

EVANS, MARTIN, PAUGAM, SERGE, and PRÉLIS, JOSEPH A. (1995), *Chunnel Vision: Poverty, Social Exclusion and the Debate on Social Welfare in France and Britain* (Discussion Paper WSP/115; London: Welfare State Programme, STICERD, London School of Economics).

FEDDERSEN, TIMOTHY, and PESENDORFER, WOLFGANG (1998), 'Convicting the Innocent: The Inferiority of Unanimous Jury Verdicts under Strategic Voting', *American Political Science Review*, 92: 23–36.

FEINBERG, JOEL (1974), 'The Rights of Animals and Unborn Generations', in William T. Blackstone (ed.), *Philosophy and Environmental Crisis* (Athens, Ga.: University of Georgia Press), 43–68.

——(1986), *Harm to Self*. Vol. iii of Feinberg, *The Moral Limits of the Criminal Law* (New York: Oxford University Press).

FIELD, MARILYN J., and GOLD, MARTHE R. (eds.) (1998), *Summarizing Population Health: Directions for the Development and Application of Population Metrics* (Report of the Committee on Summary Measures of Population Health, Division of Health Care Services, Institute of Medicine. Washington, DC: National Academy Press).

FINLAY, MOSES I. (1978), *The World of Odysseus*, 2nd edn. (New York: Viking).

FIORINA, MORRIS (1981), *Retrospective Voting in American National Elections* (New Haven, Conn.: Yale University Press).

FISHKIN, JAMES S. (1991), *Democracy and Deliberation: New Directions for Democratic Reform* (New Haven, Conn.: Yale University Press).

——(1995), *The Voice of the People: Public Opinion and Democracy* (New Haven, Conn.: Yale University Press).

——(2000), 'Citizen Juries (and Other Methods of Informed Citizen Consultation)', in *The International Encyclopedia of Elections*, ed. Richard Rose (Washington, DC: Congressional Quarterly Press), 38–9.

FOUCAULT, MICHEL (1975), *Discipline and Pubish: The Birth of the Prison*, tr. Alan Sheridan (Harmondsworth: Penguin, 1977).

FOX, J., and GUYER, M. (1977), 'Group Size and Others' Strategy in an N-Person Game', *Journal of Conflict Resolution*, 21: 323–39.

FRANKFURT, HARRY G. (1971), 'Freedom of the Will and the Concept of a Person', *Journal of Philosophy*, 68: 5–20.

FRANKLIN, MARK N., MACKIE, THOMAS T., VALEN, HENRY, *et al.* (1992), *Electoral Change: Responses to Evolving Social and Attitudinal Structures in Western Countries* (Cambridge: Cambridge University Press).

FRASER, NANCY (1994), 'After the Family Wage: Gender Equity and the Welfare State', *Political Theory*, 22: 591–618.

——(1995), 'From Redistribution to Recognition? Dilemmas of Justice in a "Post-Socialist" Age', *New Left Review*, 212: 68–93.

FRAZER, ELIZABETH, and LACEY, NICOLA (1993), *The Politics of Community: A Feminist Critique of the Liberal–Communitarian Debate* (Brighton: Harvester-Wheatsheaf).

FREY, BRUNO S., and BOHNET, IRIS (1996), 'Cooperation, Communication and Communitarianism: An Experimental Approach', *Journal of Political Philosophy*, 4: 323–37.

FRIEDMAN, MILTON (1962), *Capitalism and Freedom* (Chicago: University of Chicago Press).

FULLER, LON (1964), *The Morality of Law*, 2nd edn. (New Haven: Yale University Press).

FUNG, ARCHON (1995), 'Extended Condorcet and Experimentalist Models of Epistemic Democracy', Mimeo, Department of Political Science, MIT.

GALANTER, MARC (1984), *Competing Equalities: Law and the Backward Classes in India* (Delhi: Oxford University Press).

GAMBETTA, DIEGO (1994*a*), 'Godfather's Gossip', *Archives Européenes de Sociologie*, 35: 199–223.

—— (1994*b*), 'Inscrutable Markets', *Rationality and Society*, 6: 353–68.

GAMSON, WILLIAM A. (1995), 'Hiroshima, the Holocaust and the Politics of Exclusion: 1994 Presidential Address', *American Sociological Review*, 60: 1–20.

GARDINER, KAREN, and HILLS, JOHN (1999), 'Policy Implications of New Data on Income Mobility', *Economic Journal*, 109/1: F91–F111.

GASTIL, RAYMOND D. (1991), 'The Comparative Survey of Freedom: Experiences and Suggestions', in Alex Inkeles (ed.), *On Measuring Democracy: Its Consequences and Concomitants* (New Brunswick, NJ: Transaction Books), 21–46.

GAUS, GERALD (1997), 'Does Democracy Reveal the Voice of the People? Four Takes on Rousseau', *Australasian Journal of Philosophy*, 75/2 (June): 141–62.

GAVENTA, JOHN (1980), *Power and Powerlessness: Quiescence and Rebellion in an Appalachian Valley* (Urbana, Ill.: University of Illinois Press).

GEERTZ, CLIFFORD (1973*a*), *The Interpretation of Cultures* (New York: Basic).

—— (1973*b*), 'The Politics of Meaning', in Geertz 1973*a*: 311–26.

GEHRLEIN, WILLIAM (1983), 'Condorcet's Paradox', *Theory and Decision*, 15: 161–97.

GELMAN, ANDREW, and KING, GARY (1993), 'Why are American Presidential Election Campaign Polls So Variable When Votes are So Predictable?', *British Journal of Political Science*, 23: 409–52.

GERARDI, DINO (2000), 'Jury Verdicts and Preference Diversity', *American Political Science Review*, 94/2 (June): 395–406.

GERBASI, K. C., ZUCKERMAN, M., and REIS, H. T. (1977), 'Justice Needs a New Blindfold: A Review of Mock Jury Research', *Psychological Bulletin*, 84: 323–45.

GERBER, ELISABETH R., and JACKSON, JOHN E. (1993), 'Endogenous Preferences and the Study of Institutions', *American Political Science Review*, 87: 639–56.

GIBSON, DIANE, and GOODIN, ROBERT E. (1999), 'The Veil of Vagueness', in Morten Egeberg and Per Lægreid (eds.), *Organizing Political Institutions: Essays for Johan P. Olsen* (Oslo: Scandinavian University Press), 357–85.

GILBERT, MARGARET (1989), *On Social Facts* (London: Routledge).

GILLIGAN, CAROL (1982), *In a Different Voice: Psychological Theory and Women's Development* (Cambridge, Mass.: Harvard University Press).

GINTIS, HERBERT (1972), 'A Radical Analysis of Welfare Economics and Individual Development', *Quarterly Journal of Economics*, 68: 572–99.

GLAZER, NATHAN, and MOYNIHAN, DANIEL P. (1963), *Beyond the Melting Pot* (Cambridge, Mass.: MIT Press).

—— and —— (eds.) (1975), *Ethnicity* (Cambridge, Mass.: Harvard University Press).

—— and YOUNG, KEN (eds.) (1983), *Ethnic Pluralism and Public Policy* (Lexington, Mass.: D. C. Heath).

GOFFMAN, ERVING (1961), *Asylums* (New York: Doubleday).

GOLDMAN, ALVIN I. (1994), 'Argumentation and Social Epistemology', *Journal of Philosophy*, 91: 27–49.

GOLDTHORPE, JOHN H. (1980), *Social Mobility and Class Structure in Modern Britain* (Oxford: Clarendon Press).

GOODIN, ROBERT E. (1976a), *The Politics of Rational Man* (London: Wiley).

—— (1976b), 'Possessive Individualism Again', *Political Studies*, 24: 488–501.

—— (1980), *Manipulatory Politics* (New Haven, Conn.: Yale University Press).

—— (1982a), 'Banana Time in British Politics', *Political Studies*, 30: 42–58.

—— (1982b), *Political Theory and Public Policy* (Chicago: University of Chicago Press).

—— (1983), 'Voting through the Looking Glass', *American Political Science Review*, 77: 420–34.

—— (1985), *Protecting the Vulnerable* (Chicago: University of Chicago Press).

—— (1986), 'Laundering Preferences', in Elster and Hylland 1986: 75–101.

—— (1988), 'What is So Special about Our Fellow Countrymen?', *Ethics*, 98: 663–86.

—— (1989a), 'Do Motives Matter?', *Canadian Journal of Philosophy*, 19: 405–20.

—— (1989b), *No Smoking: The Ethical Issues* (Chicago: University of Chicago Press).

—— (1990a), 'Liberalism and the Best Judge Principle', *Political Studies*, 38: 181–95.

—— (1990b), 'Stabilizing Expectations: The Role of Earnings-Related Benefits in Social Welfare Policy', *Ethics*, 100: 530–53.

—— (1991), 'Permissible Paternalism: In Defence of the Nanny State', *The Responsive Community*, 1: 42–51.

—— (1992*a*), *Green Political Theory* (Oxford: Polity).

—— (1992*b*), 'If People were Money ...', in Brian Barry and Robert E. Goodin (eds.), *Free Movement* (Hemel Hempstead: Harvester Wheatsheaf), 6–22.

—— (1992*c*), *Motivating Political Morality* (Oxford: Blackwell).

—— (1993), 'Democracy, Preferences and Paternalism', *Policy Sciences*, 26: 229–47. Revised as Ch. 3 in this volume.

—— (1995*a*), 'Political Ideals and Political Practice', *British Journal of Political Science*, 25: 37–56.

—— (1995*b*), *Utilitarianism as a Public Philosophy* (Cambridge: Cambridge University Press).

—— (1996*a*), 'Enfranchising the Earth, and its Alternatives', *Political Studies*, 44: 835–49. Revised as Ch. 11 in this volume.

—— (1996*b*), 'Designing Constitutions: The Political Constitution of a Mixed Commonwealth', *Political Studies*, 44: 635–46.

—— (1996*c*), 'Institutionalizing the Public Interest: The Defense of Deadlock and Beyond', *American Political Science Review*, 90: 331–43.

—— (1996*d*), 'Inclusion and Exclusion', *Archives Européenes de Sociologie*, 37: 343–71. Revised as Ch. 10 in this volume.

—— (1996*e*), 'Structures of Political Order: The Relational Feminist Alternative', in *Nomos XXXVIII: Political Order*, ed. Russell Hardin and Ian Shapiro (New York: New York University Press), 498–521.

—— (1997), 'Conventions and Conversions: Or, Why is Nationalism Sometimes So Nasty?', in Jeff McMahan and Robert McKim (eds.), *The Ethics of Nationalism* (New York: Oxford University Press), 88–104.

—— (1999*b*), 'The Sustainability Ethic: Political, Not (Just) Moral', *Journal of Applied Philosophy*, 16: 267–74.

—— (1999*c*), 'Treating Likes Alike, Intergenerationally and Internationally', *Policy Sciences*, 32: 189–206.

—— (2000*a*), 'Accountability: Elections as One Form', in *The International Encyclopedia of Elections*, ed. Richard Rose (Washington, DC: Congressional Quarterly Press), 2–4.

—— (2000*b*), 'Preference Failures', paper presented to 'Fairness and Goodness' workshop, World Health Organization, Trivandrum, Kerala, India, Mar. 2000.

—— (2000*c*), 'Trusting Individuals vs Trusting Institutions: Generalizing the Case of Contract', *Rationality and Society*, 12: 381–95.

—— (2001), 'Consensus Interruptus', *Journal of Ethics*, 5: 121–31.

—— (2002), 'The Paradox of Persisting Opposition', *Politics, Philosophy and Economics*, 1: 109–46. Revised as Chs. 6–7 in this volume.

—— and BRENNAN, GEOFFREY (2001), 'Bargaining over Beliefs', *Ethics*, 111: 256–77. Revised as Ch. 4 in this volume.

GOODIN, ROBERT E. and DRYZEK, JOHN (1980), 'Rational Participation: The Politics of Relative Power', *British Journal of Political Science*, 10: 273–92.

—— and GIBSON, DIANE (1997), 'Rights, Young and Old', *Oxford Journal of Legal Studies*, 17: 185–203.

—— HEADEY, BRUCE, MUFFELS, RUUD, and DIRVEN, HENK-JAN (1999), *The Real Worlds of Welfare Capitalism* (Cambridge: Cambridge University Press).

—— PATEMAN, CAROL, and PATEMAN, ROY (1997), 'Simian Sovereignty', *Political Theory*, 25: 821–49.

—— and ROBERTS, K. W. S. (1975), 'The Ethical Voter', *American Political Science Review*, 69: 926–8.

GRANGER, GILES-GASTON (1968), 'Condorcet', in *International Encyclopedia of the Social Sciences*, ed. David L. Sills (London: Collier-Macmillan), iii. 213–15.

GRANOVETTER, MARK (1985), 'Economic Action and Social Structure: The Problem of Embeddedness', *American Journal of Sociology*, 91: 481–510.

GREENBERG, EDWARD S. (1986), *Workplace Democracy* (Ithaca, NY: Cornell University Press).

GRICE, H. PAUL (1975), 'Logic and Conversation', in Donald Davidson and Gilbert Harman (eds.), *The Logic of Grammar* (Encino, Calif: Dickenson), 64–75.

—— (1989), *Studies in the Way of Words* (Cambridge, Mass.: Harvard University Press).

GROFMAN, BERNARD (1993), 'Public Choice, Civic Republicanism and American Politics: Perspectives of a "Reasonable Choice" Modeler', *Texas Law Review*, 71: 1541–87.

—— and FELD, SCOTT L. (1988), 'Rousseau's General Will: A Condorcetian Perspective', *American Political Science Review*, 82/2 (June): 567–76.

—— and OWEN, GUILLERMO (eds.) (1986), *Information Pooling and Group Decision Making* (Westport, Conn.: JAI Press).

—— OWEN, GUILLERMO, and FELD, SCOTT L. (1983), 'Thirteen Theorems in Search of the Truth', *Theory and Decision*, 15: 261–78.

GUARNASCHELLI, SERENA, MCKELVEY, RICHARD D., and PALFREY, THOMAS R. (2000), 'An Experimental Study of Jury Decision Rules', *American Political Science Review*, 94/2 (June): 407–24.

GUSTAFSSON, GUNNEL, and RICHARDSON, JEREMY (1980), 'Post-Industrial Changes in Policy Style', *Scandinavian Political Studies*, NS 3: 21–37.

GUTMANN, AMY (1985), 'Communitarian Critics of Liberalism', *Philosophy and Public Affairs*, 14: 308–22.

—— (1987), *Democratic Education* (Princeton: Princeton University Press).

—— and THOMPSON, DENNIS (1996), *Democracy and Disagreement* (Cambridge, Mass.: Harvard University Press).

HABERMAS, JÜRGEN (1962), *The Structural Transformation of the Public Sphere*, tr. Thomas Burger and Frederick Lawrence (Oxford: Polity, 1989).

—— (1964), 'The Public Sphere', S. and F. Lennox, *New German Critique*, 3: 49–55.

—— (1973), *Legitimation Crisis*, tr. Thomas McCarthy (London: Heinemann).

—— (1992), *Between Facts and Norms*, tr. William Rehg (Oxford: Polity, 1996).

—— (1993), 'Struggles for Recognition in Constitutional States', *European Journal of Philosophy*, 1: 128–55.

—— (1995), 'Reconciliation through the Public Use of Reason: Remarks on John Rawls's *Political Liberalism*', *Journal of Philosophy*, 92: 109–31.

HADLEY, ROGER, and HATCH, STEPHEN (1981), *Social Welfare and the Failure of the State* (London: Allen & Unwin).

HALE, SIR MATTHEW (1716), *The History of the Common Law of England*, ed. Charles M. Gray (Chicago: University of Chicago Press, 1971).

HAMILTON, ALEXANDER, MADISON, JAMES, and JAY, JOHN (1787–8), *The Federalist*, ed. Jacob E. Cooke (Middletown, Conn.: Wesleyan University Press, 1961).

HAMPSHIRE, STUART (2000), *Justice is Conflict* (Princeton: Princeton University Press).

HARDIN, RUSSELL (1982), 'Exchange Theory on Strategic Bases', *Social Science Information*, 21: 251–72.

—— (1983), 'Unilateral versus Mutual Disarmament,' *Philosophy and Public Affairs*, 12: 236–54.

—— (1993), 'The Street-Level Epistemology of Trust', *Politics and Society*, 21: 505–29.

—— (1995), *One for All* (Princeton: Princeton University Press).

—— (1999), *Liberalism, Constitutionalism and Democracy* (New York: Oxford University Press).

HARDING, SANDRA, and HINTIKKA, MERILL B. (1983), 'Introduction', in Harding and Hintikka (eds.), *Discovering Reality* (Dordrecht: D. Reidel), pp. ix–xix.

HARRINGTON, MICHAEL (1962), *The Other America: Poverty in the United States* (New York: Macmillan).

HARSANYI, JOHN C. (1965), 'Bargaining and Conflict Situations in the Light of a New Approach to Game Theory,' *American Economic Review (Papers and Proceedings)*, 55 (May): 447–57.

—— (1966), 'A General Theory of Rational Behavior in Game Situations', *Econometrica*, 34: 613–34.

—— (1967–8), 'Games of Incomplete Information Played by Bayesian Players', *Management Science*, 14: 159–82, 320–34, 486–502.

HARTMANN, HEIDI (1981), 'The Unhappy Marriage of Marxism and Feminism', in Lydia Sargent (ed.), *Women and Revolution: A Discussion of the Unhappy Marriage of Marxism and Feminism* (Boston: South End Press), 1–41.

HASTIE, R., PENROD, S. D., and PENNINGTON, N. (1983), *Inside the Jury* (Cambridge, Mass.: Harvard University Press).

HAUSNER, JERZY, JESSOP, BOB, and NIELSEN, KLAUS (ed.) (1995), *Strategic Choice and Path-Dependency in Post-Socialism* (Aldershot: Elgar).

HAWTHORNE, JAMES (2001), 'Voting in Search of the Public Good: The Probabilistic Logic of Majority Judgements', Mimeo., Department of Political Science, University of Oklahoma.

HAZLITT, WILLIAM (1869), 'On Coffee-House Politicians', in Hazlitt, *Table Talk, or Original Essays* (New York: Chelsea House, 1983), 261–83.

HEAL, JANE (1998), 'Understanding Other Minds from the Inside', in O'Hear 1998: 83–100.

HELD, VIRGINIA (1987), 'Non-Contractual Society', in M. Hanen and K. Nielsen (eds.), *Science, Morality and Feminist Theory* (Calgary: University of Calgary Press), 111–38.

—— (1989), 'Birth and Death', *Ethics*, 99: 362–88.

HIBBS, DOUGLAS (1987), *The American Political Economy* (Cambridge, Mass.: Harvard University Press).

HICKS, JOHN R. (1941), 'The Rehabilitation of Consumers' Surplus', *Review of Economics Studies*, 8: 108–16.

HIRST, PAUL (1994), *Associative Democracy* (Oxford: Polity).

HOBBES, THOMAS (1651), *Leviathan* (London: Andrew Crooke).

HOCHSCHILD, JENNIFER L. (1984), *The New American Dilemma: Liberal Democracy and School Desegregation* (New Haven, Conn.: Yale University Press).

HOFFMAN, STANLEY (1981), *Duties Beyond Borders* (Syracuse, NY: Syracuse University Press).

HOLLIS, MARTIN (1977), *Models of Man: Philosophical Thoughts on Social Action* (Cambridge: Cambridge University Press).

—— (1981), 'Economic Man and Original Sin', *Political Studies*, 29: 167–80.

HONNETH, AXEL (1992), 'Integrity and Disrespect: Principles of a Conception of Morality Based on the Theory of Recognition', *Political Theory*, 20: 187–201.

HUME, DAVID (1739), *A Treatise of Human Nature* (London: John Noon).

—— (1777a), *An Enquiry Concerning the Principles of Morals* (London: Cadell).

—— (1777b), 'Of Miracles', in Hume (1777a): sec. 10.

HUNTER, FLOYD (1953), *Community Power Structures* (Chapel Hill, NC: University of North Carolina Press).

HUNTINGTON, SAMUEL P. (1997), *The Clash of Civilizations and the Remaking of World Order* (London: Simon & Schuster).

HYLLUND, AANUND, and ZECKHAUSER, RICHARD (1979), 'The Impossibility of Bayesian Group Decisions with Separate Aggregation of Beliefs and Values,' *Econometrica*, 47: 1321–36.

IONESCU, GHITA, and MADARIAGA, ISABEL DE (1968), *Opposition* (London: Watts).

JACKSON, FRANK, and PETTIT, PHILIP (1990), 'In Defense of Folk Psychology', *Philosophical Studies*, 57: 7–30.

JANIS, IRVING L. (1982), *Groupthink*, 2nd edn. (Boston: Houghton Mifflin).

JEFFERSON, THOMAS (1766–1812), *Parliamentary Pocket-Book*. Reprinted in *Jefferson's Parliamentary Writings*, ed. Wilbur Samuel Howell, 2nd ser. (Princeton: Princeton University Press, 1988), 47–162.

JENCKS, CHRISTOPHER (1994), *The Homeless* (Cambridge, Mass.: Harvard University Press).

—— SMITH, MARSHALL, ACKLAND, HENRY, BANE, MARY JO, COHEN, DAVID, GINTIS, HERBERT, HEYNS, BARBARA, and MICHELSON, STEPHAN (1972), *Inequality* (New York: Basic).

JOHNSON, NORMAN (1987), *The Welfare State in Transition: The Theory and Practice of Welfare Pluralism* (Brighton: Wheatsheaf).

JORDAN, BILL (1996), *A Theory of Poverty and Social Exclusion* (Oxford: Polity).

KAGAN, R. A. (1978), *Regulatory Justice: Implementing a Wage-Price Freeze* (New York: Russell Sage Foundation).

KAHNEMAN, DANIEL, SLOVICK, PAUL, and TVERSKY, AMOS (eds.) (1982), *Judgment under Uncertainty: Heuristics and Biases* (Cambridge: Cambridge University Press).

KALVEN, HARRY, Jr., and ZEISEL, HANS (1966), *The American Jury* (Chicago: University of Chicago Press).

KANT, IMMANUEL (1784), 'What is Enlightenment?', in *The Philosophy of Kant*, tr. and ed. Carl J. Friedrich (New York: Random House, 1949), 132–9.

KANTER, ROSABETH MOSS (1972), *Commitment and Community: Communes and Utopias in Sociological Perspective* (Cambridge, Mass.: Harvard University Press).

KETTL, DONALD F. (2000), *The Global Public Management Revolution: A Report on the Transformation of Governance* (Washington, DC: Brookings Institution).

KEY, V. O., Jr, and CROUCH, WINSTON W. (1939), *The Initiative and the Referrenda in California* (Berkeley: University of California Press).

KIEWIET, D. RODERICK (1983), *Micropolitics and Macroeconomics* (Chicago: University of Chicago Press).

KING, DESMOND S. (1995), *Separate and Unequal* (Oxford: Clarendon Press).

—— and WALDRON, JEREMY (1988), 'Citizenship, Social Citizenship and the Defence of Welfare Provision', *British Journal of Political Science*, 18/4: 415–43; reprinted in Waldron 1993: 271–308.

KIRCHHEIMER, OTTO (1969), 'Changes in the Structure of Political Compromise', in F. S. Burin and K. L. Shell (eds.), *Politics, Change* (New York: Columbia University Press), 131–59.

KLAUSEN, JYTTE (1995), 'Social Rights Advocacy and State Building: T. H. Marshall in the Hands of Social Reformers', *World Politics*, 47: 244–67.

KLEINIG, JOHN (1983), *Paternalism* (Totowa, NJ: Rowman & Allanheld).

KOSTAKOPOULAU, THEODORA (1996), 'Towards a Theory of Constructive Citizenship in Europe', *Journal of Political Philosophy*, 4: 338–59.

——(2001), *Citizenship, Identity and Immigration in the European Union* (Manchester: Manchester University Press).

KRAUSS, ROBERT M., and FUSSELL, SUSAN R. (1996), in 'Social Psychological Models of Interpersonal Communications', in E. Tory Higgins and Arie W. Kruglanski (eds.), *Social Psychology: Handbook of Basic Principles* (New York: Guilford Press), 655–701.

KREPS, DAVID M. (1990), 'Corporate Culture and Economic Theory', in J. Alt and K. Shepsle (eds.), *Perspectives on Positive Political Economy* (Cambridge, Cambridge University Press), 90–143.

——and WILSON, ROBERT (1982), 'Reputation and Imperfect Information', *Journal of Economic Theory*, 27: 253–79.

KUFLIK, ARTHUR (1977), 'Majority Rule Procedure', in *Nomos XVIII: Due Process*, ed. J. Roland Pennock and John W. Chapman (New York: New York University Press), 296–322.

KURAN, TIMUR (1998), 'Insincere Deliberation and Democratic Failure', *Critical Review*, 12: 529–44.

KVAVIK, ROBERT (1976), *Interest Groups in Norwegian Politics* (Oslo: Universiteitsforlaget).

KYMLICKA, WILL (1989), *Liberalism, Community and Culture* (Oxford: Clarendon Press).

——(1990), 'Communitarianism', in Kymlicka, *Contemporary Political Philosophy* (Oxford: Clarendon Press), 199–237.

——(1995), *Multicultural Citizenship* (Oxford: Clarendon Press).

——and NORMAN, WAYNE (1994), 'Review Article: Return of the Citizen', *Ethics*, 104: 352–81.

LACEY, NICOLA (1998), *Unspeakable Subjects: Feminist Essays in Legal and Social Theory* (Oxford: Hart).

LAHDA, KRISHNA K. (1992), 'The Condorcet Jury Theorem, Free Speech and Correlated Votes', *American Journal of Political Science*, 36/3 (Aug.): 617–34.

LAMPMAN, ROBERT J. (1974), 'What Does it Do for the Poor? A New Test for National Policy', *Public Interest*, 34: 66–82.

LASLETT, PETER (1956), 'The Face to Face Society', in *Philosophy, Politics & Society*, 1st ser., ed. P. Laslett (Oxford: Blackwell), 157–84.

——and FISHKIN, JAMES S. (eds.) (1992), *Justice between Generations: Philosophy, Politics and Society*, 6th ser. (New Haven: Yale University Press).

LASSWELL, HAROLD D. (1950), *Politics: Who Gets What, When, How?* (New York: P. Smith).

LEBLEBICI, HUSEYIN, and SALANICK, GERALD R. (1982), 'Stability in Interorganizational Exchanges: Rulemaking Processes of the Chicago Board of Trade', *Administrative Sciences Quarterly*, 27: 227–42.

LEHRER, KEITH (1976*a*), 'Rationality in Science and Society: A Consensual Theory', in Gilbert Ryle (ed.), *Contemporary Aspects of Philosophy* (London: Orel Press), 14–30.

—— (1976*b*), 'When Rational Disagreement is Impossible', *Nous*, 10: 327–32.

—— (2001*a*), 'Individualism versus Communitarianism: A Consensual Compromise', *Journal of Ethics*, 5: 105–20.

—— (2001*b*), 'The Rationality of Dissensus: A Reply to Goodin', *Journal of Ethics*, 5: 132–6.

—— and WAGNER, CARL (1981), *Rational Consensus in Science and Society: A Philosophical and Mathematical Study* (Dordrecht: D. Reidel).

LEVIN, JONATHAN, and NALEBUFF, BARRY (1995), 'An Introduction to Vote-Counting Schemes', *Journal of Economic Perspectives*, 9/1 (Winter): 3–26.

LEWIN, LEIF (1998), 'Majoritarianism and Consensus Democracy: The Swedish Experience', *Scandinavian Political Studies*, NS 2: 195–206.

LEWIS, DAVID (1969), *Convention* (Oxford: Blackwell).

—— (1979), 'Scorekeeping in a Language Game', *Journal of Philosophical Logic*, 8: 339–59.

LIJPHART, AREND (1975), *The Politics of Accommodation: Pluralism and Democracy in the Netherlands*, 2nd edn. (Berkeley, Calif.: University of California Press).

—— (1977), *Democracy in Plural Societies* (New Haven, Conn.: Yale University Press).

—— (1998), 'Consensus and Consensus Democracy: Cultural, Structural, Functional and Rational Choice Explanations', *Scandinavian Political Studies*, NS 2: 99–108.

—— (1999), *Patterns of Democracy* (New Haven, Conn.: Yale University Press).

LINDBLOM, CHARLES E. (1965), *The Intelligence of Democracy* (New York: Free Press).

—— (1977), *Politics and Markets* (New York: Basic).

LINDSAY, A. D. (1929), *The Essentials of Democracy*, 2nd edn. (London: Oxford University Press, 1935).

LIPPMANN, WALTER (1955), *The Public Philosophy* (New York: New American Library).

LIPSET, SEYMOUR MARTIN (1963), *The First New Nation: The United States in Historical and Comparative Perspective* (New York: Basic).

—— and ROKKAN, STEIN (eds.) (1967), *Party Systems and Voter Alignments* (New York: Free Press).

LIST, CHRISTIAN, and GOODIN, ROBERT E. (2001), 'Epistemic Democracy: Generalizing the Condorcet Jury Theorem', *Journal of Political Philosophy*, 9: 277–306. Revised as Ch. 5 in this volume.

LITTLE, I. M. D. (1952), 'Social Choice and Individual Values', *Journal of Political Economy*, 60: 422–32.

LLOYD, GENEVIEVE (1993), *The Man of Reason: 'Male' and 'Female' in Western Philosophy* (London: Routledge).

LOCKE, JOHN (1690), *Second Treatise of Government*, ed. Peter Laslett (Cambridge: Cambridge University Press, 1960).

LOCKWOOD, DAVID (1974), 'For T. H. Marshall', *Sociology*, 8: 363–7.

LOWENSTEIN, KARL (1938), 'Legislative Control of Political Extremism in European Democracies', *Columbia Law Review*, 38: 591–622, 725–74.

LOWI, THEODORE J. (1969), *The End of Liberalism* (New York: Norton).

LUCE, R. DUNCAN, and RAIFFA, HOWARD (1957), *Games and Decisions* (New York: Wiley).

LUKES, STEVEN (1974), *Power: A Radical View* (London: Macmillan).

LUPIA, ARTHUR (1994), 'Shortcuts versus Encyclopedias: Information and Voting Behavior in California Insurance Reform Elections', *American Political Science Review*, 88: 63–76.

——and MCCUBBINS, MATTHEW D. (1998), *The Democratic Dilemma: Can Citizens Learn What They Need to Know?* (Cambridge: Cambridge University Press).

LÆGREID, PER, and RONESS, PAUL G. (1996), 'Political Parties, Bureaucracies and Corporatism', in Kaare Strom and Lars Svasand (eds.),*Challenges to Political Parties: The Case of Norway* (Ann Arbor: University of Michigan Press), 167–80.

MACAULAY, STEWART (1963), 'Non-Contractual Relations in Business', *American Sociological Review*, 28: 55–67.

MACCALLUM, GERALD C., Jr (1966), 'Legislative Intent', *Yale Law Journal*, 75: 754–87.

MACINTYRE, ALISDAIR (1967), 'Egoism and Altruism', in *Encyclopedia of Philosophy*, ed. Paul Edwards (New York: Macmillan), ii. 462–6.

——(1981), *After Virtue* (Notre Dame, Ind.: University of Notre Dame Press).

——(1988), *Whose Justice? Which Rationality?* (Notre Dame, Ind.: University of Notre Dame Press).

MCLEAN, IAIN (1989), *Democracy and New Technology* (Oxford: Polity).

——and HEWITT, FIONA (tr. and ed.) (1994), *Condorcet: Foundations of Social Choice and Political Theory* (Aldershot: Elgar).

——and URKEN, ARNOLD B. (tr. and ed.) (1995), *Classics of Social Choice* (Ann Arbor: University of Michigan Press).

MACPHERSON, C. B. (1962), *The Political Theory of Possessive Individualism* (Oxford: Clarendon Press).

——(1973), *Democratic Theory* (Oxford: Clarendon Press).

——(1977), *The Life and Times of Liberal Democracy* (Oxford: Oxford University Press).

MADISON, JAMES (1788*a*), *Federalist*, 14, in Hamilton *et al.* 1787–8: 83–9.

——(or perhaps Alexander Hamilton) (1788*b*), *Federalist*, 55, in Hamilton *et al.*, 1787–8: 372–8.

——(1788*c*), *Federalist*, 62, in Hamilton *et al.* 1787–8: 415–22.

——(1788*d*), *Federalist*, 63, in Hamilton *et al.* 1787–8: 422–31.

—— (1840), *Notes of Debates in the Federal Convention of 1787* (New York: Norton, 1966).

MAJONE, GIANDOMENICO (1994), 'The Rise of the Regulatory State in Europe', *West European Politics*, 17: 77–101.

MALPAS, J. E. (1999), *Place and Experience* (Cambridge: Cambridge University Press).

MANIN, BERNARD (1987), 'On Legitimacy and Political Deliberation', *Political Theory* 15: 338–68.

—— (1997), *Principles of Representative Government* (Cambridge: Cambridge University Press).

—— PRZEWORSKI, ADAM, and STOKES, SUSAN C. (1999), 'Introduction', in Przeworski, Stokes, and Manin (eds.), *Democracy, Accountability and Representation* (Cambridge: Cambridge University Press), 1–26.

MANN, MICHAEL (1985), *Socialism Can Survive: Social Change and the Labour Party* (Fabian Tract, 502; London: Fabian Society).

MANSBRIDGE, JANE J. (1980), *Beyond Adversary Democracy* (New York: Basic).

—— (ed.) (1990), *Beyond Self-interest* (Chicago: University of Chicago Press).

MARCH, JAMES G. (1972), 'Model Bias in Social Action', *Review of Educational Research*, 42: 413–29.

—— (1976), 'The Technology of Foolishness', in March and Johan P. Olsen, *Ambiguity and Choice in Organizations* (Bergen: Universitetsforlaget), 69–81.

—— and OLSEN, JOHAN P. (1989), *Rediscovering Institutions* (New York: Free Press).

—— and —— (1995), *Democratic Governance* (New York: Free Press).

MARCUS, GEORGE E., and HANSON, RUSSELL L. (eds.) (1993), *Reconsidering the Democratic Public* (University Park, Pa.: Pennsylvania State University Press).

MARSHALL, T. H. (1949), 'Citizenship and Social Class', in Marshall, *Class, Citizenship and Social Development* (Chicago: University of Chicago Press, 1963), 70–134.

MARTIN, REX (1993), *A System of Rights* (Oxford: Clarendon Press).

MARX, KARL (1844), 'Economic and Philosophic Manuscripts', in Tucker 1972: 52–104.

—— (1871), 'The Civil War in France', in Tucker 1972: 526–76.

MASSEY, DOUGLAS S., and DENTON, NANCY A. (1993), *American Apartheid: Segregation and the Making of the Underclass* (Cambridge, Mass.: Harvard University Press).

MASON, SIR ANTHONY et al. (1992), 'ACT TV Ltd v Commonwealth'. *Commonwealth Law Reports*, 177: 106.

MAY, JOHN D. (1978), 'Defining Democracy: A Bid for Coherence and Consensus', *Political Studies*, 26: 1–14.

MAY, KENNETH O. (1952), 'A Set of Independent, Necessary and Sufficient Conditions for Simple Majority Decision', *Econometrica*, 20: 680–4.

MEEHAN, ELIZABETH (1993), *Citizenship and the European Community* (London: Sage).

MEIJER, HANS (1969), 'Bureaucracy and Policy Formulation Sweden', *Scandinavian Political Studies*, 4: 102–16.

MERRILL, SAMUEL, III (1984), 'A Comparison of Efficiency of Multicandidate Electoral Systems', *American Journal of Political Science*, 28/1 (Feb.): 23–48.

MERTON, ROBERT K. (1973), *The Sociology of Science*, ed. N. W. Storer (Chicago: University of Chicago Press).

——and KITT, ALICE S. (1950), 'Contributions to the Theory of Reference Group Behavior', in Robert K. Merton and Paul F. Lazarsfeld (eds.), *Continuities in Social Research* (Glencoe, Ill.: Free Press), 40–105.

MICHELMAN, FRANK (1986), 'Traces of Self-Government', *Harvard Law Review*, 100: 4–77.

MIDGAARD, KNUT, STENSTADVOLD, HALVOR, and UNDERDAL, ARILD (1973), 'An Approach to Political Interlocutions', *Scandinavian Political Studies*, 8: 9–36.

MILBRATH, L. W. (1960), 'Lobbying as a Communication Process', *Public Opinion Quarterly*, 24: 33–53.

MILL, JAMES (1823), 'Essay on Government'. Reprinted in *James Mill: Political Writings*, ed. Terence Ball (Cambridge: Cambridge University Press, 1992).

MILL, JOHN STUART (1843), *A System of Logic* (London: Longmans, Green).

——(1859), *On Liberty*, in Wollheim 1975: 5–141.

——(1861), *Considerations on Representative Government*, in Wollheim 1975: 142–423.

MILLER, DAVID (1992), 'Deliberative Democracy and Social Choice', *Political Studies*, 40/5 (Special Issue): 54–67. Reprinted in David Held (ed.), *Prospects for Democracy* (Oxford: Blackwell), 54–67.

——(1995), 'Citizenship and Pluralism', *Political Studies*, 43: 432–50.

MILLER, NICHOLAS R. (1986), 'Information, Electorates and Democracy: Some Extensions and Interpretations of the Condorcet Jury Theorem', in Bernard Grofman and Guillermo Owen (eds.), *Information Pooling and Group Decision Making*, (Greenwich, Conn.: JAI Press), 175–94.

MILLS, C. WRIGHT (1940), 'Situated Actions and Vocabularies of Motive', *American Sociological Review*, 5: 904–13.

MINNOW, MARTHA (1990), *Making All the Difference: Inclusion, Exclusion and American Law* (Ithaca, NY: Cornell University Press).

MONTAIGNE, MICHEL DE (1580), 'On the Art of Conversation', in *The Essays of Michel de Montaigne*, tr. and ed. M. A. Screech (Harmondsworth: Allen Lane/Penguin, 1991), book 3, essay 8, pp. 1044–69.

MOORE, BARRINGTON, Jr. (1967), *Social Origins of Dictatorship and Democracy* (London: Allen Lane).

——(1970), *Reflections on the Causes of Human Misery* (Boston: Beacon Press).

MORGENSTERN, OSKAR (1950), *On the Accuracy of Economic Observation* (Princeton: Princeton University Press).

MORRISS, PETER (1987), *Power: A Philosophical Analysis* (Manchester: Manchester University Press).

MUELLER, DENNIS C. (1989), *Public Choice II* (Cambridge: Cambridge University Press).

MULGAN, TIM (1999), 'The Place of the Dead in Liberal Political Philosophy', *Journal of Political Philosophy*, 7: 52–70.

MULHALL, STEPHEN, and SWIFT, ADAM (1996), *Liberals and Communitarians*, 2nd edn. (Oxford: Blackwell).

MURRAY, CHRISTOPHER J. (1996), 'Rethinking DALYs', in Murray and Alan D. Lopez. (eds.), *The Global Burden of Disease: A Comprehensive Assessment of Mortality and Disability from Diseases, Injuries and Risk Factors in 1990 and Projected to 2020* (Cambridge, Mass.: Harvard School of Public Health, for World Health Organization and World Bank), 1–98.

MYERS, D. G., and LAMM, H. (1976), 'The Group as a Polarizer of Attitudes', *Psychological Bulletin*, 83: 602–27.

MYRDAL, GUNNAR (1944), *The American Dilemma* (New York: Harper & Row).

NAESS, ARNE, CHRISTOPHERSEN, JENS A., and KVALØ, KJELL (1956), *Democracy, Ideology and Objectivity: Studies in the Semantics and Cognitive Analysis of Ideological Controversy* (Oxford: Blackwell).

NAGEL, THOMAS (1970), *The Possibility of Altruism* (Oxford: Clarendon Press).

——(1986), *The View from Nowhere* (New York: Oxford University Press).

NETZER, DICK (1978), *The Subsidized Muse: Public Support for the Arts in the United States* (Cambridge: Cambridge University Press).

NICHOLSON, LINDA (ed.) (1990), *Feminism/Postmodernism* (New York: Routledge).

——(1996), 'Identity and the Politics of Recognition', *Constellations*, 3: 1–16.

NISBET, ROBERT A. (1966), *The Sociological Tradition* (New York: Basic).

NORDHAUS, WILLIAM D. (1975), 'The Political Business Cycle', *Review of Economic Studies*, 42: 169–90.

NORTH, DOUGLASS C. (1990), *Institutions, Institutional Change and Economic Performance* (Cambridge: Cambridge University Press).

NOZICK, ROBERT (1974), *Anarchy, State and Utopia* (Oxford: Blackwell).

NUSSBAUM, MARTHA (1990), *Love's Knowledge: Essays on Philosophy and Literature* (New York: Oxford University Press).

——(1995), *Poetic Justice: The Literary Imagination and Public Life* (Boston: Beacon Press).

——(1997), *Cultivating Humanity* (Cambridge, Mass : Harvard University Press).

O'HEAR, ANTHONY (ed.) (1998), *Current Issues in the Philosophy of Mind* (Cambridge: Cambridge University Press, for the Royal Institute of Philosophy).

OLSEN, JOHAN P. (1972), 'Voting, "Sounding Out" and the Governance of Modern Organisations', *Acta Sociologica*, 15: 267–83.

——(1983), *Organized Democracy: Political Institutions in a Welfare State—the Case of Norway* (Oslo: Universitetsforlaget).

——(1995), 'The Changing Political Organization of Europe', *The European Yearbook of Comparative Government and Public Administration*, 2, J. J. Hesse and T. A. J. Toonen eds. (Baden-Baden/Boulder, Colo.: Nomos/Westview).

O'NEILL, ONORA (1988), 'Children's Rights and Children's Lives', *Ethics*, 98: 445–63.

——and RUDDICK, WILLIAM (eds.) (1979), *Having Children: Philosophical and Legal Reflections on Parenthood* (New York: Oxford University Press).

ORBELL, J. M., VON DE KRAGT, A. J. C., and DAWES, R. M. (1988), 'Explaining Discussion-Induced Cooperation', *Journal of Personality and Social Psychology*, 54: 811–19.

ORGANISATION FOR ECONOMIC CO-OPERATION AND DEVELOPMENT (1997), *Family, Market and Community: Equity and Efficiency in Social Policy* (Paris: OECD).

——(1998), 'Low-Income Dynamics in Four OECD Countries', *OECD Economic Outlook*, 64: 171–86.

OSTROM, ELINOR, BAUGH, WILLIAM, GUARASCI, RICHARD, PARKS, ROGER B., and WHITAKER, GORDON P. (1973), *Community Organization and the Provision of Police Service* (Sage Professional Papers in Administrative and Policy Sciences, 03–001; Beverly Hills, Calif.: Sage).

PAGE, BENJAMIN I. (1996), *Who Deliberates? Mass Media in Modern Democracy* (Chicago: University of Chicago Press).

——and SHAPIRO, ROBERT Y. (1992), *The Rational Public* (Chicago: University of Chicago Press).

PARSONS, TALCOTT (1965), 'Full Citizenship for the Negro American? A Sociological Problem', in Parsons and Kenneth B. Clark (eds.), *The Negro American* (Boston: Houghton Mifflin), 709–54.

PATEMAN, CAROLE (1970), *Participation in Democratic Theory* (Cambridge: Cambridge University Press).

——(1980), ' "The Disorder of Women": Women, Love and the Sense of Justice', *Ethics*, 91: 20–34.

——(1988), *The Sexual Contract* (Oxford: Polity).

PEACOCKE, CHRISTOPHER (ed.) (1994), *Simulation and the Unity of Consciousness: Current Issues in the Philosophy of Mind* (Proceedings of the British Academy, 83; Oxford: Oxford University Press for the British Academy).

PENNOCK, ROLAND J. (1979), *Democratic Political Theory* (Princeton: Princeton University Press).

PETERS, R. S. (1966), *Ethics and Education* (London: Allen & Unwin).

PETTIT, PHILIP (1982), 'Habermas on Truth and Justice', in G. H. R. Parkinson (ed.), *Marx and Marxisms* (Cambridge: Cambridge University Press), 207–28.

—— (1996), *The Common Mind*, 2nd edn. (New York: Oxford University Press).

PHILLIPS, ANNE (1995), *The Politics of Presence: Democracy and Group Representation* (Oxford: Clarendon Press).

PICO, GIOVANNI, CONTE DELLA MIRANDOLA (1486), 'Oration on the Dignity of Man' (tr. Elizabeth Livermoore Forbes), in Ernst Cassirer, Paul Oskar Kristeller and John Herman Randall, Jr. (eds.), *The Renaissance Philosophy of Man* (Chicago: University of Chicago Press, 1948).

PIKETTY, THOMAS (1995), 'Social Mobility and Redistributive Politics', *Quarterly Journal of Economics*, 110: 551–84.

PITKIN, HANNA F. (1967), *The Concept of Representation* (Berkeley, Calif.: University of California Press).

—— (1972), *Wittgenstein and Justice* (Berkeley, Calif.: University of California Press).

—— (1981), 'Justice: On Relating Private and Public', *Political Theory*, 9: 327–52.

PIXLEY, JOCELYN F. (1993), *Citizenship and Employment* (Cambridge: Cambridge University Press).

PLAMENATZ, JOHN P. (1973), *Democracy and Illusion* (London: Longman).

POCOCK, J. G. A. (1971), *Politics, Language and Time* (New York: Atheneum).

—— (1973), 'Verbalizing a Political Act: Toward a Politics of Speech', *Political Theory*, 1: 27–45.

POLANYI, MICHAEL (1958), *Personal Knowledge* (London: Routledge & Kegan Paul).

POLSBY, NELSON W. (1980), *Community Power and Political Theory*, 2nd edn. (New Haven, Conn.: Yale University Press).

POPKIN, SAMUEL L. (1991), *The Reasoning Voter* (Chicago: University of Chicago Press).

POPPER, KARL R. (1945), *The Open Society and its Enemies* (London: Routledge and Kegan Paul).

POSNER, RICHARD A. (1979), 'The Homeric Version of the Minimal State', *Ethics*, 90: 27–46.

Power and Democracy Project (2000), 'General Scheme: Power and Democracy 1998–2003', http://www.sv.uio.no/mutr/eng/scheme.html (accessed 10 Oct 2000).

PRZEWORSKI, ADAM (1998), 'Deliberation and Ideolgical Domination', in Elster 1998*a*: 140–60.

PRZEWORSKI, ADAM (1999), 'Minimalist Conception of Democracy: A Defense', in Ian Shapiro and Casiano Hacker-Cordón (eds.), *Democracy's Value* (Cambridge: Cambridge University Press), 23–55.

QUINE, W. V. O. (1961), 'Two Dogmas of Empiricism', in Quine, *From a Logical Point of View*, 2nd edn. (Cambridge, Mass.: Harvard University Press), 20–46.

QUINTON, ANTHONY (ed.) (1967), *Political Philosophy* (London: Oxford University Press).

RAE, DOUGLAS W. (1969), 'Decision-Rules and Individual Values in Constitutional Choice', *American Political Science Review*, 63: 40–56.

——(1975), 'The Limits of Consensual Decision', *American Political Science Review*, 69: 1270–94.

——(2001), 'Viacratic America: *Plessy* on Foot v. *Brown* on Wheels', *Annual Review of Political Science*, 4: 417–38.

RAIFFA, HOWARD (1982), *The Art and Science of Negotiation* (Cambridge, Mass.: Harvard University Press).

RAINWATER, LEE, REIN, MARTIN, and SCHWARTZ, JOSEPH (1986), *Income Packaging in the Welfare State: A Comparative Study of Family Income* (New York: Oxford University Press).

RANSOM, ROGER L., and SUTCH, RICHARD (1977), *One Kind of Freedom: The Economic Consequences of Emancipation* (Cambridge: Cambridge University Press).

RAWLS, JOHN (1958), 'Justice as Fairness', *Philosophical Review*, 67: 164–94.

——(1967), 'Legal Obligation and the Duty of Fair Play', in Sidney Hook (ed.), *Law and Philosophy* (New York: New York University Press), 3–18.

——(1971), *A Theory of Justice* (Cambridge, Mass.: Harvard University Press).

——(1980), 'Kantian Constructivism in Moral Theory', *Journal of Philosophy*, 77: 515–72.

——(1993), *Political Liberalism* (New York: Columbia University Press).

——(1997), 'The Idea of Public Reason Revisited', *University of Chicago Law Review*, 94: 765–807.

REGAN, DONALD H. (1986), 'Duties of Preservation', in B. G. Norton (ed.), *The Preservation of Species* (Princeton: Princeton University Press), 195–220.

RICHARDSON, HENRY (1997), 'Democratic Intentions', in Bohman and Rehg 1997: 349–82.

RIKER, WILLIAM H. (1961), 'Voting and the Summation of Preferences: An Interpretive Bibliographic Review of Selected Developments during the Last Decade', *American Political Science Review*, 55: 900–11.

——(1983), *Liberalism Against Populism* (San Francisco: W. Freeman).

RISSE, MATHIAS (2001), 'Arrow's Theorem, Indeterminacy and Multiplicity Reconsidered', *Ethics*, 111: 706–34.

RISSE, THOMAS (1999), 'International Norms and Domestic Change: Arguing and Communicative Behavior in the Human Rights Area', *Politics and Society*, 27: 529–59.

ROEMER, JOHN E. (1982), *A General Theory of Exploitation and Class* (Cambridge, Mass.: Harvard University Press).

——(1988), *Free to Lose* (Cambridge, Mass.: Harvard University Press).

——(1994), *A Future for Socialism* (Cambridge, Mass.: Harvard University Press).

ROHRSCHNEIDER, ROBERT (1988), 'Citizens' Attitudes toward Environmental Issues: Selfish or Selfless?', *Comparative Political Studies*, 21: 347–67.

ROKKAN, STEIN (1966), 'Norway: Numerical Democracy and Corporate Pluralism', in Dahl 1966: 70–115.

——(1975), 'Votes Count, Resources Decide', in Rokkan, *Makt og Motiv* (Oslo: Gyldendal Norsk Forlag), 216–24.

ROOM, GRAHAM (1995), 'Poverty in Europe: Competing Paradigms and Analysis', *Policy and Politics*, 23: 103–13.

ROUSSEAU, JEAN-JACQUES (1762), 'The Social Contract', in *The Social Contract and Discourses*, tr. G. D. H. Cole (London: Everyman/Dent, 1973), 164–278.

ROUTLEY, RICHARD, and ROUTLEY, VAL (1979), 'Against the Inevitability of Human Chauvinism', in K. E. Goodpaster and K. M. Sayre (eds.), *Ethics and Problems of the 21st Century* (Notre Dame, Ind.: University of Notre Dame Press), 36–59.

RUBINSTEIN, ARIEL (1982), 'Perfect Equilibria in a Bargaining Model', *Econometrica*, 50: 97–109.

RUDDICK, SARA (1980), 'Maternal Thinking', *Feminist Studies*, 6: 342–67.

——(1989), *Maternal Thinking* (New York: Ballantine Books).

RUGGIE, JOHN GERARD (1993), 'Territoriality and Beyond: Problematizing Modernity in International Relations', *International Organization*, 47: 139–74.

RUIN, OLOF (1974), 'Participatory Democracy and Corporatism: The Case of Sweden', *Scandinavian Political Studies*, 9: 171–86.

RUSSELL, BERTRAND (1938), *Power: A New Social Analysis* (London: Allen & Unwin).

RUSTOW, DANKWART A. (1955), *The Politics of Compromise: A Study of Politics and Cabinet Government in Sweden* (Princeton: Princeton University Press).

RYAN, ALAN (1998), 'In a Conversational Idiom', *Social Research*, 65: 473–89.

RYLE, GILBERT (1949), *The Concept of Mind* (London: Hutchinson).

SAGOFF, MARK (1988), *The Economy of the Earth* (Cambridge: Cambridge University Press).

——(1994), 'Should Preferences Count?', *Land Economics*, 70: 127–44.

SANDEL, MICHAEL J. (1982), *Liberalism and the Limits of Justice* (Cambridge: Cambridge University Press).

SANDEL, MICHAEL J. (ed.) (1984*a*), *Liberalism and its Critics* (Oxford: Blackwell).

—— (1984*b*), 'The Procedural Republic and the Unencumbered Self', *Political Theory*, 12: 81–96.

—— (1996), *Democracy's Discontent: America in Search of a Public Philosophy* (Cambridge, Mass.: Harvard University Press).

SANDERS, LYNN (1997), 'Against Deliberation', *Political Theory*, 25: 347–76.

SARTRE, JEAN-PAUL (1950), *What is Literature?*, tr. Bernard Frechtman (London: Methuen).

SAWARD, MICHAEL (1992), *Co-optive Politics and State Legitimacy* (Aldershot: Dartmouth).

—— (1998), *The Terms of Democracy* (Oxford: Polity).

SCARROW, SUSAN E. (2001), 'Direct Democracy and Institutional Change: a Comparative Investigation', *Comparative Political Studies*, 34/6 (Aug.): 651–65.

SCARRY, ELAINE (1995), 'On Vivacity: The Difference between Daydreaming and Imagining-under-Authorial-Instruction', *Representations*, 52: 1–26.

—— (1996), 'The Difficulty of Imagining Other People', in Joshua Cohen (ed.), *For Love of Country* (Boston: Beacon Press), 98–110.

SCHARPF, FRITZ W. (1999), *Governing in Europe: Effective and Democratic?* (Oxford: Oxford University Press).

SCHATTSCHNEIDER, E. E. (1960), *The Semi-Sovereign People* (New York: Holt, Rinehart & Winston).

SCHELLING, THOMAS C. (1960), *The Strategy of Conflict* (Cambridge, Mass.: Harvard University Press).

SCHMITTER, PHILIPPE C. (1977), 'Modes of Interest Intermediation and Models of Social Change in Western Europe', *Comparative Political Studies*, 10: 7–38.

SCHOBER, MICHAEL F. (1998), 'Conversational Evidence for Rethinking Meaning', *Social Research*, 65: 511–34.

—— and CLARK, HERBERT H. (1989), 'Understanding by Addressees and Overhearers', *Cognitive Psychology*, 21: 211–32.

SCHOEMAN, F. (1980), 'Rights of Children, Rights of Parents and the Moral Basis of the Family', *Ethics*, 91: 6–19.

SCHÖN, DONALD A., and REIN, MARTIN (1994), *Frame Reflection* (New York: Basic).

SCHUMPETER, JOSEPH A. (1950), *Capitalism, Socialism and Democracy*, 3rd edn. (New York: Harper & Row).

SCHUTZ, ALFRED (1943), 'The Problem of Rationality in the Social World', *Economica*, 10: 130–49.

SCHWEIKHART, DAVID (1980), *Capitalism or Worker Control?* (New York: Praeger).

SCOTT, JOAN W. (1991), 'Experience', *Critical Inquiry*, 17: 773–97.

SEARLE, JOHN R. (1969), *Speech Acts* (Cambridge: Cambridge University Press).

—— (1983), 'The Word Turned Upside Down', *New York Review of Books*, 30 (27 Oct.): 74–9.

—— (1995), *The Construction of Social Reality* (New York: Free Press).

SEIDENFELD, TEDDY, KADANE, JOSEPH B., and SCHERVISH, MARK J. (1989), 'On the Shared Preferences of Two Bayesian Decision Makers', *Journal of Philosophy*, 86: 225–44.

SELZNICK, PHILIP (1949), *TVA and the Grass Roots: A Study in the Sociology of Formal Organization* (Berkeley, Calif.: University of California Press).

—— (1992), *The Moral Commonwealth: Social Theory and the Promise of Community* (Berkeley, Calif.: Univ. of Calif. Press).

SEN, AMARTYA K. (1970), *Collective Choice and Social Welfare* (San Francisco: Holden-Day).

—— (1981), *Poverty and Famines* (Oxford: Clarendon Press).

—— (1982), *Choice, Welfare and Measurement* (Oxford: Blackwell).

—— (1983), 'Poor, Relatively Speaking', *Oxford Economic Papers*, 35: 153–69.

SHACHAR, AYELET (2001), *Multicultural Jurisdictions: Cultural Differences and Women's Rights* (Cambridge: Cambridge University Press).

SHAFFER, WILLIAM R. (1998), *Politics, Parties and Parliaments: Political Change in Norway* (Columbus: Ohio State University Press).

SHAPLEY, LLOYD S., and GROFMAN, BERNARD (1984), 'Optimizing Group Judgmental Accuracy in the Presence of Interdependencies', *Public Choice*, 43/3: 329–43.

SHAW, GEORGE BERNARD (1889), *Fabian Essays in Socialism* (London: Fabian Society).

SHKLAR, JUDITH N. (1991), *American Citizenship: The Quest for Inclusion* (Cambridge, Mass.: Harvard University Press).

SHONFIELD, ANDREW (1965), *Modern Capitalism* (London: Oxford University Press).

SIDGWICK, HENRY (1907), *The Methods of Ethics*, 7th edn. (London: Macmillan).

SIMMEL, GEORG (1908), 'The Phenomenon of Outvoting', in *The Sociology of Georg Simmel*, tr. and ed. Kurt H. Wolff (New York: Free Press, 1950), 239–49.

—— (1922), 'The Web of Group-Affiliations' (tr. R. Bendix) in Simmel 1955: 125–95.

—— (1955), *Conflict and the Web of Group Affiliations*, tr. Kurt H. Wolff and Reinhard Bendix (Glencoe, Ill.: Free Press).

SIMON, HERBERT A. (1985), 'Human Nature in Politics: The Dialogue of Psychology and Political Science', *American Political Science Review*, 79: 293–304.

SIMPSON, A. W. B. (1973), 'The Common Law and Legal Theory', in *Oxford Essays in Jurisprudence*, 2nd ser., A. W. B. Simpson ed. (Oxford: Clarendon Press), 77–99.

SINGER, PETER (1974), 'Sidgwick and Reflective Equilibrium', *The Monist*, 58: 490–517.

—— (1981), *The Expanding Circle* (Oxford: Clarendon Press).

SKINNER, QUENTIN (1971), 'On Performing and Explaining Linguistic Actions', *Philosophical Quarterly*, 21: 1–21.

SKOCPOL, THEDA (1979), *States and Social Revolutions* (Cambridge: Cambridge University Press).

SMITH, ADAM (1776), *An Inquiry into the Nature and Causes of the Wealth of Nations*, R. H. Campbell, A. S. Skinner, and W. B. Todd eds. (Oxford: Clarendon Press, 1976).

SMITH, DOROTHY E. (1987), *Everyday World as Problematic: A Feminist Sociology* (Boston: Northeastern University Press).

SMITH, GRAHAM, and WALES, CORRINE (1999), 'The Theory and Practice of Citizens' Juries', *Policy and Practice*, 27: 295–308.

SMITH, KIMBERLY K. (1998), 'Storytelling, Sympathy and Moral Judgment in American Abolitionism', *Journal of Political Philosophy*, 6: 356–77.

SNIDERMAN, PAUL M. (1993), 'The New Look in Public Opinion Research', in A. W. Finifter (ed.), *Political Science: The State of the Discipline II* (Washington, DC: American Political Science Association).

SOMERS, MARGARET R. (1994), 'Rights, Relationality and Membership: Rethinking the Making and Meaning of Citizenship', *Law and Social Inquiry*, 19: 63–112.

SOMMERLAD, FIONA, and MCLEAN, IAIN (tr. and ed.) (1989), *The Political theory of Condorcet* (Social Studies Faculty Centre Working Paper, 1/89; Oxford: Faculty of Social Sciences, Oxford University).

SPERBER, DAN, and WILSON, DEIDRE (1986), 'Loose Talk', *Proceedings of the Aristotelian Society*, 86: 153–71.

SPINNER-HALEV, JEFF (1994), *The Boundaries of Citizenship: Race, Ethnicity and Nationality in the Liberal State* (Baltimore: Johns Hopkins University Press).

SPITZ, ELAINE (1984), *Majority Rule* (Chatham, NJ: Chatham House Publishers).

STEINER, GEORGE (1963), 'Humane Literacy', in Steiner, *Language and Silence* (London: Faber & Faber, 1967), 21–9.

—— (1967), 'Literature and Post-History', in Steiner, *Language and Silence* (London: Faber & Faber), 413–24.

STEINER, JURG, and DORFF, R. (1980), *A Theory of Political Decision Modes* (Chapel Hill, NC: University of North Carolina Press).

STOCKER, MICHAEL (1982), 'Responsibility Especially for Beliefs', *Mind*, 91: 398–417.

STONE, CHRISTOPHER (1973), 'Should Trees Have Standing?', *Southern California Law Review*, 45: 450–501 at 471.

STRØM, KAARE (1990), *Minority Governments and Majority Rule* (Cambridge: Cambridge University Press).

SUNSTEIN, CASS R. (1988), 'Beyond the Republican Revival', *Yale Law Journal*, 97: 1539–90.

—— (1991), 'Preferences and Politics', *Philosophy and Public Affairs*, 20: 3–34.

—— (1993*a*), 'Democracy and Shifting Preferences', in David Copp, Jean Hampton and John E. Roemer (eds.), *The Idea of Democracy* (Cambridge: Cambridge University Press), 196–230.

—— (1993*b*), *Democracy and the Problem of Free Speech* (New York: Free Press).

—— (1995), 'Incompletely Theorized Agreements', *Harvard Law Review*, 108: 1733–72.

—— (1996*a*), 'Leaving Things Undecided', *Harvard Law Review*, 110: 4–101.

—— (1996*b*), *Legal Reasoning and Political Conflict* (New York: Oxford University Press).

—— (2001), *Republic.com* (Princeton: Princeton University Press).

—— (2002), 'The Law of Group Polarization', *Journal of Political Philosophy*, 10: 74–94.

TAAGEPERA, REIN, and SHUGART, MATTHEW S. (1989), *Seats and Votes: The Effects and Determinants of Electoral Systems* (New Haven, Conn.: Yale University Press).

TAMIR, YAEL (1993), *Liberal Nationalism* (Princeton: Princeton University Press).

TANGIAN, A. S. (2000), 'Unlikelihood of Condorcet's Paradox in a Large Society', *Social Choice and Welfare*, 17: 337–65.

TAYLOR, CHARLES (1978), *Hegel and Modern Society* (Cambridge: Cambridge University Press).

—— (1985), *Philosophical Papers* (Cambridge: Cambridge University Press).

—— (1989), *Sources of the Self: The Making of the Modern Identity* (Cambridge: Cambridge University Press).

—— (1992), *Multiculturalism and 'the Politics of Recognition'* (Princeton: Princeton University Press).

—— (1993), 'Modernity and the Rise of the Public Sphere', *Tanner Lectures on Human Values*, 14: 203–60.

TAYLOR, MICHAEL (1969), 'Proof of a Theorem on Majority Rule', *Behavioral Science*, 14: 228–31.

TAYLOR, SERGE (1984), *Making Bureaucracies Think: The Environmental Impact Statement Strategy of Administrative Reform* (Stanford, Calif.: Stanford University Press).

THERBORN, GÖRAN (1989), ' "Pillarization" and "Popular Movements"— Two Variants of Welfare State Capitalism: The Netherlands and Sweden', in Francis G. Castles (ed.), *The Comparative History of Public Policy* (Oxford: Polity), 192–241.

THOMAS, CAROL (1993), 'Deconstructing the Concept of Care', *Sociology*, 27: 649–69.

THOMPSON, DENNIS (1970), *The Democratic Citizen* (Cambridge: Cambridge University Press).

THOMPSON, JAMES D., and McEWAN, W. J. (1958), 'Organizational Goals and Environment: Goal Setting as an Interaction Process', *American Sociological Review*, 23: 23–31.

TILLY, CHARLES (1998), 'Contentious Conversation', *Social Research*, 65: 491–510.

TILTON, TIMOTHY A. (1990), *The Political Theory of Swedish Social Democracy* (Oxford: Clarendon Press).

TOCQUEVILLE, ALEXIS DE (1835), *Democracy in America*, tr. George Lawrence, J. P. Mayer and Max Lerner eds. (New York: Harper & Row, 1966).

TORGERSEN, ULF (1970), 'The Trend towards Political Consensus', *Acta Sociologica*, 61: 159–72. Reprinted in Erik Allardt and Stein Rokkan (eds.), *Mass Politics* (New York: Free Press, 1970), 93–104.

TRONTO, JOAN C. (1987), 'Beyond Gender Difference to a Theory of Care', *Signs*, 12: 644–63.

——(1993), *Moral Boundaries: A Political Argument for an Ethic of Care* (London: Routledge).

TUCKER, ROBERT C. (ed.) (1972), *The Marx-Engels Reader* (New York: Norton).

TULLY, JAMES (1995), 'Constitutional Demands for Cultural Recognition', *Journal of Political Philosophy*, 3: 118–40.

——(1999), 'The Agonic Freedom of Citizens', *Economy and Society*, 28: 101–22.

TUSHNET, MARK (2001), 'Non-Judicial Constitutional Review', paper presented to Workshop on 'Human Rights Protection', Melbourne, 14 Dec.

TYLER, TOM R. (1990), *Why People Obey the Law* (New Haven, Conn.: Yale University Press).

UHR, JOHN (1998), *Deliberative Democracy in Australia* (Cambridge: Cambridge University Press).

VAN ALSTYNE, MARSHALL, and BRYNJOLFSSON, ERIK (1996), 'Could the Internet Balkanize Science?', *Science*, 274/5292 (29 Nov.): 1479–80.

——and——(1997), 'Electronic Communities: Global Village or Cyberbalkans?', paper presented to 17th International Conference on Information Systems, Cleveland, Ohio.

VAN KERSBERGEN, KEES (1995), *Social Capitalism: A Study of Christian Democracy and the Welfare State* (London: Routledge).

VAN PARIJS, PHILIPPE (1998), 'The Disfranchisement of the Elderly, and Other Attempts to Secure Intergenerational Justice', *Philosophy and Public Affairs*, 27/4 (Fall): 292–333.

VINSON, FRED M. (1948), 'Opinion of the U.S. Supreme Court', *Shelley v. Kramer*, 334 US 1, 4–23.

WALDRON, JEREMY (1989), 'Democratic Theory and the Public Interest: Condorcet and Rousseau Revisited', *American Political Science Review*, 38/4 (Dec.): 1322–8.

——(1991), 'Homelessness and the Issue of Freedom', *UCLA Law Review*, 39/2: 295–324. Reprinted in Waldron 1993: 309–38.

——(1993), *Liberal Rights* (Cambridge: Cambridge University Press).

——(1995), 'Legislators' Intentions and Unintentional Legislation', in Andrei Marmor (ed.), *Law and Interpretation* (Oxford: Clarendon Press), 329–56.

——(1999*a*), *The Dignity of Legislation* (Cambridge: Cambridge University Press).

——(1999*b*), *Law and Disagreement* (Oxford: Clarendon Press).

WALKER, R. B. J. (1993), *Inside/Outside* (Cambridge: Cambridge University Press).

WALLERSTEIN, IMMANUEL (1979), *The Capitalist World-Economy* (Cambridge: Cambridge University Press).

WALZER, MICHAEL (1968), 'A Day in the Life of a Socialist Citizen: Two Cheers for Participatory Democracy', *Dissent*, 15/3: 243–7. Reprinted in Walzer 1970: 229–41.

——(1970), *Obligations* (Cambridge, Mass.: Harvard University Press).

——(1983), *Spheres of Equality* (Oxford: Martin Robertson).

——(1987), *Interpretation and Social Criticism* (Cambridge, Mass.: Harvard University Press).

——(1993), 'Exclusion, Injustice and the Democratic State', *Dissent*, 40/2: 55–64.

——(1994), *Thick and Thin: Moral Argument at Home and Abroad* (Notre Dame, Ind.: University of Notre Dame Press).

WARING, MARILYN (1988), *If Women Counted: A New Feminist Economics* (New York: Harper & Row).

WARNER, FLOYD (1953), *Community Power Structures* (Chapel Hill, NC: University of North Carolina Press).

WASSERSTROM, RICHARD (1964), 'Rights, Human Rights and Racial Discrimination', *Journal of Philosophy*, 61: 628–41.

——(1977), 'Racism, Sexism and Preferential Treatment', *UCLA Law Review*, 24: 581–662.

WATSON, GARY (1977), 'Skepticism about Weakness of Will', *Philosophical Review*, 86: 316–39.

WEBER, EUGEN (1976), *Peasants into Frenchmen: The Modernization of Rural France, 1870–1914* (Stanford, Calif.: Stanford University Press).

WEILER, J. H. H. (1991), 'The Transformation of Europe', *Yale Law Journal*, 100: 2403–83.

——(1995), 'The Reformation of European Constitutional Law', paper presented to 'Workshop on Constitutionalism', University of East Anglia, Norwich, Sept.

WEISS, DONALD D. (1973), 'Wollheim's Paradox: Survey and Solution', *Political Theory*, 1/2 (May): 154–70.

WENDT, ALEXANDER E. (1987), 'The Agent-Structure Problem in International Relations Theory', *International Organization*, 41: 335–70.

WHITE, STEPHEN K. (1991), *Political Theory and Postmodernism* (Cambridge: Cambridge University Press).

WHORF, BENJAMIN LEE (1956), *Language, Thought and Reality* (Cambridge, Mass.: MIT Press).

WIKLER, DANIEL (1979), 'Paternalism and the Mildly Retarded', *Philosophy and Public Affairs*, 8: 377–92.

WILLIAMS, BERNARD (1973), 'Deciding to Believe', in Williams, *Problems of the Self* (Cambridge: Cambridge University Press), 136–51.

WILSON, BRYAN (ed.) (1970), *Rationality* (Oxford: Blackwell).

WIT, JÖRGEN (1998), 'Rational Choice and the Condorcet Jury Theorem', *Games and Economic Behavior*, 22: 364–76.

WITTGENSTEIN, LUDWIG (1958), *Philosophical Investigations*, tr. G. E. M. Anscombe (Oxford: Blackwell).

——(1974), *Tractatus Logico-Philosophicus*, tr. D. F. Pears and B. F. McGuinness (London: Routledge & Kegan Paul).

WITTMAN, DONALD (1995), *The Myth of Democratic Failure: Why Political Institutions are Efficient* (Chicago: University of Chicago Press).

WOLFF, ROBERT PAUL (1980), 'There's Nobody Here But Us Persons', in Carol C. Gould and Marx W. Wartofsky (eds.), *Women and Philosophy* (New York: Putnam), 128–44.

WOLLHEIM, RICHARD (1962), 'A Paradox in the Theory of Democracy', in *Philosophy, Politics and Society*, 2nd series, P. Laslett and W. G. Runciman ed. (Oxford: Blackwell), 71–87.

——(ed.) (1975), *John Stuart Mill, Three Essays* (Oxford: Clarendon Press).

——(1984), *The Thread of Life* (Cambridge: Cambridge University Press).

WORDSWORTH, WILLIAM (1820), 'Observations Prefixed to "Lyrical Ballads"', in *What is Art?*, Alexander Sesokske ed. (New York: Oxford University Press, 1965), 261–74.

WORLD BANK (1994), *Averting the Old Age Crisis: Policies to Protect the Old and Promote Growth* (New York: Oxford University Press).

World Health Organization (2000), *The World Health Report: Health Systems: Improving Performance* (Geneva: WHO).

WYATT-BROWN, BERTRAM (1982), *Southern Honor: Ethics and Behavior in the Old South* (Oxford: Oxford University Press).

YANAY, URI (1995), 'Personal Safety and the Mixed Economy of Protection', *Social Policy and Administration*, 29: 110–21.

YANKELOVICH, DANIEL (1991), *Coming to Public Judgment: Making Democracy Work in a Complex World* (Syracuse, NY: Syracuse University Press).

YOUNG, H. PEYTON (1988), 'Condorcet's Theory of Voting', *American Political Science Review*, 82/4 (Dec.): 1231–44.

——(1995), 'Optimal Voting Rules', *Journal of Economic Perspectives*, 9/1 (Winter): 51–64.

YOUNG, IRIS MARION (1990), *Justice and the Politics of Difference* (Princeton: Princeton University Press).

——(1995), 'Together in Difference: Transforming the Logic of Group Political Conflict', in Will Kymlicka (ed.), *The Rights of Cultural Minorities* (Oxford: Oxford University Press), 155–77.

——(1997), 'Communication and the Other: Beyond Deliberative Democracy', in Young, *Intersecting Voices* (Princeton: Princeton University Press), 60–74.

——(2000), *Inclusion and Democracy* (Oxford: Oxford University Press).

——(2001), 'Activist Challenges to Deliberative Democracy', *Political Theory*, 29: 670–90.

YOUNG, ORAN R. (1967), *The Intermediaries: Third Parties in International Crises* (Princeton: Princeton University Press).

——(ed.) (1975), *Bargaining: Formal Theories of Negotiation* (Urbana, Ill.: University of Illinois Press).

INDEX

Note: An '*n*' after the page number indicates a footnote.